William Taylor Adams

Isles of the Sea

Young America - A Story of Travel and Adventure

William Taylor Adams

Isles of the Sea
Young America - A Story of Travel and Adventure

ISBN/EAN: 9783744712996

Printed in Europe, USA, Canada, Australia, Japan

Cover: Foto ©Andreas Hilbeck / pixelio.de

More available books at **www.hansebooks.com**

Thomas Speers is Promoted. Page 18.

ISLES OF THE SEA;

OR,

YOUNG AMERICA HOMEWARD BOUND.

A Story of Travel and Adventure.

BY

WILLIAM T. ADAMS

(*OLIVER OPTIC*),

AUTHOR OF "OUTWARD BOUND," "SHAMROCK AND THISTLE," "RED CROSS,"
"DIKES AND DITCHES," "PALACE AND COTTAGE," "DOWN THE
RHINE," "UP THE BALTIC," "NORTHERN LANDS,"
"CROSS AND CRESCENT," "SUNNY SHORES,"
"VINE AND OLIVE," ETC.

BOSTON:
LEE AND SHEPARD, PUBLISHERS.
NEW YORK:
CHARLES T. DILLINGHAM.
1877.

Electrotyped and printed by
Rand, Avery, and Company,
117 *Franklin Street,*
Boston.

To My Friend,

P. WOODBURY DODGE, Esq.,

OF AMHERST, N.H.,

BENEATH WHOSE HOSPITABLE ROOF IT WAS WRITTEN,

This Volume

IS RESPECTFULLY DEDICATED.

YOUNG AMERICA ABROAD.

By OLIVER OPTIC.

A Library of Travel and Adventure in Foreign Lands. First and Second Series; six volumes in each Series. 16mo. Illustrated.

First Series.

I. *OUTWARD BOUND;* OR, YOUNG AMERICA AFLOAT.
II. *SHAMROCK AND THISTLE;* OR, YOUNG AMERICA IN IRELAND AND SCOTLAND.
III. *RED CROSS;* OR, YOUNG AMERICA IN ENGLAND AND WALES.
IV. *DIKES AND DITCHES;* OR, YOUNG AMERICA IN HOLLAND AND BELGIUM.
V. *PALACE AND COTTAGE;* OR, YOUNG AMERICA IN FRANCE AND SWITZERLAND.
VI. *DOWN THE RHINE;* OR, YOUNG AMERICA IN GERMANY.

Second Series.

I. *UP THE BALTIC;* OR, YOUNG AMERICA IN NORWAY, SWEDEN, AND DENMARK.
II. *NORTHERN LANDS;* OR, YOUNG AMERICA IN RUSSIA AND PRUSSIA.
III. *CROSS AND CRESCENT;* OR, YOUNG AMERICA IN TURKEY AND GREECE.
IV. *SUNNY SHORES;* OR, YOUNG AMERICA IN ITALY AND AUSTRIA.
V. *VINE AND OLIVE;* OR, YOUNG AMERICA IN SPAIN AND PORTUGAL.
VI. *ISLES OF THE SEA;* OR, YOUNG AMERICA HOMEWARD BOUND.

PREFACE.

"Isles of the Sea" is the sixth and last volume of the second series of "Young America Abroad," and contains the history of the academy squadron during its voyage, "homeward bound," across the Atlantic. The title of the book, "Isles of the Sea," indicates the character of the foreign travel in which the students of the institution were engaged; and in the pursuit of knowledge they visit the Madeira Islands, the Canaries, the Azores, the Bermudas, and one vessel of the fleet extends its cruise to the Cape Verd Islands. As in its predecessors, the professor of geography and history has something to say about each of the islands visited, and the surgeon and sanitary officer continues to enlighten the young gentlemen who seek his companionship in their rambles on shore. The field of geography and history is not so extensive as in the preceding volumes of the series; and for this reason the story occupies a larger place in the book.

Of the story, Mr. Tom Speers is the central figure, or at least one of the most prominent characters. Possibly he may be deemed a rather eccentric character for one under age; but, as the author has so often expressed himself before, it does not so much matter what else a young man may be, if he only has high aims, and a resolute purpose to carry out his ideal of what is noble, good, and true. Tom is a high-toned young man, as are all the other characters with whom the young reader is at all likely to sympathize, and in whose fortunes he is most certain to be interested.

As to the innate probability of a few of the leading incidents, they are suggested by actual occurrences in maritime history, which may be recalled by those who have kept themselves familiar with the subject. In regard to the long search of the Ville d'Angers for the academy squadron, which extended nearly across the Atlantic, the recorded experience of those who have traversed the ocean on similar ventures shows how difficult it is, away from the telegraph and the ship news, for one vessel to find another.

The first volume of the first series of "Young America Abroad" was published in 1866, by the publishers whose imprint is on the present and last of the series. It is therefore eleven years that the author has been engaged in this pleasing work. These books have been received with a degree of favor which the writer is proud and happy to acknowledge, and for which he returns his sincere thanks. He is especially grateful that his life has been spared to complete the work begun; and every year has increased his interest in the host of young friends to whom these books have introduced him in all parts of the country. He regrets, that, in this particular field of travel and adventure, his task has reached its conclusion. He has crossed the Atlantic four times, and travelled in every country of Europe, in preparing himself for the work; and the pleasant memories of the "lonely ocean" and the far-distant lands he has visited will always be retained and cherished, in their association with the multitude of young people in whose delightful service he voyaged and travelled.

TOWERHOUSE, BOSTON, Nov. 3, 1877.

CONTENTS.

		PAGE
I.	THE TELEGRAPHIC DESPATCH	11
II.	THE LETTER FROM LONDON	25
III.	AN APPROACHING SQUALL	39
IV.	A VESSEL IN DISTRESS	53
V.	BOARDING THE WRECK	67
VI.	A VOLUNTEER SHIP'S COMPANY	81
VII.	THE INVALID YOUNG LADY	95
VIII.	THE VILLE D'ANGERS	109
IX.	THE NEW SHIP'S COMPANY	123
X.	SOMETHING ABOUT THE MADEIRA ISLANDS	137
XI.	BUDDING VINES AND ORANGE GROVES	151
XII.	CONCERNING THE MISSING STEAMER	165
XIII.	A MUTINY IN THE FIRE-ROOM	180
XIV.	THE WRECK OF THE CASTLE WILLIAM	194
XV.	A CHANGE OF DESTINATION	200
XVI.	THE WINE-ROOM OF THE VILLE D'ANGERS	222
XVII.	STRIKING WHILE THE IRON IS HOT	236

CONTENTS.

		PAGE
XVIII.	A Trip to the Canary Islands	250
XIX.	Walks and Talks about the Canary Islands,	263
XX.	"A Yankee Ship and a Yankee Crew"	276
XXI.	The Sprigs of Nobility	292
XXII.	What the Students saw in the Azores	306
XXIII.	Carrying out the Programme	319
XXIV.	A Hasty Run to the Cape Verds	333
XXV.	The Last of the Isles of the Sea	348
XXVI.	Young America Homeward Bound	363

ISLES OF THE SEA.

ISLES OF THE SEA;

OR,

YOUNG AMERICA HOMEWARD BOUND.

CHAPTER I.

THE TELEGRAPHIC DESPATCH.

"ALL hands, pipe to muster!" shouted the boatswain of the Tritonia.

At the same moment the shrill whistle and the sharp cry sounded through the American Prince and the Josephine. The squadron was at anchor in Gibraltar Bay; and since seven bells in the first watch, the signal, "Assign rank," had been displayed on the American Prince, the flag-ship of the fleet.

It was the first day of April. The merit marks of the students had been added since the last recitations, and the offices were to be given out at eight bells. The squadron had visited all the ports of the Spanish Peninsula, and several trips to the interior had been made. The fleet was to sail to Seville to witness the scenes of Holy Week; and this excursion was to finish the cruise, not only in the waters of Spain and Portugal, but in those of Europe. The vessels would then be homeward bound, but by the way of the "Isles of the Sea."

There was no little excitement in all the vessels of the squadron. Though the students could keep their own reckoning tolerably well, so far as the literary pursuits were concerned, they were wholly in the dark in relation to the marks for seamanship, navigation, and conduct. Some had strong hopes and expectations, based upon their own earnest efforts; and these were seldom greatly disappointed, though their rank was sometimes not so high as they anticipated. But, as a rule, the whole matter was a great mystery, which it was not possible to find out.

Sometimes there would be very little change in the rank of the officers for several months; and then came a general turn-over of every thing. The rise from the steerage to the cabin was almost uniformly slow and regular, though sometimes a student jumped over the heads of the half-dozen who had stood next above him. This sudden elevation of an officer or seaman had a tendency to produce bad feeling among his rivals in the race for honors, for the boys continued to be human in spite of the discipline of the service.

Possibly the interest on the present occasion was intensified by the fact that the squadron was so soon to sail for home; and doubtless many of the students were thinking of the uniform in which they should be presented to their friends on their return to the American shores. On board of the Tritonia it was known among the closer observers of events, that several of the students had been putting forth extraordinary exertions; and this circumstance fully accounted for the unusual excitement of the day. Among them was Bark Lingall, who had attempted to run away, but had voluntarily returned. He appeared to be thoroughly reformed, and, from one of the most indifferent and vicious boys in the vessel, had become a model of propriety in all things, as well as a very diligent and faithful scholar.

There was a certain class of students in the steerage of the Tritonia, as there always is in any large company of boys, who affected to despise one who had turned away from his evil habits and associations, and reformed his life and character. Lingall had his trials with this class of students; but he was resolute in his purpose to continue in the good way. Under the influence of Raymond, who had inspired him with the desire to do his whole duty, he kept his temper under his persecutions; and in no instance was he provoked to subject himself to discipline by the jeers and taunts of the disaffected.

Another student in the Tritonia, who had not distinguished himself by any misconduct, though he had been an easy-going fellow, suddenly began to exert himself without any apparent stimulus for such action. He was a high-minded boy, but rather peculiar in his ways of thinking and doing. His name was Thomas Speers. He was twenty years old, though he did not show his years, and one might easily have mistaken him for sixteen.

For the reason that they were doing their best in seamanship and the studies, Bark Lingall and Tom Speers excited a great deal of remark, not to say feeling, among the students. Bark had one of the highest numbers in the vessel, which indicated that his rank was among the lowest. He had never done any work he could avoid doing since the first two or three months of his service in the vessel. He had been a conspirator against the discipline and even the safety of the schooner, and was considered a bad boy by the vice-principal in charge and the professors.

Tom Speers had no particular record. He was considered a good fellow by the students in general; and, though he was noted for his independence, he had never wilfully broken the rules of the vessel. He was a first-class seaman; and his ability as a student was discovered to be of the highest order as soon as he chose to exert himself.

While the boatswain of the Tritonia was still piping his call to muster through the vessel, a shore boat approached the gangway. A man in the stern hailed the vessel; and Marline, the adult boatswain, went down on the accommodation steps to see what he wanted, for visitors were not admitted at this time.

"Is there a man by the name of Thomas Speers on board of this craft?" asked the man in the boat.

"We have a young man of that name on board," replied Marline.

"Can I see him for a moment?"

"For a moment you can; but he will be wanted very soon."

The boatswain returned to the deck, and, calling Speers, sent him to the gangway. As the student had no friends in Gibraltar, he wondered who could wish to see him. He hastened to the steps, and went down to the platform at the foot of them. Marline remained at the rail, to see that nothing improper passed between Speers and the man; but he was called away before the student had communicated with the boat.

"Telegraph despatch from San Roque," said the messenger, handing the document to Speers.

"It can't be for me," protested the student, surprised that such a message should come to him. "I don't know any one in San Roque."

"It is directed to Thomas Speers, and there is the name of this vessel on it," persisted the messenger, pointing to the address. "But it is not from San Roque the message comes: that is the nearest telegraph station."

"Where did it come from?" asked Speers, turning the message over and over in his hand.

"I don't know: you can tell by opening it."

"I don't want to open it, if it is not for me."

"If your name is 'Thomas Speers, it is for you. I have done my errand, and I have nothing more to say about it," added the man, as he shoved his boat off from the platform.

"All hands on deck!" shouted an officer at the gangway.

Speers put the message into his pocket. He seemed to have no curiosity in regard to its contents. He was more interested in the distribution of the offices on board of the Tritonia; but he did not believe the message was for him. He hastened back to the deck, and took his station in the waist.

He hoped his place would be on the quarter-deck for the new term. He had made a desperate struggle with all his studies, and he was not conscious that he had failed in any thing. Mr. Pelham, the vice-principal, took his position at the heel of the main-mast, with the list of officers and seamen in his hand. Most of the students looked very anxious, though a few of the "marines" affected to make fun of the occasion, and pretended that they did not care what positions fell to their lot.

The vice-principal made the usual introductory speech, pointing the moral the occasion suggested. The record for the last month indicated some very important changes; and he hoped they would cause no ill feeling either in the cabin or the steerage. The merit marks strictly represented the conduct and work of the students; and the result of the addition of the figures had caused as much surprise among the professors as it would among the young gentlemen.

Mr. Pelham then announced the name of Wainwright as captain. This officer had held the position for many months; and, as he was very popular on board, the announcement was received with hearty applause. Greenwood was first lieutenant again; and his name was well received by the ship's company. Scott, who had been fourth lieutenant during the preceding month, came in as second; and, as the joker had always been a favorite, his promotion produced a very decided sensation.

"I congratulate you, Mr. Scott," said the vice-principal, with a smile.

"Thank you, sir. For the good of the Tritonia, I am glad this thing has happened," replied the joker.

"Modesty is a cardinal virtue," added Mr. Pelham.

"I know it, sir; and that is the reason I am so heavily loaded with it," returned Scott, making a face which caused a tremendous laugh on the quarter-deck.

If there was anybody that did not laugh, it was Alexander, who had formerly been first lieutenant; and his name was not yet called. But it came in next as third lieutenant; while O'Hara, the "Oyrish Oytalian," was again the fourth lieutenant.

"No great change in that," said Richards, the **first** master, who had been struggling for a lieutenant's place for months.

"No; but that shows the changes are yet to be mentioned," replied Blair, the fourth master, to whom the remark had been addressed. "It looks as though there was a chance for some of us to take a berth in the steerage. Perhaps you are the one to go down, Richards."

"What makes you think so, Blair?" asked the first speaker anxiously.

"I don't think so: I have no opinion at all about it. If there are to be great changes, some of us will have to go down," added Blair.

So it proved; but not just as the fourth master had indicated. The vice-principal paused a long time before he read the next name; and the hearts of many beat violently as the moment came that might dash down all their hopes for the present.

"**First** master," said the vice-principal at last, "**Thomas** Speers."

The announcement was received in silence and in blank amazement. The students who had observed that Speers was making an effort thought it possible he might be coxswain of the captain's gig, captain of the after-guard, or something of that sort; but they had not the slightest expectation that he would get into the cabin, to say nothing of his jumping over the heads of four masters who had been in the cabin for months. The experience of the past demonstrated that a fellow who once got into the cabin very seldom allowed himself to be shoved out of it. If he had the ability to get there, he had the ability to stay there. Besides, the constant presence of the professors had a tendency to stimulate him to do his best.

"Speers, I congratulate you on the great promotion you have won," said Mr. Pelham, breaking in upon the silence into which the ship's company had been surprised by the mention of the name of Speers in connection with so high a position.

"I thank you, sir," replied Tom Speers, bowing and blushing.

Then came the most tumultuous applause from the seamen in the waist. One of their own number had gone up; and, though they had no particular sympathy with Speers, his elevation indicated that one of the present officers would be reduced to the steerage. There were enough among them to rejoice at the fall of a superior; for it was quite impossible to repress entirely the spirit of envy and jealousy excited by the elevation of the few above the many.

This subject had early attracted the attention of Mr. Lowington, the principal of the academy squadron; and he had done all he could to moderate and expel the feeling among the students. But they were all human beings, subject to the infirmities of the flesh; and they could not be wholly different from the more mature actors on the stage of life. They were fully instructed and warned in regard to the effect of cherishing this vicious spirit; but that was all that could be done. The boys were to meet and encounter the same circumstances in the great world as on board of the vessels of the academy fleet; and they received all the preparation for the ordeal it was possible to give them.

"That proves that one of us will have to go down," said Blair, while the seamen in the waist were applauding the promotion of Speers.

"I don't believe in this thing," added Richards, with no little excitement in his tones and manner. "Who ever heard of such a thing as a fellow in the steerage leaping over the heads of all the masters?"

"It is done; and it's no use to talk about it," continued Blair. "Speers's marks give him that place, or he would not have it."

"There is something wrong about it."

"What can be wrong?"

"It looks as though the books of the professors had been doctored. Didn't the vice-principal say it was as great a surprise to the faculty as to fellows?"

"That only shows that they have had their eyes open; and, if there was any thing wrong about the books, they would have discovered it."

"It would have been easy enough for Speers to alter half a dozen figures on the book," Richards insisted.

"I don't believe Speers is a fellow of that sort," Blair objected. "If he had done such a thing, the professors could see that the figures had been changed."

"I don't understand it; and I can't explain it in any other way," added Richards, shaking his head.

"Second master," the vice-principal proceeded, "Henry Raymond. He is absent, but the principal instructs me to hold his position the same as last month."

Raymond's absence was explained, as it was in all the vessels of the fleet; and it was satisfactory to all except Ben Pardee and Lon Gibbs, of the "marines," who had been engaged in an attempt to run away. The vice-principal glanced at his list again, and the students waited with intense interest for the name of the next officer.

"Third master," said he; and there was another long pause. Blair and Richards were holding their breath in their anxiety to hear the next name, for there were only two chances more for the cabin.

"Third master," repeated the vice-principal, "Barclay Lingall."

If the name of Tom Speers had produced a sensation among the officers and crew, that of Bark Lingall made a greater one. Three months before, he had run away from the vessel with a fellow so bad that the latter was expelled; and on his return, though he came back of his own accord, having been reformed by the influence of Raymond while both were absent, his lost lessons could not be made up; and he was given the highest number in the vessel, which placed him below all the others. From that low position he had suddenly risen to be the third master of the Tritonia. The case seemed to be so singular, and so contrary to the past experience of the students, that the vice-principal deemed it necessary to explain it. He took the occasion to illustrate that almost any student who was thoroughly in earnest in his studies could obtain any position his ambition coveted. When he saw that Lingall was doing so well, he anticipated a high position for him, though not quite so high as he had attained.

"I am disgusted," said Richards, when one more chance had slipped away from him. "I feel sure that the books have been doctored. Two fellows from the steerage have got into the cabin."

"And we are about at the end of the rope. Either you or I must go down now, and perhaps both of us," replied Blair, shrugging his shoulders.

"That's so; but I don't believe we are to be sent down by any sort of fair play," growled Richards.

"There is no help for it. I don't think I did as well last month as I should have done if I had supposed there was any danger of being shoved out of the cabin," continued Blair frankly.

"I have no doubt I could have done better; but I believe now that I have done well enough to keep my place."

"What are you going to do about it? get up a mutiny?"

"I feel like doing something about it."

"Wait a minute before you do it," laughed Blair. "You may be all right yet."

"I can't be any thing better than fourth master, and below Speers and Lingall."

"Fourth master," continued the vice-principal, when the excitement of the last announcement had in a measure subsided; and then he paused again, not to prolong the agony of the students, but to make sure that no mistake was made.

"We shall know all about it in another minute," said Blair; "and you will learn whether or not you need go on with your mutiny."

"I haven't said any thing about a mutiny: you said that, Blair."

"Mutinies don't pay in this squadron: besides, we shall be homeward bound in a few days," laughed Blair.

"Fourth master, Richards," read the vice-principal from his list.

"There you are, Richards!" exclaimed Blair.

"And you are counted out," added the new fourth master.

"I am; but I shall not cry about it. You are an officer, and I am a seaman now; and, if I conclude to get up a mutiny at your suggestion, I shall not say any thing to you about it."

Blair shrugged his shoulders, and, making a merit of necessity, he stepped down from the quarter-deck into the waist. A few minutes later his name was read as one of the highest of the petty officers. There was not much consolation in this position, as he was turned out of the cabin.

The rest of the numbers were given out in the order of merit. As usual, there was considerable grumbling, while not a few were elated over the rank they had won. Before noon the officers put on their uniform, though two of them were absent.

Tom Speers in his frock-coat and cap was a good-looking officer. He was well received by the other occupants of the cabin,—possibly with the exception of Richards, who could not wholly forgive him for getting above him. Tom had quite forgotten the telegraphic despatch he had received, till he put on his uniform, and changed the contents of his pockets into those of the new dress.

He was not much interested in the document: his big promotion monopolized all his thoughts. He had no time to look at it; for, as soon as the rank was assigned in the squadron, the signal for sailing appeared on the American Prince. When the fleet was under way, the second part of the port watch to which Tom Speers belonged was off duty, the first part being in charge of the vessel.

O'Hara, the fourth lieutenant, was his associate watch officer. The Irish Italian had treated him very handsomely from the moment the rank of the newcomer into the cabin was announced. They were to spend days and nights together in charge of the deck, and it was pleasant to be on good terms with each other. They had a long talk together as soon as the Tritonia was clear of the Bay of Gibraltar.

While they were thus engaged, Speers took from his pocket the telegraph despatch, which got into his hand by accident rather than by design. He had been too much interested in the conversation with O'Hara to think of it before. He took it from his pocket that he might not forget it again, and not with the intention of opening it in the presence of his companion; but it attracted the attention of the fourth lieutenant.

"What have you there, Speers?" asked O'Hara. "A letter from home? We have had no mail in the ship for a fortnight."

"No: it is not a letter," replied Tom Speers very indifferently.

"Not a letter? isn't it in an envelope?" demanded O'Hara, more interested in the matter than the owner of the document.

"It is a telegraph despatch, which was brought to me just as all hands were piped to muster this morning."

"I hope none of your friends are sick or dead," added the lieutenant, with a show of sympathy.

"I have no near friends to die or be sick."

"Who sends you the despatch, then?"

"I don't know: I haven't opened it yet."

"You haven't? What is the telegraph for but to hurry up things? and you haven't opened the envelope yet!" exclaimed the impulsive young Irishman.

"I will open it now," said Tom, as he broke the seal.

"Faix, you are mighty cool about it," laughed O'Hara. "Where is it from?"

"From London. I will read it to you, O'Hara, if you will keep it to yourself."

"Oh, no! I don't ask to hear what's in it."

"But I want you to hear it."

"Then I will keep your secret."

"'Uncle dead; letters sent: come to London quick.
RODWOOD.'"

This was the despatch.

CHAPTER II.

THE LETTER FROM LONDON.

"I THOUGHT you said you had no friends to die or be sick," said O'Hara, when Tom Speers had read the neglected despatch.

"I said I had no near friends," explained Tom.

"Don't you call your uncle a near friend, especially if you have no others?"

"I should say that would depend upon circumstances. I never lived with my uncle, and I never saw a great deal of him. He was a very rich man: I have heard it said that he was worth five or six millions."

"Murder! what an uncle!" exclaimed O'Hara. "Five or six millions! that's a power of money. How many children had he?"

"None at all; not a chick nor a child," replied Tom, amused at the manner of his companion, who always indulged in the brogue when he was excited.

"Howly St. Patrick! five or six millions of money, and not a child in the world? What has he done with it all?"

"I don't know," replied Tom coolly.

"How many brothers and sisters had he?" asked

O'Hara, opening his mouth with the interest he felt in the case.

"None at all."

"How can he be your uncle, then? That's what bothers me."

"My father was his only brother, and they had no sisters. My father died when I was ten years old; and my mother died two years ago, just before I joined the academy ship."

"Begorra, then you are the heir of the five or six millions!" shouted O'Hara, as excited as though all the money were coming to him. "Faix, I'm glad to be in the same watch with you! I shall make it the business of my loife to cultivate your frindship."

"I don't think it will pay for you to do so, for I never saw my uncle a dozen times in my life; and I am confident he has given his money to some other person," answered Tom, laughing at the enthusiasm of his companion. "He never did a thing for me, and, what is worse, he never did a thing for my mother when she needed help; and so it isn't likely that he has left any of his money for me."

"Whose name is it signed to the despatch?"

"Rodwood; Judge Rodwood. He always was a great crony and adviser of my uncle; and now I suppose he is the executor or administrator."

"Why should he telegraph to you if your uncle didn't lave you the money?" demanded O'Hara warmly.

"I don't know: I may get the letters he sent before we sail for home."

"But he says you are to go to London quick; and I shall not have you in my watch, after all."

"Yes, you will; for I shall not go to London," added Tom decidedly.

"Howly Mother! not go, when there is five or six millions of money waiting for you to put your hand to it?" gasped O'Hara.

"I don't know that there is even a single dollar waiting for me; and if I knew there were a million I wouldn't go," answered Tom, laughing at his friend's zeal.

"You wouldn't! what are you made of? You are cowlder than a frozen brickbat! What's the rayson you won't go?" inquired the lieutenant.

"I'll tell you why. My father died worth only about five thousand dollars. My mother kept this money for me; and she took care of me with only an income of three hundred and fifty dollars a year. She asked my uncle for a little help, and he took no notice of her letter. This was a year before she died, and she wanted to send me to college. Then she went to see him, thinking he might not have got the letter. He put her off for a time; but he finally told her he would do nothing for her. I never went to see him after that, though he often sent for me. He did not like my mother, and he never invited her to his house.

"After my mother died, I made up my mind that I wanted to go to sea, and work my way up to be captain of a ship. My mother's brother was my guardian, and he consented to use my little fortune in paying my expenses in this institution. Now I am here; and I have just got waked up as I never was before. At one bound, I have become first master of the Tritonia. I like the berth; and I am going to do a great deal better than I have yet. Now, do you think I will leave this high place in the vessel at the call of one I don't care a straw about? I never even saw Judge Rodwood, though I have heard enough about him."

"He may be your guardian under the will."

"I don't care if he is: I have only one guardian that I know any thing about, and that's my uncle on my mother's side. I like this situation too well to leave it," continued Tom, independent as a basket of chips.

"But the money?" suggested O'Hara.

"I don't know that my rich uncle has left me any money; and, in fact, I don't care if he has. I have not quite forgiven him for refusing to help my mother."

"You might take his money, whether you forgive him or not."

"Now he is dead, I am willing to forgive him; but I don't ask any favors of him or his estate."

"Faix, you are moighty indepindint."

"I love the Tritonia with all my heart just now; and I wouldn't leave her for filthy lucre any more than I would cast off the girl that loved me for it. Judge Rodwood is a great boatman, and has a steam yacht, though I believe my uncle owned it; so that I might have a chance to go to sea in good shape if I went to him. But I like my place on board this vessel better; and I mean to stay here as long as I can. I have told you all about my affairs, O'Hara; and now you will not blow on me, will you?"

"Faix, I won't, thin! Not a word shall pass my lips," protested the warm-hearted Irishman.

"If the vice-principal should see this message, or hear of it, he would tell Mr. Lowington; and he might make me go to London, whether **I am** willing or not," added Tom rather anxiously.

"I'm sure he would make you go to London for your own good. But not a word will I spake till I have your permission to do so."

"Thank you, O'Hara: **I** am sure we shall be **good** friends."

"You may bet your life on that! You are a broth **of a boy,** with five or six millions, more or less, **in your** trousers-pocket; and you may depind upon it, I'll stick **to you like a brother,"** said O'Hara, with a wild laugh.

"Don't **consider me an** heir **till** we have further information. But we were very good friends before I read this message to you."

"Faix, we were!"

The conversation was continued till the two officers were called to attend to their duties, when the first part **of the** watch was relieved. The following week was spent at Seville, and then the squadron returned **to** Gibraltar. The vessels had hardly anchored before Mr. Lowington's agent came off with a mail for the students and others on board. There was a letter for Tom Speers.

He put it into his pocket without stopping to read it, though not till he had seen that the post-mark was London. This was the letter alluded to in the telegraphic despatch; and doubtless it contained full par**ticulars of the death of his uncle, and** an explanation of the reason why he **was summoned to London.** Tom was not inclined to read it, for he did not wish **to be** told of any thing that would call him away from the Tritonia. His ambition was thoroughly aroused, and he was resolved to win the highest position in the vessel.

All who had received letters from home were busy reading them, and the discipline of the squadron was sufficiently relaxed to permit them to do so without interruption; but Tom Speers put his letter into his pocket. O'Hara had news from home, and he was busy digesting it, so that he could not speak to him about his affairs. He felt the need of counsel, while he dreaded to receive it lest it should oblige him to abandon the Tritonia and the brilliant hopes of the future.

Perhaps his uncle had left him a fortune, for there were a dozen fortunes in the vast pile of wealth the dead man had left behind him. It was even probable, in Tom's estimation, that he had done so, for he had been named after his uncle; and, if he did not care for his nephew, he might desire to have his name live after he could no longer bear it except upon the costly monument that marked his last resting-place. The young man felt no deep affection for his uncle, and had no great respect for his memory. A few thousands given to his mother while she was pinching herself to bring up her boy would have been better than as many hundred thousands to him now that she was gone.

Tom felt that he was alone in the world, and he had only to look out for himself. While he cherished no spite or ill-will towards his departed uncle, he did not quite like the idea of being made a rich man by his bounty. He was very proud and independent; and to accept a fortune from his uncle, seemed almost like treachery to his mother. It was the sentimentalism of the young man, which a few years of contact with the world would obliterate.

The letter from Judge Rodwood was in his pocket, and it seemed to burn there. He was curious to know its contents, but he did not wish to be influenced by any thing it might contain. He did not like to be tempted by wealth to give up his present ambitious prospects. He thought every minute, as he looked at his shipmates reading their letters from home, that he would open the one from the judge; but he did not. He sat upon the quarter-deck, gazing listlessly at all the objects in sight, from the lofty rock bristling with guns and batteries, to the scenes which were transpiring on board of the schooner; but he could not decide to do any thing to settle the present problem of existence.

He had made up his mind to be a sailor. He had longed for a "life on the ocean wave" since he was a small boy, and read the tales of the sea; but his devotion to his mother did not permit him to mention the subject after he had observed her shudder when he alluded to it for the first and last time. But he had dreamed, all the time, of roaming the seas, and visiting the distant lands of the earth. He had put himself in the way to realize these visions as soon as he had in a measure recovered from the deep grief occasioned by the death of his mother. Now, when he had almost reached the pinnacle of his hopes, came this command of his uncle's executor — as he supposed the judge was — to abandon his delightful mission.

But Judge Rodwood was not his guardian, so far as he knew; and he was not willing to recognize his right to order him to London. Perry Bowman, his mother's brother, was all the guardian he could recognize. This gentleman had possession of his little fortune, or what was left of it; for his expenses in the academy squadron had already absorbed a considerable portion of the principal, besides the income.

While he was thinking of the subject, unable to come to a decision in regard to the letter, which he was confident was a repetition of the order for him to hasten to London, he saw a boat leave the American Prince, and pull first to the Josephine, and then to the Tritonia. The officer in charge of it delivered a note to each vice-principal, and then returned to the steamer, which was still taking in coal at the station.

All the preparation for the voyage among "The Isles of the Sea" had been completed on board of the two consorts. All the water-tanks and spare casks had been filled with water, and an abundance of fresh and salt provisions had been taken on board. The compasses had been adjusted, and the chronometers had been regulated; and every thing was in readiness for sailing at a moment's notice, though the steamer would not have received all her coal till after dark.

The boat which brought the note had hardly returned to the flag-ship before the signal for sailing appeared at the mainmast of the Tritonia. Word was passed along among the officers, that the two schooners would sail at ten, leaving the American Prince to follow in the evening.

"We are off in ten minutes," said O'Hara, disturbing the meditations of Tom Speers, as soon as the news had been circulated among the students.

"I am not sorry that we are not to wait all day in port for the steamer," replied Tom. "You have had letters from home, O'Hara. I hope your friends are all well."

"First class," replied the fourth lieutenant. "And did you get the letters from London of which you were advised in the despatch?"

"I got one letter, but it is a very thick one, and very likely the envelope contains two or three of them."

"Well, what is it all about? How much money has your uncle left you?" asked O'Hara glibly, but with deep interest manifested in his bright eyes.

"I don't know: I haven't opened the letter yet," replied Tom, with a smile.

"Haven't opened it!" exclaimed the lieutenant, holding up both hands in amazement. "Upon my sowl, you are a lunatic, Speers! you haven't a head upon your shoulders at all, at all!"

"Now, I think I have," added Tom, laughing heartily at the earnestness of his companion. "Did you open your letters?"

"To be sure I did."

"Why did you open them?"

"Why did I open them? Howly Mother, what a question! Why did I open them? To see what was in them. What else would I open them for?"

"For nothing else. You wanted to know what was in them; and the right thing for you to do was to open them. I don't want to know what is in mine; and for that reason I don't open them. Isn't my way of doing it just as sensible as yours?" demanded Tom, satisfied with his logic.

"You don't want to know what is in them! By the powers, that's the rayson why you are a lunatic! I don't know but I ought to report you to the vice-principal before we sail, that you may have proper medical tratement before we get out of the raych of the docther."

"Don't do that, if you please, O'Hara," said Tom earnestly. "I told you the reason why I did not wish to be sent to London."

"Never you fear. Sure, it's joking I was. I wouldn't mutther the first taste of a sound to bother you; but, upon my sowl, you are the quayrest boy I ever met in the whole course of my life. You don't care a straw how much money your rich uncle has left you!"

"I don't think I do. If he had given my poor mother a hundredth part of his big fortune when she was alive, I would have blessed his memory, and heeded his slightest wish, alive or dead."

"Then the executor of your uncle must go down on his knees, and beg you to take the fortune he has left you!" exclaimed the lieutenant. "If you don't want it yourself, take the money, and hand it over to the poor, myself among the number."

"I suppose I shall take whatever my uncle has left me; and I shall try to make a good use of it. But when I came into the academy squadron, I had made up my mind that I would be the architect of my own fortunes. I came here to learn the arts of seamanship and navigation as the means to earn my own living. I don't feel like turning away from my plan yet. I love the sea."

"But with all the money your uncle will leave you, can't you sail all over the world in your own yacht; and that yacht a steamer like the American Prince, or a full-rigged ship like the Young America? What are you talking about?"

"But I want to finish my course in the Tritonia; and, if you won't laugh at me, I mean to be the captain of her before she reaches the shores of the United States," said Tom, with enthusiasm.

"Oh, murther! is that what's the matter wid you?" ejaculated O'Hara, with a laugh. "I had that same fayver; and, when I first got into the Tritonia, I said to myself that I would be the captain of her in six months; and now it's more than a year I'm in her, and I'm only fourth lieutenant."

"If I fail, I fail; but I shall do all I can to win the position."

"But don't be a lunatic any longer! Open the letter, and see what's the matter. Faix, I'm dying with curiosity to know what's in it," continued the lieutenant.

"One reason why I did not open it before was that I wanted to talk with you about it; for I believe you are the best friend I have in the ship," said Tom earnestly; for he had a great admiration for his fellow watch-officer.

"Thank you for that. Upon my sowl, I think you are a good fellow, if you are a lunatic on the letter. Take the advice of your best friend on board, and see what's in that envelope immejitly."

"I will, since you advise it," replied Tom, taking the letter from his pocket.

While O'Hara was glancing at the superscription, the boatswain's whistle sounded through the ship.

"All hands, up anchor!" shouted that officer, after he had piped the call.

Tom Speers grasped the letter, and returned it to his pocket. At the next instant he was at his station, for with his lofty ambition he could not afford to be the last in his place. The first lieutenant was in position on the quarter-deck, with the speaking-trumpet in his hand, though it was an emblem of authority, rather than a useful implement in a quiet time.

"Man the capstan!" said this high official, in moderate tones, considering the magnitude of the position he filled.

The order was repeated by the other officers till it came to the forecastle. Every seaman knew precisely what he was to do in the operation of weighing the anchor; and in a moment the bars were shipped and swiftered. All hands were then in position, and waiting for the next order.

"Heave around! Heave in the cable to a short stay!" added the first lieutenant; and the order went forward as before.

The first master had been directed to inform him when the cable had the proper scope, which had been indicated to him.

"Avast heaving!" said Tom Speers. "Cable at a short stay, sir," he added to the first lieutenant.

"Pawl the capstan! Unship the bars!" continued the executive officer.

The cable was well stoppered, or secured where it was. About three-fourths of the whole of the cable which had been run out was hauled in by the operations described. The wind was moderate in the harbor, and only enough was now out to hold the vessel while the rest of the preparations were made for getting under way. The part out was "up and down," and a few turns of the capstan would have lifted the anchor clear of the bottom.

The length of cable used in anchoring, or in holding the vessel at a short stay, requires the exercise of discretion and judgment; but the young officers were required to determine for themselves all these questions. The harder it blows, or the swifter the tide, the greater the scope of cable needed. It is true, the adult boatswain was always on hand to see that the work was properly done on the forecastle; and the vice-principal, who was the only adult seaman in the cabin, closely observed the manœuvres made; but they never interfered, unless the safety of the vessel required them to do so. If the young officers were at fault, they were criticised afterwards, when the crew were not present.

"Stations for loosing sail!" said the first lieutenant, when the cable was at a short stay.

The fore-topsail was shaken out, the foresail and mainsail were set; and the order was given to man the jib and flying-jib halyards, and to ship the capstan bars again.

"Anchor a-weigh, sir!" reported the first master on the forecastle.

Tom Speers saw that the anchor was clear of the bottom when the hands at the capstan had heaved a few turns.

"Let go the downhauls, and hoist away!" added the executive officer; and at the order up went the jib and flying-jib.

The wind was about north, and the sails were trimmed as they filled. As soon as the Tritonia was fairly under way, her fore-topmast-staysail, fore-top-gallant-sail, and main-gaff-topsail were set. At the same time the order was given to cat and fish the anchor, or hoist it up to the cat-head, and then put it in its usual position when the vessel was at sea.

As the beautiful craft swung around, and the breeze filled her sails, ringing cheers came from the shore and from the men-of-war in the harbor; all of which were returned with vigor by the young tars. With the wind on the beam, the two schooners stood out of the bay, and in a short time were passing through the Strait of Gibraltar. As they went out into the broad ocean, the wind freshened till they were making ten knots an hour. It was study time for the port-watch, and Tom had no chance yet to read his letter.

CHAPTER III.

AN APPROACHING SQUALL.

THE port-watch were on duty from twelve till four in the afternoon; but the second part had their off time for the first two hours. The Tritonia was jumping at a lively pace in the white-capped sea, headed west, a quarter south. O'Hara had been impatiently waiting for this time to come to dive into the mysteries of that London letter. He was more anxious to know the contents of the envelope than Tom was.

As soon as the starboard watch had piped to dinner, the fourth lieutenant led the way to a place on the lee-side of the quarter-deck where they could be alone. Tom produced the important letter, and broke the seal. As he had surmised, it contained two other letters, one of them addressed to Mr. Lowington, the principal of the squadron, and the other in the handwriting of his maternal uncle.

"Sure, you can't deliver that one to Mr. Lowington now," said O'Hara, looking back to the distant land which would soon be out of sight.

"I am not anxious to deliver it; for I can guess the substance of what it contains," replied Tom.

"Well, what's in the letter from London?" asked the lieutenant impatiently.

Tom Speers unfolded the sheet. It was a brief business-like document, hardly covering a page of the paper, though written in a very open hand. It was dated on board steam-yacht Marian, at Southampton, though it had been mailed in London.

Thomas Speers, the millionnaire uncle of the first master, had died six weeks before. He had given about half of his immense fortune to charitable institutions, and the other half to his nephew. Judge Rodwood was appointed guardian and trustee, so far as this property was concerned. The judge had come to England in his steam-yacht in order that he might follow the academy squadron, if, as he feared, it had left Europe on its return voyage to America.

"Give me your hand, Speers!" said O'Hara with enthusiasm. "I was dead sure your uncle had made a *millionnaire* of you!"

"I was rather afraid he had," replied Tom moodily, as he glanced at the letter again. "He gives me no particulars of the death of my uncle, or in relation to the fortune."

"Upon my sowl, you are the quarist mortal that iver came into the world, or will iver go out of it after getting quare in it. You are afraid your uncle has made a millionnaire of you! Where is your gratitude?"

"I don't carry it in my trousers-pocket. The whole of it is, O'Hara, I am too much interested in the voyage of the Tritonia to care much about the contents of this letter. I have just become an officer, and I don't want to give up my position."

"I understand that; but what's the use of running away from the fortune that is waiting for you?"

"I don't intend to run away from it. I think it will keep till the Tritonia returns to the United States."

"Another of those letters is addressed to you. Will you leave that till to-morrow before you open it?"

"Not at all. This one is from my uncle, Perry Bowman; and I am always glad to hear from him," replied Tom, as he opened the letter. "'Wonderful news for you, my dear boy,'" continued the first master, reading from the letter: "'your uncle is dead, and has left you at least three millions of dollars: so much for bearing his name, for he wanted to preserve it after he was gone. You are to have the income of your money till you are twenty-five, and then a million every five years till you get the whole of it into your own hands. I have resigned my guardianship of you in favor of Judge Rodwood. I offered to pay over to him about four thousand dollars in my hands; but he declined to take it till you had formally named him as your guardian, as you have the right to do, so far as personal care is concerned. He advised me to pay over the money to you at once; and I send you a letter of credit for the amount. You may want it more before you get home than afterwards.'"

"Howly St. Patrick!" exclaimed O'Hara, as Tom opened the valuable document alluded to. "You are measly with money."

"That paper will be convenient, wherever I happen to be," said Tom, with a smile, as he put the letter of credit into his pocket-book. "I could have made a better use of it six months ago than I can now. I was poor as a church-mouse then, when most of the fellows were made of money."

"You can buy them all out now," added O'Hara. "Now, what are you going to do about this business, my lad?"

"I can't do any thing now: it is too late for me to go to London," replied Tom with a smile.

"I see you are satisfied with the matter as it is."

"I am."

"But Judge Rodwood is over here in his steam-yacht for the purpose of following the squadron, if he don't find it in European waters," added the lieutenant.

"I am willing he should follow it."

"When he begins to look into the matter, anybody in Gibraltar can tell him the fleet has gone to Madeira; and all he has to do is to follow you."

"I don't object."

"Of course you don't; but when he finds you, he will take you out of the vessel."

"I don't believe he will, if I am not ready to leave her. Don't my uncle Perry say I have the right to name my own guardian? if the judge don't do the right thing, I will not consent to name him as my guardian. But when I tell him I prefer to stay in the Tritonia, if he is a reasonable man, as I think he is, he will not object."

"But you are not doing the right thing yourself, my boy," protested O'Hara. "What kind of a way was it to put a telegraphic despatch in your pocket, and not open it? And what kind of a way was it to lave your letter unopened till it was too late to do what you were told by your guardian? Don't your uncle Perry tell you to come home as soon as ever you can?"

"He has resigned as my guardian; and the other one has not been properly appointed," said Tom, laughing at his own ingenuity in devising an excuse.

"How do you know what's in the letter to Mr. Lowington?" demanded the lieutenant.

"I have no doubt it contains an order for my discharge from the academy squadron," replied Tom. "I would deliver it, if the principal were only here; for I have no right to keep his letters back, whatever I do with my own."

"I think you had better give the letter to the vice-principal."

"I am willing to do that."

"I am afraid the powers that be will blame you for not opening the letter before we sailed," continued O'Hara.

"I am willing to bear the blame for what I have done," replied Tom; and, seeing the vice-principal coming up from the cabin, he delivered the letter to him as he reached the deck.

"Where did you get this?" asked Mr. Pelham, surprised to see a sealed letter to the principal so soon after leaving port.

"It was in a letter to me, which I did not open till just now," replied Tom.

"And why didn't you open it before the ship sailed?" demanded Mr. Pelham, quite as much astonished as the fourth lieutenant had been.

"I didn't care to open it, sir," answered Tom, wondering how he could get out of the scrape without telling the whole truth.

"That is very strange."

"I had some idea of what the letter contained," added Tom, with a smile.

"And that was the reason you didn't open it?"

"I was not interested in it."

"There seems to be something under all this, Speers," continued the vice-principal, looking into the honest face of the young man. "What is it?"

"A telegraph-despatch, sir," replied Tom, handing the document to Mr. Pelham.

Tom found, after due consideration, that there was no way out of the scrape; and he explained the whole matter in full.

"I don't care to have my shipmates know about this, sir," said Tom, when he had told the whole story.

"It is your private affair, and you have a right to keep it to yourself if you choose," replied Mr. Pelham; "and I shall respect your wishes."

"I have told O'Hara about it, but no one else."

"But it cannot be long concealed that we have a millionnaire on board," added the vice-principal, laughing. "Judge Rodwood will follow the squadron to Madeira."

"When I see him I hope he will permit me to remain in the Tritonia; and till that time I don't care to have any thing said."

"Very well. But I think you ought to have opened your letter before the vessel sailed. It was hardly treating Judge Rodwood with proper respect, to take no notice of his telegraphic despatch."

"Perhaps it was not, sir; but I did not know what to do. I suppose the whole of it is, that I didn't want to leave the vessel; and I was afraid if I answered the despatch, or opened the letters, I might have to go," pleaded Tom honestly. "I have no doubt that letter to Mr. Lowington contains a request for my discharge."

"Probably it does; but I don't see that any thing can be done about it now. The vessel is almost out of sight of land," said Mr. Pelham, smiling; and he looked as though he rather sympathized with the first master in the trials and tribulations cast upon him by his coming fortune. "I will consult with Mr. Fluxion, who is my senior in rank, as soon as possible; though the sea is rather too heavy just now to communicate with the Josephine, except in a case of emergency."

"I am in no hurry to have any thing done," replied Tom, laughing and shrugging his shoulders.

"The last log gave us ten knots, and the wind is increasing. At this rate we may get to Madeira before the American Prince overhauls us," added the vice-principal.

"I am willing," chuckled Tom.

Mr. Pelham descended to the steerage to resume his duties as instructor in navigation. Tom was very well satisfied with the result of his interview, and joined O'Hara on the lee side of the vessel. His position was safe, for the present at least; and he hoped Judge Rodwood would be reasonable enough to allow him to complete his course in the academy squadron.

"Well, my boy, did you get a black eye from the vice?" asked O'Hara, who had been watching the conference with the most intense interest.

"Not a bit of it: Mr. Pelham knows how it is himself, and he behaved very handsomely," replied Tom cheerfully.

"I suppose the news will be all over the ship now before the dog-watches are out," added O'Hara.

"Three of us have the secret now; and I think we are strong enough to keep it."

"Then it can't be kept."

"If you keep a stopper on your jaw-tackle, O'Hara, it will be safe till Judge Rodwood arrives at Madeira, though I am not without a hope that we shall be gone when he comes."

"That is your little game, is it?"

"There is no game about it. It is only a hope I have; and I shall do nothing wrong about it."

"Of course you won't do any thing wrong: you are not the fellow for that," added O'Hara, with a little taste of Irish blarney.

"I am not so high-toned as Raymond; but, if I intend to be captain of this vessel, of course I can't afford to be on the wrong side of any question; for it is a matter of marks as well as of morality," replied Tom, with a laugh.

The matter was settled, for the present at least, so far as the student was concerned. But the vice-principal was not quite satisfied with the situation. The letter to Mr. Lowington ought to have been delivered before the vessel left Gibraltar. It might contain something more than an application for the discharge of the first master. He was very anxious to consult with the senior vice-principal; and, as soon as the recitation he had in hand was finished, he went on deck to take a look at the weather.

The quarter-watch had been changed, and O'Hara and Tom Speers were in charge of the deck. They had no opportunity to converse together now, for it was contrary to the rule for officers on duty to do any unnecessary talking. But they noticed the nervous manner of the vice-principal as he looked up to windward. The wind had been increasing since the Tritonia sailed in the forenoon. Though it still looked squally and threatening, as it had for the last three hours, there seemed to be a brief lull in the force of the wind, though the barometer was falling.

The Josephine was abreast of the Tritonia; for the two vessels were very equally matched, though each had its peculiar advantage in different points. The former could hug the wind a little closer, and the latter could gain a trifle on the other going free. Each ship's company bragged of its own craft, because each had got a little ahead of the other on its best course.

"Signal on the Josephine, sir," reported the lookout on the weather cat-head.

"Signal on the Josephine, Mr. O'Hara," repeated the first master in the waist.

"Call the signal-officer," added the fourth lieutenant.

The box containing the signals was opened; glasses were in demand; and the signal which the Josephine displayed was promptly examined.

"Do you make it out, Mr. Lingall?" asked O'Hara, rather impatiently, for it was an unusual thing for one vessel of the squadron to communicate with another under like circumstances.

"'Have you any'"—replied Lingall, who was the signal-officer, and who had carefully studied his duties since his unexpected promotion. "Reply that the signal is understood, quartermaster."

The proper flag was set, whereupon the Josephine began to display single letters, indicating that the article for which she desired to ask was not contained in the signal code. The process was slow, but it was sure in the end.

"How far have you got?" asked O'Hara.

"C-h-l-o," replied Lingall.

"By the powers, you have made a mistake, Mr. Lingall!" said the fourth lieutenant, with a laugh.

"I think not, sir: I take down each letter as it comes," replied Lingall.

"You have misplaced the letters: it is c-h-o-l they mean; and they want to ask if we have the c-h-o-l-i-c, colic."

"I think not, sir; for I don't believe that is the way they spell 'colic' on board of the Josephine," added Lingall, with a smile, and not quite sure that it was prudent to expose the blunder of his superior.

"Faix, you have me there! I see you have learned your spelling-lesson well, Mr. Lingall."

"'R,'" continued the signal-officer, adding another letter to the unfinished word.

"Chlor," said O'Hara. "That's not a nautical word, to be sure."

"No: it looks more like a medical term," added Mr. Pelham, who had joined the group gathered around the signal officer.

"'O,'" continued Lingall, as another letter was indicated.

"Chloro: that must be chloroform. The professors on board are going to perform a surgical operation."

"I think not: there is no doctor on board of the Josephine," added Mr. Pelham.

"It must be some doctor's stuff," persisted the fourth lieutenant.

"If you are patient for a few moments longer, you will not be under the necessity of guessing what is wanted. I am satisfied the word is chlorodyne," said the vice-principal.

"Chlorodyne!" exclaimed O'Hara. "Is that a rope, or something to eat?"

"Neither: it is a medicine with which all the vessels of the squadron are provided; and I have had occasion to administer it several times."

"If it's physic I've nothing to say; but if there is a rope in the ship that I don't know, I feel guilty," said O'Hara, with a mock sigh of relief.

"'D,'" continued Lingall, taking down the next letter of the word.

"That's enough," interposed Mr. Pelham. "The article wanted is chlorodyne; reply 'understood,'— yes."

This signal was transmitted, for the Tritonia had an abundant supply of the medicine named; and Mr. Pelham wondered how the Josephine happened to be out of the article, since it was Dr. Winstock's favorite remedy in all cases of colic or severe pain in the bowels.

"Heave to, and wait for a boat," was the next message interpreted from the signals.

The signal was duly reported to the captain, who

was studying his lessons in the cabin. He directed the officer of the deck to obey the order, which was regarded as coming from the senior vice-principal. Simultaneously the two vessels came up into the wind, backing their fore-topsails.

Mr. Pelham went down into the cabin as soon as the Tritonia was brought to; but he returned in a few moments, wearing his pea-jacket.

"This will afford me an opportunity to consult with the senior vice-principal in regard to your matter, Speers," said Mr. Pelham to the first master in the waist.

"I hope we shall not be ordered back," replied Tom, not a little annoyed at the prospect.

"I think there is no danger of that, Speers; but I feel obliged to make the case known to Mr. Fluxion: he will at least share the responsibility with me," replied Mr. Pelham.

Tom felt easier after this assurance. The vessel pitched very heavily in the sea when she was hove to; and, if the junior vice-principal had any doubt about the propriety of leaving the Tritonia at such a time, he did not express it to any one on board. Certainly the indications of the weather, as gathered from the barometer and the appearance of the heavens, were any thing but favorable.

The second cutter of the Josephine was hoisted out with its crew on board. The fact that the adult boatswain was sent in the boat, in addition to the usual crew, seemed to indicate that Mr. Fluxion would not send the boat unless he considered the occasion an emergency. It was probable that one of the students in the vessel was very sick, and that Mr. Fluxion believed the weather was better now than it was likely to be for some hours to come.

The cutter from the Josephine cast off from the schooner. The young oarsmen gave way with a will, and the boat began to rise and to plunge into the heavy sea. The two vessels were not more than a couple of cable-lengths apart; but the passage from one to the other occupied a considerable time.

The officer of the cutter skilfully brought his boat under the lee of the Tritonia. It was a perilous position, and it was in great danger of being dashed to pieces against the counter of the vessel. A rope was thrown to the bowman, who promptly secured it, and made it fast by catching a turn over the fore thwart.

The first master of the Josephine, who was in charge of the cutter, was a lithe little fellow; and, taking to the rope as a cat runs up a tree, he climbed to the deck of the Tritonia in the twinkling of an eye.

"That was well done, Mr. Pepper," said Mr. Pelham when the little officer stood before him, drenched to the skin by the seas that had broken over him. "You want chlorodyne."

"Yes, sir: we had a large bottle of it, but the steward dropped it on the floor of the steerage, and spilled the whole of it," replied Mr. Pepper. "Boyle is very sick with colic, or something of that sort; and Mr. Fluxion has no proper medicine for him."

"I shall go on board of the Josephine with you; and I have the bottle in my pocket," added the junior vice-principal, as he slid down the rope into the Josephine's cutter.

Mr. Pepper followed him, and the boat pulled back. As it was evident that she must return to the Tritonia, she was brought up under the counter of the Josephine. Mr. Pelham was the first to board the vessel.

"I am surprised that you should leave your charge, Pelham," said the senior vice-principal anxiously, and in a low tone, as his junior presented himself on the deck.

It took Mr. Pelham five minutes to tell the story of Tom Speers as briefly as it could be told.

"Never mind Speers or his letters," said Mr. Fluxion impatiently. "Return to the Tritonia at once!"

It was too late. A fearful squall was driving down upon the two vessels.

CHAPTER IV.

A VESSEL IN DISTRESS.

MR. PELHAM saw that he had made a mistake in leaving the Tritonia at such a time, though he would not have thought of doing so if the senior vice-principal had not sent the boat. But it was a case of severe sickness which had induced his superior to send out a boat in such a sea. The squall, which might prove to be a hurricane, was already roaring in the distance. In a moment more it would break upon the vessels.

"Get your boat in quick!" said Mr. Fluxion to the officer of the deck, in sharp tones, though not loud enough to be heard by the seamen. "Call all hands!"

At the same moment the senior vice-principal seized the speaking-trumpet in the hands of the officer of the deck, and, leaping into the main rigging, shouted,—

"Fill away! fill away!"

Whether, in the roar of the tempest, the officer in charge of the Tritonia heard him or not, the vessel immediately filled away. O'Hara was too good a sailor to be caught napping at such a time. He had sent for the captain as soon as he saw the squall coming; and, as this was a case of emergency in which the officer of the deck was authorized to act without waiting for orders, he had braced up the fore-yards on his own responsibility.

Capt. Wainwright came on deck before the schooner was fairly under way again. All hands were called, the lessons of the professors in the steerage were promptly abandoned, and almost in the twinkling of an eye the canvas was reduced to a storm staysail.

The Josephine had a bigger problem to solve: the officer of the deck sent for Capt. Vroome, but, without waiting for his coming, ordered the cutter to be hauled under the lee of the schooner; and it was hoisted up at the davits, carefully secured, and swung inboard.

As soon as the boat was clear of the water, the fore-braces were manned, and the yards trimmed, the vessel filling away as this was done. The orders came very rapidly from the first lieutenant for a moment; but they were executed as fast as they were given, and the vessel was soon under the same short canvas as the Tritonia.

The squall came down upon the little squadron, and the vessels reeled under it. But this was one of the emergencies which the students, especially the officers, of the academy squadron, had been faithfully trained to meet. The ships' companies had executed the manœuvre just completed, hundreds of times, in still water and at sea in a fresh breeze.

Though the fury of the squall lasted but a short time, it was succeeded by a severe gale, which had been sufficiently prognosticated by the barometer and the aspect of the heavens. When the first fierceness of the tempest had somewhat abated, the Josephine set her foresail, close reefed, and hoisted her jib. The wind still came from the north-west, and she resumed her course for the Madeira Islands.

Capt. Wainwright followed the example of his senior; and the two vessels were again standing on their course, which was still west, a quarter south. All went well till dark, though the vessels labored heavily in the ugly sea. The captain of the Tritonia was somewhat anxious about his craft, as he had no vice-principal on board upon whom he could lean if the situation became more trying. He walked the deck, keeping his gaze fixed to windward most of the time.

Since the squall a full watch had been kept on duty. Scott was in charge of the deck when the darkness, deep and dense, settled down upon the scene. Even with only the jib and the double-reefed foresail, the Tritonia rolled till the water frequently came in over her high bulwarks, while the seas broke in heavy sheets over the top-gallant forecastle.

"This will be a nasty night, Scott," said the captain, pausing in his walk on the weather side of the vessel.

"I never saw any thing worse," replied the second lieutenant. "But I think we shall be able to keep most of the water on the outside of her."

"She is wetter on deck than I ever saw her before," added Capt. Wainwright.

"Or behind either."

"I am afraid we shall lose sight of the Josephine before morning."

"If we do, I suppose, like any other old wine-bibbers, we can find our way to Madeira."

"But I am very sorry that Mr. Pelham was unable to return," continued the captain.

"I think he will feel worse about it than any one else," answered Scott.

"It is for his sake that I am sorry."

"I don't object to a cruise on our own account as long as we keep within the strict line of duty."

"I am not alarmed, though in such a night as this I cannot help feeling a little anxious about the vessel," said Capt. Wainwright. "I had no idea that we should have such a storm as this proves to be. I don't see the lights of the Josephine."

"I saw her starboard light within five minutes," added Scott, as he peered through the gloom of the night in the direction the consort had last been seen. "She can't be far from us."

"I see it now," added the captain. "The tops of the waves shut it out from our view at times."

"Now we have lost it again."

The Tritonia rolled and pitched fearfully, and of course the Josephine was doing the same. The night was a long and dismal one. Twice it became necessary to call all hands to lay the vessel to under the storm staysail. Even the jib and reefed foresail were too much for her.

Shortly after the captain and second lieutenant were observing the lights of the Josephine, they disappeared, and were not seen again. A very heavy rain began to pour down, and it was thought that the thickness of the weather alone prevented them from seeing her. Capt. Wainwright declared that it was the worst night he had seen since he had been in the Tritonia; and Mr. Marline confirmed his view of the matter,

The morning broke dull and heavy, with a fierce rain-storm still battering against the rigging. The captain had been on deck about all night, and had turned in at eight bells in the morning when the watch was changed, leaving the first lieutenant in charge of the deck.

"Heard a gun off the port bow," reported the lookout on the top-gallant forecastle.

"Are you sure it was a gun?" asked Richards, the fourth master, to whom the report was made.

"It was a good way off; but I'm pretty sure it was a gun," replied the seaman. "There it is again! I am sure of it now."

Richards heard the gun himself this time, though it was only a dull report, evidently coming from a great distance. He reported it to the officer of the deck.

"I haven't heard it," said Greenwood.

"You can hardly make out the sound above the roar and swash of the sea. I heard it myself just now," added Richards.

They listened attentively for some minutes, but without hearing the gun again. The first lieutenant concluded that the officer and seaman had been mistaken, and he sent the fourth master back to his station. All hands forward listened again for some time; but the gun was not heard.

"I was sure I heard it," said Richards to the second master.

"There are so many strange sounds in a storm like this, that you can't be sure of any thing," replied Raymond. "I hope you didn't hear a gun, for it can only be a signal of distress in such a storm."

But Richards was piqued at the idea of having made a false report, and he kept his ears wide open for the next hour. Once he thought he heard the sound again, but he did not mention it, though the lookout glanced at him to indicate that he had heard something.

It was too thick and dark to see any thing, even if there had been a sinking ship within a cable's length of the Tritonia. Nearly half an hour later he heard the sound again. It was a sort of dull and indistinct "thud," which might have been made by a wave under the counter of the schooner; but it came from a distance, and from the same direction as before.

"Gun on the weather-bow, sir," repeated the lookout; and this time he spoke so confidently that the fourth master deemed it his duty to report again to the officer of the deck.

"I imagined I heard it myself this time," replied Greenwood, looking very anxious. "But it might have been a gun, and it might not."

"I think it was a gun; and I have heard it several times," answered Richards.

"I don't like to call the captain, after he has been on deck all night, for nothing," continued the first lieutenant, looking very much troubled, as he wiped the spray from his face.

"If it is a gun, it can only mean that some vessel is in distress," added Richards. "I think we had better err on the side of humanity."

"No doubt of it; but we are not running away from the direction you report the sound as coming from."

"If the vessel is disabled, she is drifting this way;

and we can hardly work to windward in this weather."

"Remain on the quarter-deck, if you please, Mr. Richards, and see if you can make out the gun again," continued Greenwood.

"I hardly expect to hear it again for half an hour; for it is that time since I heard it last," said Richards, as he climbed into the weather main rigging.

Greenwood continued to walk the deck along the life line, which had been extended fore and aft for the safety of the officers and seamen on duty. As the fourth master had suggested, the sound was not heard again till nearly another half-hour had elapsed. Then it was heard, and so distinctly that Richards thought there could be no mistake about it this time.

"I heard it myself," said the officer of the deck when the report was made to him. "I will thank you to call the captain, and inform him that signal-guns have been heard on the weather-bow."

Richards came down from his perch in the weather rigging, and went below. Wainwright awoke from a heavy slumber at the knock on his door; but he was himself at once, and inquired carefully into the matter of the report till he had satisfied himself that guns had really been heard. Hastily putting on his pea-jacket, he went on deck.

All hands gazed earnestly at him as he appeared, and watched his movements with intense interest. The vice-principal was not on board, and Capt. Wainwright was the supreme authority. Mr. Primback, the senior professor, who was nominally the head of the institution in the absence of the vice-principal, knew no more about a ship, or about nautical matters, than a man that had never seen the ocean. The adult boat-swain and carpenter were seamen, and were competent advisers; but they were without authority in the absence of Mr. Pelham.

While Capt. Wainwright was inquiring into the situation, the signal-gun was repeated; and this time it could be plainly heard by all on deck. It was more nearly on the beam than before. The Tritonia was on her course. The wind, which had been rather variable during the night, was now from the north, veering to the west. The vessel in distress was therefore almost dead to windward.

"Brace her sharp up, Mr. Greenwood," said the captain, as soon as he had fully taken in the situation.

The first lieutenant gave the necessary orders in detail to carry out the command of the captain. The Tritonia promptly answered her helm, and, coming up into the wind, rose upon the tremendous sea, and then darted down into the trough, while the crest of the wave broke upon her top-gallant forecastle.

"We can't make much beating to windward under a double-reefed foresail, in such a sea as this," said Greenwood.

"I am afraid not," replied the captain, as he returned to the cabin to inform the senior professor of the action he had taken.

"How do you know it is a ship in distress?" asked Mr. Primback, greatly disturbed by the announcement.

"Ships at sea don't fire guns for nothing in such a sea as this," answered Wainwright.

"It may be an engagement between a French and a

German vessel; for France and Germany are unhappily at war with each other at this time," suggested the professor.

"I think not, sir; for vessels in action would be likely to fire oftener than once in half an hour," replied the captain.

"Very true: I think they would be likely to discharge their guns more frequently than this," added Mr. Primback, looking wise. "You feel confident that the guns are from a ship in distress?"

"I feel reasonably sure of it, sir."

"Then I suppose it is quite proper to go to her assistance," said the professor, with an inquiring look at the young commander.

"Entirely proper, Mr. Primback."

"I am sorry that some other vessel does not have this duty imposed upon it. Nevertheless, as the sea is very stormy, and the violence of the motion does not permit the conducting of the regular recitations, I dare say that no great loss of time will result from this deviation from the true course of the vessel."

"I should say not, sir," added the captain.

"Have you consulted with Mr. Marline, in the unfortunate absence at this time of Mr. Pelham?"

"I have not done so, sir. Mr. Marline turned in, and"—

"Did what? Do me the favor to speak the English language when you address me," interposed the professor, who could not tolerate even the mildest of nautical terms.

"He went to bed, sir."

"Ah, he retired?"

"Yes, sir: he turned in when " —

"Retired, if you please."

"Yes, sir: he retired from the deck when I did; and I have not seen him since the signal-guns were reported to me."

"Mr. Marline is a prudent mariner; and I request that you confer with him before any decided steps are taken."

"But I have taken the decided step already; for I have hauled her up " —

"How can that be when the vessel is far out of sight of the land? You speak in enigmas," interrupted Mr. Primback.

"We braced her up " —

"In English, sir," said the professor rather sternly.

"I don't know that I can describe nautical manœuvres in any other than nautical language," said Wainwright. "We were going with the wind free before, sir " —

"The wind is always free, Wainwright: no one can control it."

"Well, sir, I caused the schooner to be turned so that she is headed as near as she can go in the direction from which the wind comes."

"That is quite intelligible. I thank you."

"The vessel is now headed as near as can be towards the ship in distress. If you wish me to speak to Mr. Marline I will do so, sir; but I think it is better to let him sleep, after being on deck as he was all night."

"He must be somewhat fatigued; and you may wait till he gets up from his bed."

Wainwright withdrew from the cabin of the professor, and went on deck again. It was still too thick to make out the vessel in distress; and, when he had directed the first lieutenant to call him if occasion should require, he went to his state-room to obtain the rest he needed.

The guns were repeated every half-hour as before; and it was evident that the two vessels were coming nearer together. The rain had ceased, but a thick fog had settled down upon the ocean, and concealed the two craft from each other. But the captain could not sleep, weary as he was, in his anxiety about the wreck to windward of the Tritonia. He went on deck. The gun sounded as though the vessel in distress was not more than a mile distant.

There was no gun on board of the schooner, or he would have used it to inform the sufferers that assistance was at hand.

The Tritonia had tacked several times in the heavy sea; and, after the captain came on deck the second time, he had ordered the addition of a close-reefed mainsail to the vessel, for the wind seemed to have abated a trifle.

"I see her!" shouted the lookout forward.

"Where away?" demanded the fourth master, springing upon the rail of the vessel, ready to get into the fore-rigging.

"Sharp on the weather-bow."

"I see her," added Richards, as he made out the dim outline of the craft in the fog, which had lifted a little as if to reveal the presence of the sufferer.

"She is a steamer!" shouted Richards, as he

jumped down upon the deck, and hurried aft as rapidly as the uneasy motion of the Tritonia would permit.

He reported to the first lieutenant the position of the steamer; and immediately all the officers leaped upon the rail, and looked intently to windward to obtain a view of her.

"What do you make of her, Mr. Greenwood?" asked Capt. Wainwright, who was of course too dignified to leave the quarter-deck.

"She is a steamer, barkentine rig. She is heeled over to port, with her stern settled deep in the water," replied the first lieutenant.

"Down from the rail!" shouted the captain.

The order was repeated by the officer of the deck, and the momentary panic caused by the appearance of the wreck gave place to the usual order on board of the schooner. The captain sent the fourth master to call Marline; and this old salt was greatly surprised when he learned what had been done while he slept.

"How do we happen to be headed to the nor'ard, captain?" asked he, after he had glanced at the compass.

"We have been working to windward for the last four hours in search of this vessel, for we heard her signal-guns at two bells in the morning watch," replied the captain, with a smile at the blank look of astonishment on the face of the boatswain. "Mr. Primback desired me to confer with you as soon as you came on deck."

"Why was I not called before?"

"I thought it best not to disturb you after you had been all night on deck."

"And you were on deck all night also."

"I was; but I was called at two bells. I propose to lie to under the lee of the steamer, and send a boat on board of her as soon as practicable," continued the captain. "What do you think of that idea?"

"I don't think much of it," replied the old sailor bluntly. "Do you think of sending a boat on board of the wreck at once?"

"Do you think it is safe to get out a boat?"

"I don't think it is safe; and for that reason I shouldn't lay her to."

"What would you do?" asked Capt. Wainwright, rather nettled by the disapproval of the boatswain.

"I should run as near the wreck as possible, hail them, and say we will stand by them; then stand off and on till the weather moderates a little. A boat might live now; but the steamer floats, and don't seem to be in any immediate danger of going down," said Mr. Marline, when he had examined the condition of the wreck as well as he could in the fog.

"I like that plan," replied the captain; "but I thought we might be able to reach the wreck in a boat."

"If there was any need of it, we might," added the boatswain, now getting a better view of the steamer. "She has a hole in her starboard bow; she has been run into by another vessel. I think the water poured into that hole in the beginning, flowed aft, and settled her down by the stern so as to lift the opening out of the water. That is what saved her. It was a miracle."

The Tritonia tacked again, and then stood under the stern of the wreck. Only one man, whose gray locks were streaming in the fresh wind, could be seen on board of her.

"We will stand by you!" shouted Greenwood through the trumpet, as the Tritonia passed within a few fathoms of the steamer.

"Two ladies on board!" yelled the man in response to the hail.

"We will save them!" replied Greenwood.

The Tritonia passed out of hailing distance.

CHAPTER V.

BOARDING THE WRECK.

"THERE seems to be but one man on board the wreck," said Wainwright, when the Tritonia had passed out of hailing distance.

"And he says there are two women on board," added Marline. "It seems to me that I have heard that man's voice before."

"He speaks plain English, at any rate," continued the captain. "Have you any idea what has become of the Josephine, Mr. Marline?"

"It was easy enough to lose her in such a night as the last. She may have carried sail while we were laying to, or we may have carried sail while she was doing so. She may have been within a few miles of us when we changed our course to the nor'ard."

"But, if she had been anywhere near us, she would have heard the guns on this steamer," suggested Wainwright.

"I think we shall have a change of weather soon, and we shall find out where she is."

"The barometer is rising; and I am confident, if the Josephine's people heard those guns, she will follow them up, and we shall see her in the course of the forenoon."

"No doubt of it," replied Marline. "The fog is lifting now."

"The steamer seems to be in no danger of sinking," added Wainwright, as he brought his glass to bear upon her. "Her stern is well down in the water, but her bow is clear up in the air."

"She won't go down unless the weather gets worse. It is moderating very rapidly."

"What can we do with the steamer after we get on board of her?" asked the captain, who had been considering this question since the wreck was first discovered.

"I don't know that we can do any thing but save the passengers," replied Marline.

"But the vessel seems to be in good condition; and it may be possible to take her into port."

"It may be; but I think we have not force enough to handle her, if the crew have deserted her."

"If we save her, won't she belong to us?" inquired Wainwright, who had been a seaman on the Josephine when she picked up a Dutch vessel in the North Sea, in a sinking condition.

"No; but the judges of the Marine Court, or whatever they call it over here, decide what part of the value of the vessel shall be given to those that save her."

"It is a case of salvage, then. I didn't know but the vessel, if she had been wholly abandoned, might go to those who picked her up."

"I am no sea-lawyer, and I don't know much about

it; but my notion is, that if the owners claim her, they take her by paying the salvage decreed by the court. I am sorry Mr. Pelham is not here to settle all the questions that may come up concerning this steamer."

"I think we shall be able to settle them somehow or other," replied Wainwright confidently. "It would be a big thing for the Tritonia to send that vessel into port."

"So it would; but it will be a bigger thing to save the passengers on board of her. Though we see but one man on board of her, there may be a dozen or twenty," added Marline.

"What are they about, if there are any others in her?"

"That's more than I know; but men lose their heads in times of trouble. The crew may have broken into the rum-barrels, and got drunk. A crew is very likely to do such a thing after the discipline of the vessel is lost."

"Do you suppose that is the case?"

"I don't suppose any thing about it: I have known just such things to happen," answered Marline, who evidently did not care to continue the conversation, for he did not wish to commit himself to any thing.

The sea was still too heavy, when the port watch came on duty at eight o'clock, to allow any recitation to be conducted in the steerage. Professor Primback, with his supreme contempt for all things nautical, was unable to keep on his legs, and was therefore incompetent to sustain the dignity of his position. He knew that the students would laugh if a smart sea should upset him, or cause him to reel, during his demonstration at the blackboard; and he was unwilling to tempt them. For this reason it was usually vacation time in very stormy weather. The seamen not on duty were reclining in their berths, or wedged into various corners where they could save themselves from being pitched about by the savage plunging of the vessel. Every movable thing had been secured by the stewards, for neither tables nor stools would stay upon their legs.

Professor Primback was very nervous and uneasy in the absence of the vice-principal; for he did not place any great confidence in the good judgment and discretion of the young officers of the vessel. He perversely refused to inform himself in regard to seamanship and maritime custom and law; and he was no better than a child outside of the duties of an instructor. He remained in his berth till after nine o'clock in the morning, because he would not trust himself to the uneasy deck. But he was not satisfied with the action of the young commander, even after the latter had consulted with Mr. Marline.

After he had carefully considered the situation without being able to reach any conclusion, he decided to go on deck, — if he could get there, — and examine for himself into the condition of affairs. He got out of his berth with no little difficulty, and by sundry darts and plunges reached the companion-way. While he had the baluster under his hand he did very well, and succeeded in reaching the quarter-deck without any disaster.

Seeing Capt. Wainwright on the weather side, he waited a moment till the vessel was on an even keel, and then started for him. If he had known any thing about the motions of a ship, or had understood the meaning of the order given, "Ready about," as he appeared at the companion-way, he would not have undertaken the feat of crossing the deck at that particular moment.

"Hard down the helm!" shouted Scott, the second lieutenant, who was then in charge of the deck.

The Tritonia threw her head up into the wind as the hands at the wheel obeyed the order. As she fell off she met a tremendous wave, which broke over the topgallant forecastle, and, as the bow of the vessel rose upon the sea, sent tons of water rolling along the lee side of the deck. The officers and seamen, as taught to do by experience, seized the life-lines, and held on for a moment till the water had poured out through the scuppers. But Mr. Primback was either too ignorant or too dignified to depend upon any support but his legs, and was knocked from his feet, and carried over to leeward. Mr. Marline and some others had warned him in season of his danger; but unfortunately they used sea-slang in doing so, and the professor did not comprehend the warning.

The boatswain sprang to his assistance, and picked him up. He conducted him to one of the life-lines, where he was content to hold on. The foresail and the mainsail went over, and as soon as they filled the motion of the schooner was easier.

"What do you mean, sir?" demanded the professor angrily, as Scott passed by him in the discharge of his duty.

"I don't mean any thing, sir," replied the joker demurely, and was about to continue on his way to the waist.

"Stop, sir! What do you mean by playing a trick

upon me when I come on deck?" foamed the worthy instructor.

"I beg your pardon, sir, if I have done any thing wrong," added Scott, shrugging his shoulders like a Frenchman. "I did not mean to do any thing out of the way."

"You tipped the ship so as to throw me down," added the irate professor.

"I didn't tip the ship, sir."

"You gave the order to have it done, as soon as you saw me come on deck."

"The captain ordered me to tack ship, and I gave the order to the watch on deck, sir. I only did what the captain told me to do."

"This isn't the first time you have played such a trick upon me," continued Mr. Primback, who honestly believed that Scott was the author of his misfortune.

The professor considered that any person who was capable of making a joke would not scruple to do a wicked deed; and for this reason Scott was not a favorite with the professor.

"I never played a trick upon you in my life, sir," pleaded the second lieutenant, with his cheerful smile.

"Don't contradict me, Scott!" said Mr. Primback, waxing more indignant as he saw the smile. "I will report you for discipline to the vice-principal as soon as he returns."

"I beg your pardon, Mr. Primback," interposed the captain, "but I do not think Mr. Scott was to blame."

"I did not ask your opinion, Wainwright: I hold *Mr.* Scott responsible for his own acts," snapped the professor.

"He only obeyed the order I gave him to tack ship, and it was not his fault that she made a lee lurch."

"You will use none of that gibberish to me! And I will tolerate no interference when I speak to a student."

"I only desired to explain, sir," added the captain, with the utmost deference and respect.

"Then do it in English."

"When the vessel turned so that the wind did not press upon the sails, the heavy waves caused her to roll and pitch violently," continued the captain.

"And Scott turned the vessel just as he saw me come on deck."

"I gave him the order to turn her."

"He could have waited a moment till I had reached a secure position. He has been guilty of disrespect to the senior professor of the vessel. — Scott, you will go down into the cabin, and settle this case with me," continued Mr. Primback, who was certainly more irritable than usual.

Wainwright was confounded by this order. It was plain that the professor had forgotten the regulation of the principal, which ought to have governed him in the present emergency. In the absence of the vice-principal, he had no control whatever over the captain in regard to the management of the vessel. He was taking the course pursued by another professor in the squadron, who had been sent home for interfering with the discipline of the ship.

"Mr. Scott is the officer of the deck, sir," said the captain, greatly embarrassed by the situation.

"I don't care if he is: he will obey my order, or I

will suspend him from duty," replied Mr. Primback stoutly.

"You will excuse me, sir, if I call your attention to the regulation bearing upon this case," continued the captain.

"Is my order to be obeyed, or not?" demanded the professor.

"I hope you will revoke the order till you have looked at the regulations, sir."

"This is insolence, Wainwright. I am the acting vice-principal of this vessel in the absence of Mr. Pelham. I stand in his place; and he is authorized to suspend an officer for cause."

"If you will be kind enough to read the regulations, I think you will see that you are mistaken," added the captain in a low tone.

"I am not mistaken," persisted the professor.

"We shall have to tack again in a moment, Mr. Primback; and the vessel will roll and pitch as badly as before."

"I think you had better go below, sir," said Mr. Marline, coming up to the professor at this moment, hoping to make an end of the disagreeable controversy. "The sea is very heavy, and she may roll herself full of water up to the rail."

"Mr. Marline, you will see that Scott obeys my order," replied Mr. Primback, creeping along the life-line towards the companion-way.

The boatswain made no reply, but took the arm of the "philosopher," as he insisted upon calling all the professors, and helped him down the steps. He deposited him on a sofa where he could preserve his equilibrium. The learned gentleman was very glad to be in a safe position again; but he could not forget the fancied injury to which he had been subjected.

"I ordered Scott to come into the cabin, and settle his case with me, Mr. Marline. He hasn't come yet," said the professor, wiping the salt spray from his face.

"I beg your honor's pardon, but you are all wrong in this matter," replied Marline bluntly, for he saw that nothing but plain speech would answer his purpose.

At the same time he took from his pocket a copy of the regulations which had been printed on board of the Young America, and slowly unfolded the document.

"How can I be all wrong, when, in the absence of the vice-principal, I am in his place, and my authority is supreme?" asked the professor in great astonishment.

"Your honor is no sailor."

"I thank the stars that I am not."

"The regulations say that you cannot interfere with the management of the vessel, or with the officers and seamen in the discharge of their duty. If the vice-principal is not on board, the professors can't meddle with the navigation of the ship. That's the law; and all we have to do is to obey it."

Mr. Primback took the regulations, adjusted his glasses, and proceeded to read the articles relating to his own duties. The boatswain was right; but the professor was unwilling to admit the fact.

"Am I placed at the mercy of these boys?" demanded Mr. Primback, as he removed his glasses, and looked at the boatswain.

"So far as handling the vessel is concerned, I don't see that you have any thing to do with them."

"They are my scholars, but they may insult me if they choose."

"But they don't choose to do any thing of the kind. It was no more Scott's fault that you were rolled into the scuppers, than it was mine; and I'm sure I had nothing to do with it," added Marline.

"I don't believe it: the fellow laughed in my face when I spoke to him. If he comes into the cabin, as I directed him to do, and makes a suitable apology for his conduct, I will pass over his offence as lightly as possible."

"Scott obeyed orders, and he couldn't help himself."

"He did not want to help himself," persisted Mr. Primback. "I will resign my position before I will submit to such treatment."

Just then the Tritonia tacked, and the vessel gave a tremendous lurch, as if to illustrate the argument of the boatswain. The professor was hurled from his seat, and Marline helped him up.

"You don't think that I did that, do you, Mr. Primback?" asked the old salt.

"Of course you did not. Have you any control over these boys, Mr. Marline?" inquired the professor in a tone of contempt.

"None at all in the absence of the vice-principal," answered the boatswain.

"Then they may take us anywhere, and do what they please with us, if I understand the situation."

"I suppose so, sir."

"Then I never comprehended my position before," added the professor, with increasing disgust.

"The trouble, if there is any, is all on account of

the absence of the vice-principal, who is authority in all matters."

"I had trouble enough with these boys before he came on board. I supposed in his absence that I took his place."

"But your honor is no sailor; and you couldn't handle the vessel if you tried."

"I have no desire to handle the vessel; but, if these boys can insult me with impunity, it is time for me to know it."

The conversation, which did not promise to end in any happy result, was interrupted by the appearance of third master Lingall, who politely touched his hat, and stood waiting to deliver his message.

"What do you want?" demanded Mr. Primback.

"The captain desires to see Mr. Marline on deck," said Lingall.

"Tell the captain that Mr. Marline is engaged with me," interposed the professor testily.

"I will report to the captain myself," added Marline, who was in a better frame of mind than the "philosopher."

"Wait till I have done with you."

"I beg your honor's pardon, but I always obey the captain," replied the boatswain; and touching his hat, and scraping his right foot across the floor, he hastened on deck.

"Stop!" called Mr. Primback. "I have something more to say to you."

"I will see your honor as soon as I can," added the boatswain; and he ran up the steps.

Mr. Marline could see that the professor was very

unreasonable, considering there was a steamer in distress depending upon the Tritonia for assistance. He touched his hat to the captain, and waited for further orders.

"What do you think of the sea now, Mr. Marline?" asked Wainwright.

"It has improved a good deal during the last hour."

"Do you think it is prudent to get out a boat?"

"I think it is as good weather as we are likely to have for some time," replied Marline, looking at the sky and the sea.

"Then we will board the steamer."

The captain gave the order to call all hands; and, as soon as the ship's company had mustered, the vessel was heaved to. The second cutter was cleared away, and her crew piped into her. O'Hara was detailed to take charge of her; and Mr. Rimmer, the carpenter, was directed to go in the boat, not only to render any assistance that might be required in boarding the steamer, but to examine into her condition.

The cutter was lowered into the water, with the crew in her, under the direction of Mr. Marline. It was no easy task to accomplish this work in the heavy sea. The boat rose and fell on the angry waves; but it was so well managed that very little water was taken in. Under the lee of the drifting steamer the water was comparatively smooth. The man who had hailed the Tritonia threw a line to the cutter, which Mr. Marline secured to the fore-thwart.

"Are we to lower the ladies into the cutter?" asked O'Hara, when the boat was fast to the steamer.

"I can't say what's to be done till we have boarded her," replied the boatswain.

"'Then I'll do that same at once," added the fourth lieutenant; and, suiting the action to the word, he ran up the line like a cat.

"Well, good gracious! this is one of the academy squadron!" said the man on board of the steamer, as O'Hara leaped down from the rail. "I thought so the minute I laid eyes on her; but, seeing her out here all alone, I gave up the idea at once."

"Mr. Frisbone!" exclaimed the lieutenant, as he recognized the gentleman who had presented the American Prince to the principal of the academy squadron.

"Well, you boys are smart sailors; and you are an honor to your country," added Mr. Frisbone.

"I thought you had given up going in any steamers, after your experience in the American Prince."

"We went to Liverpool to meet my wife's sister, who came over here for her health. The doctors said Malaga was the place for her to spend the winter; and we started for Spain. When I got into France, I found the Germans had got almost over to the sea-shore; and we took this steamer at Havre for Cadiz. Last night she was run into by another vessel, and had a hole knocked in her bow. We were the only passengers on board; and the crew jumped on board of the other vessel as soon as they found she had a hole in her."

"But didn't they try to save you and your wife?" asked O'Hara indignantly.

"Yes, they did; but my wife and her sister were both sick in their berths; and, when I got them out, the crew had deserted her, and the other vessel was out of sight in the fog. The fact was, they were so flurried they didn't know what they were about."

"We will take them on board of the Tritonia."

"I don't believe we could ever get them into that boat," added Mr. Frisbone, as he glanced at the cutter, which was almost swamped in every sea that swept by her.

"The steamer don't seem to be in any present danger of going down," said O'Hara.

"She won't sink this time; and, if her crew had only stuck by her, they might have saved her."

"She is not very heavily loaded."

"She has some machinery or something of that sort in her; and it must have shifted so as to bring that hole out of the water. If I had some help I could right her."

O'Hara asked Mr. Rimmer to come on board.

CHAPTER VI.

A VOLUNTEER SHIP'S COMPANY.

THE carpenter of the Tritonia climbed up the rope, and reached the deck of the steamer. The moment he saw Mr. Frisbone, he recognized him, and saluted him with nautical politeness.

"Mr. Rimmer, the carpenter of the Tritonia," said O'Hara, by way of introduction.

"I am glad to see an American seaman on board of this steamer," replied Mr. Frisbone heartily. "You are the carpenter of the Tritonia, and you can soon tell whether this vessel is worth saving."

"She don't seem to be in very bad condition with the exception of that hole in her starboard bow," added Mr. Rimmer, as he cast his eyes about him.

"I wish you would look her over; and then we can decide what is best to be done."

The carpenter began his survey of the vessel, accompanied by Mr. Frisbone and O'Hara. They visited every part of her, examining very carefully into her condition.

"I suppose I know as much about the engine as anybody; and I can say that it is in good order," said Mr. Frisbone, as they passed the door of the engine-room.

"I don't know any thing about engines," added the carpenter modestly. "But I can say that the vessel is in first-rate condition; and that hole in her bow can be stopped so that she will live in any sea. The opening is above the water-line, so that there will be no great pressure upon it."

"Then we can save the vessel," replied the American Prince, as he claimed to be, and as he had named his steam-yacht. "That will be a feather in the caps of you boys."

"I should like to take a hand in the game," said O'Hara, his face lighting up at the prospect.

"But we want help; and there is a great deal of hard work to be done," continued Mr. Frisbone. "How many hands have you in your boat?"

"Ten besides Mr. Rimmer."

"If they are good stout hands, we may do something with them."

"But I must report the condition of the vessel, and wait for further orders," interposed O'Hara.

"Quite right," added the Prince, with a smile. "I forgot that you live on your discipline."

"But the boat came off to take you and the ladies on board the Tritonia."

"I think we are safe enough here for the present; and I know the women-folks won't think they can get into that boat while it is bobbing around like corn in a popper. Return to your ship, and give my respects to the captain and the old folks on board, and tell them I think the steamer can be saved."

O'Hara tried to explain how easy it would be to get the ladies into the cutter; but Mr. Frisbone seemed to be unwilling to leave the steamer while there was a chance to save her. He conducted the young officer into the cabin, the door of which opened from the main deck.

"Here, Maggie," said the Prince, calling to his wife, who was in her state-room. "One of the vessels of the academy squadron has come to get us out of this scrape."

Mrs. Frisbone came out of the state-room, looking very pale and sick. She was followed by her sister the invalid, who, however, looked better than the Prince's wife.

"This is Lieut. O'Hara, of the Tritonia; Mrs. Frisbone."

The young officer took off his cap, and bowed politely to the lady.

"Miss Louise Rodwood, my wife's sister," continued the prince.

O'Hara thought she was a very pretty girl, and he indulged in an extra flourish as he saluted her.

"With the compliments of the captain, I beg to tender you the hospitalities of the Tritonia," said the lieutenant, when he had formally greeted the ladies.

"Good!" roared the American Prince. "That is a very pretty way to address a couple of shipwrecked women; and it is a credit to your bringing-up."

"I beg to place our vessel at the disposal of the ladies; and whatever else we may not be able to do for you, we will keep the ship right side up."

"That's handsome; and the boat is all ready to take you to the steamer, Maggie."

"I would rather drown where I am than attempt to

get into that boat," protested Mrs. Frisbone. "I saw it from the window in my room; and it jumps about like a wild horse."

"I am sure I can't slide down a rope into the boat as I saw that man come up," added Miss Rodwood.

"All right; and we will stay where we are for the present," said Mr. Frisbone.

"We can rig a whip, and lower the ladies into the cutter without any difficulty," persisted the young officer, who perhaps thought it would be pleasant to have such a passenger as the younger lady.

"If we are in no danger here, as Mr. Frisbone says we are not, I prefer to stay where I am," replied Mrs. Frisbone; and her sister was of the same mind.

"All right, lieutenant," added the Prince. "I thought the women would rather stay where they are; and I think you had better return to your ship, and report to the captain. If he will send as many men as he can spare, I believe we can put this craft into sailing trim in a few hours."

"I will do so, sir. But you forget that we have no engineers on board of the Tritonia to run the engine," suggested O'Hara.

"I will run the engine myself. I never went to sea much, but I have run an engine on a river and bay steamer enough to understand the business," replied the American Prince. "If you will find firemen, I will look out for the engine."

"I will report all you say to the captain."

"Let me see: you have a vice-principal, or something of that sort, in each of the consorts. Of course he will direct in this matter."

"We have no vice-principal in the Tritonia just now;" and O'Hara explained how they happened to be without one.

"Then I suppose the professors attend to this business."

"No, sir: the captain attends to it in the absence of the vice-principal. The professors have nothing to do with the management of the vessel, for they are not sailors."

"And I would rather trust the young gentlemen in matters of seamanship than the professors," added Mr. Rimmer, with a chuckle.

O'Hara bowed to the ladies, and retired from the cabin. He tried to be dignified and graceful; but the heavy rolling of the steamer interfered sadly with the poetry of motion. Both of the ladies were holding on with all their might at the brass rods which extended the entire length of the cabin on each side, except across the doors of the state-rooms. Every thing seemed to be in good order, and every article was lashed so that it could not move at the motion of the vessel.

O'Hara and Rimmer slid down into the boat, which was protected from the full force of the sea by being under the lee of the steamer. The cutters were all life-boats, and when well handled would keep right side up in any ordinary sea. The crews had been thoroughly disciplined in the roughest weather in which it was safe to launch a boat; so that they were perfectly at home on the present occasion.

The second cutter pulled under the davits, and the falls were hooked on. This feat was accomplished not without great difficulty, and only by watching for the favorable moment. A blunder might have smashed the boat, and thrown its crew into the sea. When the falls were fast, the hands on deck hoisted the boat up to the davits.

O'Hara reported to the captain, and explained why the passengers on board the wreck had not come off in the boat. Wainwright was not a little surprised to learn that Mr. Frisbone, the munificent donor of the American Prince, was on board of the steamer with his wife. He knew precisely what Mr. Lowington would do if he had been within hail, and precisely what he would wish to have done in his absence.

"Mr. Frisbone desires you to send as many hands as you can spare; and with help enough he is confident we can save the steamer, and take her into port," continued the fourth lieutenant.

"How many of our ship's company can we spare, Mr. Marline?" asked the captain, turning to the adult boatswain, who had been called to hear the report of the lieutenant.

"We can get along well enough with one watch," replied the old salt.

"That was just my view of the matter," added the captain. "But I will not detail either watch as a whole. There will be a great deal of hard and dirty work to be done on board of the steamer, and I will call for volunteers."

All hands were piped to muster in form, for they had already come on deck to witness the expected arrival of the passengers from the wreck. The seamen laid hold of the life-lines and such parts of the vessel as afforded them a hold, and waited impatiently to learn what was to be done. Capt. Wainwright made a speech in which he explained the situation on board of the steamer. She was to be saved and sent into port if possible. This announcement was greeted with yells and cheers.

"I purpose to select a **crew to** man the steamer," continued Wainwright. "**The work** on **board of** her will be difficult, and **some of it very dirty and** disagreeable. I shall therefore call for volunteers."

"Stop, Wainwright!" suddenly interposed Mr. Primback, who had crawled on deck in season to hear the last part of the captain's speech, after one of the stewards had informed him what was transpiring on board.

"I beg your pardon, Professor Primback; but this business admits of no delay," replied the captain, vexed at the interruption of the "philosopher."

"What do you mean, Wainwright, by sending half the students out of the vessel without saying a word to me?" demanded the irate instructor.

"I have consulted with Mr. Marline, as you desired, sir; and I don't think there is any other way to do."

"But I object. You have taken the ship a long way out of her course; and here you are wasting your time and mine in some Quixotic adventure."

"Have you been informed that Mr. Frisbone, the gentleman **who** presented the American Prince to the principal, is on board of that steamer, with his wife and her sister, sir?"

"I have been so informed; but that don't affect the case at all. You sent a boat to convey them on board of this vessel, which was a very proper thing to do, as it involved the possible saving of human life. To that I did not object: I do not now object to such just and proper action as may be necessary to insure the safety of any persons on board of the unfortunate vessel," continued Mr. Primback, whose speech became more precise and dignified as he cooled off. "I do not propose to interfere with the management of the vessel; but when you indicate your intention to send away one-half of my pupils on a boyish expedition of very doubtful practicability, I feel it to be my duty to interfere as one having authority."

"I shall be very sorry to do any thing without your approval, Professor Primback," replied Wainwright, in a very respectful tone.

"Do I understand you to mean by that, you intend to proceed with the plan you have just announced without my sanction, and even in opposition to my direct prohibition?" demanded Mr. Primback, controlling his wrath as well as he could.

"I hope you will not compel me to do any thing of the kind, sir."

"I understand you perfectly, Wainwright. You are prepared, I see, to set at defiance my authority," continued the professor, biting his lips to repress his anger.

"I should like to speak with you a few moments, brother Primback," interposed Dr. Crumples, the other instructor of the Tritonia.

"I am ready to hear any thing you have to say, doctor," replied Mr. Primback coldly.

Though the two professors never quarrelled, or exhibited any signs of variance, before the students, there was no sympathy whatever between them. Dr. Crumples was a genial, good-natured man, rather fond of a joke; while the other cared for nothing but Greek, Latin, science, and philosophy.

"I have been reading the regulations, and I have come to the conclusion that you and I have nothing to do or say about the nautical affairs of this vessel," said the doctor, in a low tone, not intended for the ears of the students.

"Do you intend to sustain the boys in their resistance to my authority, Dr. Crumples?" demanded the philosopher, straightening himself up to the full height of his dignity.

Unfortunately for him, in doing this he let go of the life-line; and a sudden jerk of the vessel would have pitched him down into the scuppers if Marline had not seized him by the arm, and held him. He came down from his dignity all in a heap. The students turned away to hide the laugh they could not suppress.

"I certainly do not intend to sustain the boys in their resistance to your authority, for the simple reason that I don't believe you have any authority in the premises. If you will come into the cabin, where both of us will be more at ease than on this unstable deck, I shall be happy to explain my view of the case," replied Dr. Crumples, when his associate was fairly planted on his legs again.

"I do not care to know your opinion of the case, Dr. Crumples," added Mr. Primback tartly.

"You know it already, professor," chuckled the doctor.

"I am the senior professor of the ship, with full powers to direct every thing" —

"In the scholastic department," interposed the doctor.

"Do you suppose I am placed here to follow the lead of a boy?" demanded Mr. Primback, pointing at the captain of the Tritonia in the most contemptuous manner.

In releasing his hold upon the life-line he was in great danger of being upset again, and Marline grasped his arm, this time so vigorously that the professor groaned with pain. Possibly the old salt was disgusted with the "philosopher," and expressed his feeling in this way.

"Do you mean to break my arm, Mr. Marline?"

"I beg your honor's pardon, but I was afraid you were going to be shied into the scuppers again," pleaded the boatswain.

"I shall call for volunteers, my lads," Capt. Wainwright continued, resuming his speech to the ship's company where he had left off.

"You will not call for volunteers, Wainwright!" interposed Mr. Primback warmly. "I forbid you to call for volunteers! I forbid any student to volunteer! It is my order that you proceed on the voyage to Madeira, according to the direction of the principal."

"Shall I leave Mr. Frisbone and the ladies to perish on the wreck?" asked the captain mildly.

"I have already given you permission to bring them on board of the Tritonia. You may still do that," replied the senior professor.

"But the ladies decline to get into the boat while the sea is so rough."

"Is it possible to get the ladies into the boat, Mr.

Marline?" asked the professor, turning to the boatswain.

"I suppose we could hoist them into the boat by main force; but they said they preferred to drown where they were, rather than slide down on a rope into the cutter," replied the boatswain, rather doggedly. "If we can save the steamer we ought to do it, in my judgment."

"We have nothing to do with saving the vessel. We are not out upon the ocean for any such purpose."

"Just as your honor pleases."

"If the ladies will not get into the boat, you must either force them to do so, or leave them where they are," added Mr. Primback.

Wainwright said nothing more. It could make no difference to him if the senior professor did forbid any further action towards the saving of the steamer. His action was approved by all the other adults on board; and he was confident that the officers and seamen would obey his orders, possibly with greater readiness than if the head of the scholastic department had not forbidden them to do so.

The Tritonia had filled away again on the return of the second cutter from the wreck. By this time it was necessary to come about again, and stand towards the steamer. Wainwright politely notified Mr. Primback that the vessel was about to "go in stays;" hoping that he would retire to the cabin, and permit him to finish the business of the hour.

"Go in stays! Will you ever speak English, Wainwright? Do you mean to insult me by using that gibberish to me when I have forbidden you to do so?"

"That is the proper nautical expression for what we are about to do," replied the captain.

"Do you mean that you are going to turn the vessel?"

"That is substantially what we intend to do; but sailors would not understand me if I called it turning the vessel."

"Do you presume to instruct me in the use of language, Wainwright?"

"By no means, sir; but I use nautical language as I was instructed to use it by Mr. Lowington and the other instructors in seamanship and navigation. — Mr. Greenwood, let the vessel go in stays," continued the captain, turning to the first lieutenant.

"Man the fore and main sheets!" called the executive officer. "Ease down the helm!"

As the vessel came up into the wind in obedience to her helm, the fore and main sheet began to bang and thrash as the pressure was removed.

"Haul in on the sheets," called the first lieutenant; and the order was repeated by the other officers in charge of the sheets.

"I'm afraid you will get hit by the sheet-blocks if you stand here any longer, sir," said Mr. Marline to Professor Primback. "Excuse me, sir, but you had better go below, or the vessel will shake you up badly as she catches the wind on the other tack."

The professor made a dive at the companion-way. As the vessel at that instant was on an even keel, he succeeded in reaching his destination. The line of seamen "walking away" with the fore-sheet then crowded upon him, and he fled to the cabin in disgust. The Tritonia gave a terrible lurch as the sails filled on the port tack; and the grouty professor, losing his hold of the stair-post, was pitched down to the lee side of the cabin. One of the stewards picked him up; but his temper got the better of him. Dr. Crumples tried to comfort him; but he would not be comforted.

The Tritonia was again headed towards the steamer. The captain took some time to consult with Mr. Marline and Mr. Rimmer in regard to the detail of officers and seamen for duty on the disabled vessel. Then he had a talk with O'Hara, though no one could hear what passed between them. All hands were again called; and every one on board volunteered, as the captain had told Marline they would.

"Perhaps, when I have explained the duties of the crew on board of the steamer, you will not be so willing," said the captain, with a laugh. "It will be necessary for a portion of the volunteers to act as firemen; and I need not tell you that the fire-room of any steamer is a very hot and dirty hole. But this work will be fairly divided among all the seamen."

"But not among the officers," added a young salt, laughing.

"Certainly not: I shall detail two officers for duty in the engine-room; but I select them simply because they understand the business," replied the captain. "Lieut. O'Hara will act as captain of the steamer; first master Speers as chief officer; second master Raymond as second officer."

These names were received with cheers by the seamen; but the three lieutenants whose names had not been mentioned thought it a little strange that they had been passed over, though the third lieutenant, Alexander, was competent to run an engine, which explained why his name had been omitted.

"Lieut. Alexander will act as chief engineer, and fourth master Richards as assistant," continued the captain, reading from a paper he had made out.

The names of eighteen seamen and petty officers were then read; and Wainwright desired any one who had any objections to make, to make them now, for it would be too late when the party had gone on board of the steamer. No one made any objections; and the order was given to clear away the second and third cutters. They were lowered into the water, one at a time, and their crews pulled for the steamer. Mr. Rimmer, the second cook, and two stewards were sent with them.

CHAPTER VII.

THE INVALID YOUNG LADY.

WHEN Professor Primback heard the noise of lowering the boats into the water, he wrote a formal order to the captain not to send away any portion of the ship's company, unless it was to bring off the passengers of the steamer. He signed his name in full to this document, and sent it on deck by one of the stewards. Wainwright took the paper, read it attentively, and then put it into his pocket. He took no further notice of it.

The senior professor evidently supposed that no notice would be taken of the order, and he seemed to be aware that he had no means of enforcing his commands; for he went to his state-room, and made no further demonstration. He did not even speak to Dr. Crumples about the matter.

As the crew of the steamer had taken the boats with them when they abandoned her, the second and third cutters of the Tritonia were to be retained by the party. In half an hour they were all on board the steamer, with the boats hoisted up at the davits. O'Hara reported what had been done on board of the Tritonia to Mr. Frisbone, and informed him that he had been appointed captain of the steamer, or, at least, of the party sent to assist in saving her.

"Capt. O'Hara, I greet you! and the captain of the Tritonia could not have selected a better captain, without speaking ill of the other officers; for I know how well you managed some very difficult business in Italy last fall," said Mr. Frisbone. "Now will you introduce me to the rest of your officers?"

O'Hara presented them one at a time, and the American Prince shook hands with each. When he came to Mr. Alexander, he gave one of his loud and hearty laughs.

"I thought I was to be chief engineer," said he, wringing the hand of Alexander; "but I am willing to place myself under your orders, Mr. Chief Engineer."

"He is the chief engineer as far as our party is concerned," O'Hara explained. "Though Capt. Wainwright is the commander of the Tritonia in name and in fact, so far as doing duty is concerned, yet the vice-principal is really the captain. If you please, Mr. Frisbone, we shall all regard you as the principal, on board of the steamer."

"All right, Capt. O'Hara," replied the Prince, who seemed to take great delight in giving the young officers their full titles, and using them often.

"I shall be glad to take my orders from you; and the chief engineer will do the same," added O'Hara.

"Possibly the chief engineer knows more about running an engine than I do; and I know more about building them than I do of running them."

"Of course I shall give in to you, sir," said Alexander.

"Thank you; but do you really know any thing about an engine, Mr. Alexander?" asked Mr. Frisbone, in his teasing tone.

"Two years ago I was assistant engineer on a screw steamer about the size of this one," answered Alexander.

"And how old were you two years ago?"

"I was eighteen, sir. My father received a legacy from an uncle in Scotland, which made him a rich man; and then I was sent to this institution to finish my education. I had worked two years in a machine-shop before I went to sea at all. I think I can run an engine, sir."

"I have no doubt you can; in fact, I believe these young gentlemen can do any thing that anybody can," added Mr. Frisbone, laughing heartily; and sometimes no one could imagine what he was laughing at.

"The second engineer ran a stationary engine when he was twelve years old, in his father's shop," continued O'Hara, when he had presented this officer.

"And I was engineer of a small steam-yacht when I was fourteen," added Richards.

"All right, young gentlemen; and 'I shall have nothing to do but sleep in the cabin, and take care of the women-folks," chuckled the Prince.

"I think some of our officers will be quite willing to assist you in that part of your duty," said O'Hara lightly. "Upon my loife, the young lady is as beautiful as the lovely Giulia Fabiano; and, by the powers, that's saying a great dale!"

"By the way, now I think of it, is there a young gentleman in the squadron by the name of Speers,— Tom Speers?"

"There is, sir; and he is one of our party," replied O'Hara. "Where are ye, Tom Speers?"

Tom had been introduced; but the Prince evidently did not notice the name, for he had called him "Mr. Spear," when he addressed him. Tom came forward when his name was called.

"How is it you happen to be here, Mr. Speers?" asked the Prince.

"I was detailed to act as chief officer of this vessel, by the captain of the Tritonia, sir," replied Tom, wondering how Mr. Frisbone happened to know any thing about him.

"I know; but you were sent for by my friend Judge Rodwood, to go to England."

"I did not go, sir."

"Well, we won't stop to talk about that now. We must go to work on the steamer at once, and have her in good condition in case another storm comes on," said Mr. Frisbone, suddenly changing his tone and manner.

But, before the officers left the cabin, he introduced them to his wife and her sister; then the party took a look at the vessel below. Mr. Rimmer had been studying the hole in the starboard bow since he came on board, and by this time he was hard at work repairing the damage. Two seamen, who had a taste for carpentry, were detailed to assist him. Until the hole was stopped, nothing could be done towards righting the vessel; for she lay just in the proper position to enable the carpenter to do his work to the best advantage.

Mr. Rimmer intended to do the job in a much more thorough manner than he had at first proposed, for the reason that he found the materials for it on board. He proceeded to splice the broken ribs, and then to plank them over, as the work would have been done in a ship-yard. A stage was rigged, and lowered over the side; and, while the carpenter was getting out his stock, his assistants removed the broken planking. The heavy rolling of the vessel interfered very much with operations on the stage; but the workmen were very zealous, and made good progress in spite of all the disadvantages.

In the mean time Mr. Frisbone and the rest of the ship's company were preparing to right the steamer, and pump the water out of her, as soon as this work could be undertaken. The steam-pump was put in good order; and every thing about the vessel was restored to its usual condition, so far as it was possible to do so.

In the afternoon the wind abated almost to a calm, and a boat came from the Tritonia to pay the steamer a visit. Mr. Marline was in it, with one of the stewards who had been a ship-carpenter. Both of them went to work with Mr. Rimmer, and before dark the hole was planked over. As there were some indications of bad weather again, the Tritonia's boat returned, and Mr. Rimmer and his assistants proceeded to calk the seams by the light of the lanterns. By midnight the job was completed, even to coppering the part below the water-line.

Before eight bells in the evening, the ship's company had been divided into two watches, as in the merchant service. One watch had turned in at eight bells; but all hands were called at midnight, when the repairs were finished. At this time the steam-pump was started, and it discharged the water at a very rapid rate. Mr. Rimmer followed the water as it receded in the hold, to ascertain if there was any leak in the bottom; but none was found.

The steamer had for a cargo the parts of an iron bridge, and the labels upon them indicated that it was consigned to a firm in Barcelona. One of the heaviest of the pieces had shifted from its position in the hold, throwing others out of place, till their weight had heeled the vessel over as the party had found her.

"Well, Capt. O'Hara, do you think you can stow this cargo over again so as to right the vessel?" asked Mr. Frisbone, when the pump had worked long enough to afford them a full view of the condition of the hold.

"I have no doubt I can," replied O'Hara confidently.

"But some of those pieces weigh several tons," suggested the Prince.

"But we have a donkey-engine on deck; and, with snatch-blocks, we can apply the power in any direction we desire."

"Precisely so: I see that you are master of the situation."

The captain had already caused the necessary blocks and rigging to be collected in the hold. The assistant engineer was stationed at the donkey-engine, the snatch-blocks were arranged for moving the heaviest piece of the bridge, and the rope was adjusted. A chain sling was attached to the iron, and the line made fast to it.

"Go ahead!" said O'Hara, when every thing was ready; and the order was passed along the line of seamen until it reached the officer in charge of the donkey-engine.

The rope straightened and strained as the power was applied; and then the huge mass of iron began slowly to move in the required direction. Mr. Rimmer and his gang placed the skids, and in the course of half an hour the piece was moved to the place indicated by the carpenter. The steamer came up on an even keel as the heavy weight changed position.

"But she is down too much by the stern," said Mr. Rimmer, when the piece had been blocked securely in its place.

"I see why that is," added the Prince. "Half a dozen of those tube pieces have rolled out of the places where they were first stowed."

These were restored to their original beds as indicated by the blocking; and they had doubtless been thrown out of place by the shifting of the larger piece.

"The vessel is in good trim now," said Mr. Rimmer, wiping the perspiration from his brow. "Those pieces will not move again unless the steamer goes over on her beam-ends."

The party left the hold, and hastened on deck. The weather was still mild, though the sky was clouded over. The captain sent an order to the chief engineer, directing him to get up steam. The fires had been started in the furnaces; but only steam enough had been made to work the donkey-engine, which was not furnished with a separate boiler, as in many vessels.

The amateur firemen had been fully instructed in their duties by Mr. Frisbone, who remained in the fire-room till morning. Thus far the seamen considered the hot and dirty work as good fun; but they were not likely to hold this opinion for any length of time. Four hands had been detailed from each watch to serve as firemen; and these were to work two at a time, so that only two hours' service were required of each, or six hours a day. The fire-room was well ventilated, so that it was not so intensely hot as in many steamers. A lot of cast-off woollen shirts and trousers had been brought from the Tritonia for the use of the firemen.

Mr. Frisbone did not like the looks of the quarters occupied by the French sailors and firemen; and he insisted that the seamen should be berthed in the cabin. There were state-rooms enough to accommodate them all; but the part of the cabin used by the officers was separated from that of the seamen by a curtain sliding on a brass rod.

The steamer was the Ville d'Angers. She was evidently a nearly new vessel, of about six hundred tons. Unlike most of the English steamers, she had a pilot-house forward, as in American vessels of this kind. Her cabin was handsomely fitted up, and she appeared to be a first-class steamer in every respect.

O'Hara went into the pilot-house, when the work below was completed. Tom Speers followed him, for there was nothing more to be done till the engineer should report that he had steam enough to start her.

"This will be a big spree, my boy," said the captain, as he seated himself by the wheel.

"The biggest that ever happened. I am amazed to find myself in it," replied Tom. "I don't see how I came to be appointed to the second place on board, when there are so many fellows above me that wanted to take a hand in this business."

"You don't see it? Then I'll tell you, my boy," added the captain with a jolly laugh, as though he enjoyed the situation.

"I suppose you helped me into the place."

"Troth, I did, thin! You see, when a fellow like you, rotten with stamps, with millions in prospect, and a letter of credit for thousands in his trousers-pocket, comes along, it is well to get on the right side of him," continued O'Hara, laughing all the time.

"I don't believe the money had any thing to do with it," protested Tom. "You are the farthest from a selfish fellow of all the ship's company; and I won't believe what you say of yourself."

"Thank you for so much, my lad. But I'll bet a hackle, if the fellows knew how rich you are, they would say that's the rayson. When Capt. Wainwright told me beforehand that he should give me the command of the steamer, which he didn't do till he had talked it over with Mr. Marline, he asked me to tell him who I wanted for officers. Your name was the first I gave him; so don't forget me when you make your will."

"I certainly will not if I have any thing to leave," replied Tom.

"Steam up!" shouted Alexander through the speaking-tube which connected with the engine-room.

"Then we are all ready to go ahead. Have you seen the Tritonia's lights lately, Tom?" said O'Hara, looking out in the direction from which they had been last seen.

"I have not: we have all been so busy that we have not thought of her. She has been standing off and on all night, I suppose."

"There she is, astern of us," added O'Hara. "We must run down and report the state of things on board to the captain. Call the quartermaster and a seaman to take the wheel, if you please, Tom."

The two hands were called into the pilot-house, and the quartermaster was given the charge of the wheel. The other hand was required to assist him, for the officers had not yet learned how much force was needed to steer the steamer.

"Do you know any thing about these jinglers, Burley?" asked the captain, as the quartermaster took the wheel.

"Yes, sir: the chief engineer told me all about them," replied Burley.

"Start her, then," added the captain.

The quartermaster pulled the bell-handle on the wheel-frame. The hissing steam was heard below; the vessel jarred a little; and then she went ahead.

"The course, if you please?" inquired the quartermaster.

"Run for the Tritonia; but be sure you don't run over her," replied O'Hara. "She is astern of us now."

"For the Tritonia, sir," repeated Burley, as he threw the wheel over.

"We are actually moving!" said O'Hara, as he left the pilot-house, followed by Speers.

"I think there is no doubt of that," replied the chief officer. "Have you any idea where we are going?"

"Not the least in the world; but, the nearer the port,

the shorter our term of office. I wish we were bound to New York, or some other port on the other side of the ocean; for I should like a long cruise under present circumstances."

"So should I; but I suppose we shall have only a day or two of it at the most."

"We shall soon know where we are going; for I suppose Capt. Wainwright has been studying on that question since he sent us on board of the steamer."

O'Hara then directed that the starboard watch, which had been on duty all night, should be relieved. It was two o'clock in the morning, and they were to be called at four. This was Tom Speers's watch; but he was not inclined to turn in before the captain had reported to the Tritonia. Raymond was now in charge of the deck, and Tom had nothing to do. He went into the cabin, and to his surprise found that Miss Rodwood was there.

Tom touched his cap to her, and remarked that she was up late. There had been so much noise in the hold, that she could not sleep, and she had got up. The officer seated himself on a divan, and he could not keep his eyes off the fair passenger.

Miss Rodwood was walking up and down the cabin; and Tom could not help thinking again that she was a very pretty girl. She was very pale, and no doubt her recent experience on shipboard had been a severe trial to her nerves. Tom noticed that there was something very strange about her expression. He could not explain it; but he was confident that she was suffering from some cause. She did not seem to be in bodily pain. The motion of the vessel was tolerably easy compared with what it had been, so that she had no difficulty in walking on the cabin floor. The curtain partition was open on one side of the table, so that the lady extended her walk to the entire length of the apartment.

She kept quickening her pace till she was going almost at a run; but she moderated it as she approached the young officer. Tom watched her with increasing interest, as she appeared to grow more excited. He was sure now that something was the matter with her; and he felt that something ought to be done for her.

"The weather has been very favorable for our work," said Tom, desiring to ascertain something more about the lady's condition through the medium of conversation.

"I suppose it has," she replied, with a nod, and continued her walk.

Tom saw that her eye looked a little wild. He decided that he ought to inform Mr. Frisbone of her condition, though he hardly understood enough of such matters to determine whether any thing was the matter with her.

While he was thinking of the case, he saw Miss Rodwood ascend a flight of stairs in the forward part of the cabin, leading to the hurricane-deck. He rushed out at the main entrance, and ran up the ladder. The lady was walking very fast towards the stern of the vessel. He concluded that she had come up to take the air; and she would certainly regard it as impertinent for him to follow her. He paused to consider what he should do.

He saw O'Hara planking the main deck from the waist forward. He would speak to him, and ask him to send for Mr. Frisbone. He descended to the main deck, and hailed the captain.

"I thought you had turned in, my boy," said the captain lightly.

"No: I thought I would stay up till you have communicated with the Tritonia," replied Tom. "Have you noticed any thing strange about the young lady on board, O'Hara?"

"Upon me sowl, I haven't, except that she is as pretty a girl as I have set eyes on for seven years; and that's saying a great dale," answered the captain.

"Don't joke, please, just now, O'Hara. I think something ails the young lady; and I'm afraid it's something serious," added Tom.

"You don't mane it! What could ail a girl as pretty as she is?"

Tom took five minutes to tell what he had observed in the cabin.

"Is it crazy she is? Is that what you mane?" demanded O'Hara, not a little excited by the inference he drew from what his companion had said.

"You needn't call it by any such name as that. I believe she is an invalid; and, after all she has been through during the last twenty-four hours, it wouldn't be very strange if she were a little out of her head. I don't like to lose sight of her. There she is, walking up and down the poop-deck as though she were running a race with her own shadow. Will you send one of the watch down to tell Mr. Frisbone how it is with her, or ask him to come on deck without saying what is wanted?"

"Troth, I'll do so myself!" replied the captain, hurrying down through the engine-room.

He had hardly disappeared before Miss Rodwood started to run with all her might towards the stern of the steamer. Tom Speers leaped up the ladder to the hurricane-deck in season to see her spring over the low railing into the sea.

"Man overboard! man overboard! Stop her!" cried Tom at the top of his lungs; and they were not feeble lungs.

He cut loose the life-buoy which was lashed to the railing, and threw it overboard. But Tom was not content with this action: he kicked off his shoes, and stepped out of his heavy pea-jacket and coat at the same moment, and plunged into the sea.

CHAPTER VIII.

THE VILLE D'ANGERS.

"HELP, help! Save me!" cried Miss Rodwood in the water, at some distance from Tom Speers.

As the girl had voluntarily thrown herself into the sea, Tom could not understand why she called for assistance. He had struck the water only a few seconds after she sprang overboard, and she could not be at any great distance from him. He was a strong swimmer, and the sea was very smooth. He heard the cry of the girl repeated as he came up with the life-buoy he had thrown overboard. Placing it before him, he swam with all the speed he could make, and reached the sufferer when she was quite exhausted by her efforts. She could swim a little herself, and had more confidence in the water than most persons who had never tried to do so.

"Don't be afraid!" cried Tom, when he saw in the gloom of the night that she was still struggling to keep afloat.

In a moment more he reached her, and placed her hands upon the life-buoy, which was buoyant enough to support both of them.

"You are perfectly safe now," said Tom, as he assured himself that she had a good hold upon the buoy.

She was too much exhausted to make any reply; and, whatever she had intended in the beginning, it was clear enough to Tom that she had no present desire to end her young life.

Capt. O'Hara had hardly entered the engine-room, when he heard the energetic cry of Tom Speers; and he realized in an instant that the worst his friend feared had come to pass.

"Man overboard! Stop her, Alexander!" he shouted to the chief engineer, who was watching the motions of the machinery.

The captain told the engineer to pass the word for Mr. Frisbone. He returnd to the main deck; but Raymond, the second officer, had heard the startling cry. Already the third cutter was swung out, and all the watch on deck were in the boat. The officers and seamen had been thoroughly trained to this sort of service, and there had been no more delay than if they had been on board of the Tritonia. The crew lowered themselves into the water, as there was no difficulty in doing in a smooth sea. The falls were cast off, and the cutter shoved away from the steamer. The four oars were shipped, and the crew pulled with all their muscle.

"Pull directly astern of the vessel!" shouted O'Hara, who had gone upon the hurricane-deck, where he could see all that was done.

"Ay, ay, sir!" replied the quartermaster, who, as the highest in rank, had taken the place of the coxswain; for the boat-service of the steamer was not yet organized, and it was not the practice in the vessels of the squadron to wait for the regular officers and crew of the boats in any emergency.

"Call all hands, Mr. Raymond," said the captain to the officer of the deck.

As there was not another seaman left on the deck of the Ville d'Angers, Raymond performed this duty himself.

"Man overboard! All hands on deck!" cried Raymond, as he passed into the cabin, and proceeded to open the doors of all the state-rooms occupied by the crew.

"What is the matter?" asked Mrs. Frisbone, coming out of her room.

"Man overboard, madam," replied the second officer.

"Man overboard! Who is it?" asked the terrified lady.

"I'm sure I don't know who it is, madam."

As it was a "man overboard," it did not occur to her that the unfortunate person could be her sister; but, fearing that the invalid might be alarmed at the unusual noise, she went to her room, and found she was not there.

"Where is my sister?" asked Mrs. Frisbone, very much startled by the discovery she had made.

"I don't know, madam," replied Raymond. "I saw her walking on the hurricane-deck a while ago. I will see if she is there now."

The second officer left the cabin; and, finding the captain on the upper deck, he asked if he had seen Miss Rodwood.

"She is overboard," replied the captain.

"My sister overboard!" exclaimed Mrs. Frisbone, who had followed Raymond from the cabin.

"I am sorry to say she is, madam," added O'Hara; "but I think she will be saved. Mr. Speers leaped in after her only a few seconds after she went over."

"Did she fall into the water?" demanded the excited lady.

"She jumped over the railing herself, madam," answered O'Hara, as gently as he could utter the disagreeable words.

"Impossible! She could not have intended to end her life," groaned the agonized sister.

The captain was explaining what had passed in the cabin before the catastrophe, when Mr. Frisbone joined them. He was astounded at the intelligence conveyed to him.

"Have you suspected that she was out of her head, Maggie?" he inquired.

"I have not seen a single indication of any thing of the kind," she replied.

"I was on my way to the fire-room to call you, at the request of Mr. Speers, who was sure something was the matter with her, when I heard the cry of 'Man overboard,'" added O'Hara.

"I wish he had called me," said Mrs. Frisbone, with a shudder.

"Don't be alarmed, madam: I am confident she will be saved," continued the captain, looking out into the darkness astern of the ship.

"I am sure I did not suspect any thing of this kind. She seemed to be quite cheerful and happy when she retired," mused Mrs. Frisbone.

"Hurrah! hurrah!" shouted the boat's crew, in the gloom, where they could not be seen.

"That means good news," said the captain. "They have her in the boat by this time."

The party on the deck listened for further sounds in the direction from which the cheers had come. In a few moments they heard the measured stroke of oars at some distance from the ship. Raymond had ordered up all the lanterns on board, which were taken to the gangway.

"Hurrah! hurrah! hurrah!" shouted the crew of the third cutter, as the boat approached the steamer.

The party descended from the hurricane-deck, and gathered at the gangway, where the accommodation steps had been rigged by Raymond's directions. The cutter came up to the platform; and Tom Speers, taking the shivering invalid in his arms, bore her up the steps, and into the cabin.

She was too cold, and exhausted by her struggles in the water, to speak. Tom laid her in the berth, and all retired but her sister. Her wet clothing was removed, and she was wrapped in blankets. In half an hour she was warm and comfortable. Her improved condition was reported by the Prince to the interested officers.

"What induced you to do such a thing?" asked Mrs. Frisbone. "Are you tired of living, Louise?"

"Far from it, Maggie! I don't know what made me do it. I can't explain it. I certainly had no intention of jumping overboard. An impulse came over me, and I could not resist it. I have hardly slept a wink for two nights, and I was very nervous."

This was all the explanation the invalid could give

of the rash act she had attempted. She insisted that the bath had done her good, and that she was no longer vexed by the morbid fancies which had troubled her since the collision. She expressed her gratitude in the strongest terms to the young gentleman who had gone to her assistance; and she was sure she should have drowned without his aid, for she felt that she was sinking when he brought the life-buoy to her.

Mrs. Frisbone would not leave her again that night, though the invalid declared that she should go to sleep at once; and she did as soon as the explanations were finished. In the mean time Tom Speers had gone to his state-room, and changed his wet clothes for dry ones, and was no worse for his bath.

"Mr. Speers, you have laid me and my wife under a load of obligation that I shall never feel like getting rid of," said the Prince, as the young hero came out of his room. "I like that girl as though she was my own daughter; and you have done more for me than any living man could do, unless it was to save my wife from drowning in the same way."

"I am sorry you feel that way about it, sir," replied Tom, laughing; "for I don't like to have anybody feel that he owes me too much."

"You are more than ten times the feller I supposed you was, Mr. Speers; and I have heard a good deal about you within the last week or two."

"What have you heard about me, sir?" asked Tom curiously.

"I'll tell you some other time," answered the Prince. "I must go and look out for the firemen, for they are very green in their new duties, and I'm afraid they will catch cold when the watch is shifted: it is just like boys to go on deck to cool off when they leave the fire-room."

Mr. Frisbone disappeared in the engine-room, and Tom went forward. He had a long talk with O'Hara about the adventure of the night, in which the captain did not spare the praise he felt that the bold fellow deserved.

"Upon my sowl, the Prince would make you a rich man if he could; but, by the powers, you have got ahead of him, and it'll be no use. You are richer than he is, and he can't do any thing for you in that way."

"I hope not; for I should feel insulted if a man offered me money for that sort of service," replied the high-toned young officer. "I feel as much at home in the water as I do on this deck; and, if I saw anybody in the water, I couldn't help going in after him, if he needed help."

"That's the ginerous nature you have, my boy! It's a wonder you wasn't born in ould Ireland or Italy."

"The Tritonia is close aboard of us," said the officer of the deck, touching his cap to the captain.

"I see she is: slow down, if you please, Mr. Raymond," replied O'Hara. "We shall soon know now to what port we are bound."

"I think I can go to sleep when I know that," added Tom.

The Tritonia had made a long tack in standing off and on; and, when she was at the greatest distance from the Ville d'Angers, the wind had died out. She was rolling in the long swells with all sail set, but making no progress through the water. The Ville d'Angers ran across her wake, and within hailing distance of her.

"On board of the steamer!" called the officer of the deck.

"On board the Tritonia!" replied Raymond, prompted by the captain.

"The captain desires Mr. O'Hara to report in person," added the officer of the schooner.

"All ready with the third cutter," said the captain.

The boat was lowered into the water, and pulled off with O'Hara on board. In a few moments he was on the quarter-deck of the Tritonia. Capt. Wainwright had been called when the steamer was made out by the watch, and he immediately came on deck.

O'Hara reported in full concerning his action since he had taken possession of the steamer. He declared that the Ville d'Angers was in good seaworthy condition in every respect. She was abundantly supplied with coal, water, and provisions.

"It seems very remarkable that we should pick up Mr. Frisbone and his wife in a disabled vessel," said Capt. Wainwright, when O'Hara had finished his report, which closed with the catastrophe of Miss Rodwood. "It would perhaps have been better if the American Prince had happened to come to the relief of the Ville d'Angers."

"But better the Tritonia than neither," added O'Hara.

"There would have been a certain fitness in the American Prince saving her former owner from the perils of the sea."

"Indade there would!" exclaimed the captain of the steamer.

"But I suppose you want your orders; and I confess that I have been in a great deal of doubt. Professor Primback is so much incensed against me, that he won't speak to me. I have asked his advice in regard to what to do; but he will not say any thing. He says I am in the attitude of rebellion against his authority. He insists that I shall call back the students I have sent away, and let the steamer go to the bottom, if that was to be her fate. Mr. Marline thinks I had better send her to the nearest port, which would be Cadiz."

"That would be a sensible way to dispose of her," interposed O'Hara, who was in favor of an independent cruise.

"Then I find I differ from all others. I am neither in favor of sending her to Cadiz, or of letting her go to the bottom," added the captain of the Tritonia decidedly. "And, as I am to be responsible for my action, I shall follow my own plan. Mr. Primback annoys me very much, and I wish to put an end to this state of things as soon as possible."

"You did not state your plan, captain," suggested O'Hara nervously; for the independent cruise seemed to be no longer probable.

"I worked over the dead reckoning last night, after the calm settled down upon us; and I make it out that the Josephine cannot be more than forty or fifty miles to the southward of us. She must have laid her course sooner than we did, or we should not have lost sight of her in the night."

"The American Prince must have sailed some time in the evening, if she was not delayed by the storm;

and she may have overhauled the Josephine before this time."

"Possibly; but the two vessels got so much off their course during the blow, that I hardly expect to see the Prince till we reach Funchal," replied Capt. Wainwright. "All I care for is to get the vice-principal on board again; and then he can settle all disputed questions, and order the Ville d'Angers to Funchal or to Cadiz, as he pleases; and I shall be relieved of all responsibility."

"I see," said O'Hara; but he did not see what he wished to see.

"The Josephine must be becalmed, as we are, within fifty miles of us; and, as the weather is clear now, we shall be likely to see her," continued the captain. "So, Mr. O'Hara, you will range your steamer ahead of the Tritonia, and take on board our best hemp cable. In other words, you will take the schooner in tow. When you have made fast our line, you will make your course south south-west, and run under full steam."

"South south-west, under full steam," repeated O'Hara, not at all pleased with the prospect; for he did not like the idea of having the Ville d'Angers changed into a tow-boat, as he contemptuously expressed it afterwards.

"It is now nearly eight bells in the morning," continued Wainwright. "You will take the course given you; and if by meridian we don't see any thing of the Josephine, I shall be ready to give you new orders."

O'Hara returned to his boat, and was pulled to the steamer. She went on, and took a position ahead of the schooner, and as near as it was safe to lie. The second cutter carried the tow-line to her stern, and the end was hauled on board. It was made fast under the direction of Mr. Rimmer, for there were no proper bitts for the purpose.

"Are you all ready?" shouted the captain of the Tritonia.

"All ready, sir," replied O'Hara, when the hawser had been secured.

"Then go ahead," responded Capt. Wainwright.

The bells in the engine-room sounded; and in a few minutes the Ville d'Angers was going ahead at full speed, towing the Tritonia in the direction indicated by the captain of the latter.

Mr. Frisbone was informed of the use to be made of the steamer; but he offered no objection. He had heard that Madeira was a good place for invalids; and very likely his wife's sister would do as well as, if not better than, at Malaga so late in the season. He was as willing to go to Funchal as to Spain. He staid in the fire-room till six o'clock, when he had thoroughly trained both watches of firemen in their duties.

During the forenoon Tom Speers saw Miss Rodwood for the first time since the stirring event of the early morning. She expressed her gratitude to him in the warmest terms, and Tom thought she was prettier than ever.

"You bear a name which has been familiar to me for some years, Miss Rodwood," said Tom, trying to turn the conversation from his own gallant deed. "Judge Rodwood was my uncle's most intimate friend, but I have no acquaintance with his family; and possibly you are his daughter."

"I am not his daughter: he has no children. Judge Rodwood is my uncle; and he is a very intimate friend of Mr. Frisbone."

"Yes; and he was very anxious to find you, young man," said the Prince, who joined the party in the cabin at this moment.

"He was more anxious to find me than I was to have him find me," replied Tom, laughing.

"Your uncle has left you a big fortune, and appointed the judge your guardian. Didn't you get a despatch and some letters from him?" asked the Prince.

"I received a despatch and a letter from him," replied Tom.

"Then, why under the sun didn't you answer it, or go to London at once?" demanded the Prince, who supposed he had not received any thing from the judge.

Tom honestly explained why he had not opened the letter.

"If you have any influence with Judge Rodwood, I hope you will use it to induce him to allow me to remain in the academy squadron," continued Tom.

"I certainly will; for I believe it is the best institution in the world," replied the Prince heartily.

"Sail on the starboard bow!" shouted the lookout in the foretop of the Tritonia, loudly enough to be heard on board of the steamer.

This announcement put an end to the conversation, for all were anxious to know whether or not the sail was the Josephine. All the glasses on board were pointed at the white spot on the ocean in the distance. A gentle breeze was blowing from the south-east, and the vessel had all sail set; but she was too far off for the officers of the steamer to determine what she was.

"On board the Ville d'Angers!" shouted the officer of the deck on the Tritonia.

Raymond answered the hail; and the order came from Capt. Wainwright, to head the steamer to the south-west. This course was directly towards the distant sail. At six bells in the forenoon watch, all hands were assured that the sail was the Josephine. Wainwright ordered three guns to be fired on board of the steamer, to attract the attention of her people; for the wind was freshening, and the chase was likely to be prolonged. Mr. Frisbone, who had fired the guns which answered as signals of distress, attended to this duty, though the students were very anxious to assist, especially in pulling the lock-string.

The signals were heard on board of the Josephine; and she came about, and stood towards the steamer and her tow. In half an hour the vessels were within hailing distance.

"Steamer ahoy!" shouted Robinson, the officer of the deck on board of the Josephine.

"On board of the Josephine!" replied Raymond.

"What steamer is that?"

"The Ville d'Angers, towing the Tritonia."

While this conversation was going on, the crew of the Josephine were getting out the second cutter; and, when it was lowered into the water, Mr. Pelham stepped on board. The boat pulled for the Tritonia, which had been cast off by the steamer, and had heaved to under the lee of the Josephine. The vice-principal boarded her, and was received by Capt. Wainwright, cap in hand.

"I am very glad to see you, Mr. Pelham," said Wainwright, as they shook hands.

"I did not expect to see the Tritonia again till she arrived at Funchal," replied the vice-principal.

"I am glad you have come, sir," said Professor Primback in a severe tone. "I am sorry to be obliged to charge Wainwright with gross insubordination during your absence, Mr. Pelham."

"I will hear your complaint at another time, Mr. Primback," replied the vice-principal.

"I think it would be more proper to hear it at the present time," added the professor. "I have suspended Wainwright and Scott from duty; and I wish to know whether or not my authority is to be sustained. No attention whatever has been paid to my directions. If you have any orders to give, you will please regard Greenwood as the captain, and Alexander as the first lieutenant."

The professor then retired to the cabin.

CHAPTER IX.

THE NEW SHIP'S COMPANY.

THE vice-principal was very much perplexed at the condition of things he found on board of the Tritonia. He was greatly annoyed that his involuntary absence had raised a tempest in the vessel. He was astonished to find the schooner in tow of the steamer; and, before he made any inquiries into the case of discipline, he listened to the report of the captain of the events which had transpired since the consorts parted company.

Before Wainwright had proceeded far with his account, the cutter which had conveyed Mr. Pelham on board returned with Mr. Fluxion. The two vice-principals heard the story, and then retired to the cabin to consult together in regard to it. Mr. Primback was called; and his charges against the captain and the second lieutenant were heard.

Wainwright and Scott were questioned in the presence of the professor; and, when they had retired, the charge against Scott was declared to be frivolous, as any sailor could see that it was.

"I think if you will read the regulations, Professor Primback, you will see that you had no authority to suspend the captain or the second lieutenant," said Mr. Fluxion, who was disgusted with the conduct of the instructor.

"I admit that the regulations give me no authority over the officers of the vessel in purely nautical matters," replied Mr. Primback. "I take pride and pleasure in acknowledging that I know nothing about a ship or its management."

"It would be better if you knew enough about nautical matters to understand the duty of the officers," added the senior vice-principal. "It is very unpleasant for me to decide against you; but the case is so very plain, that I can't do otherwise."

"I think you have not fully examined the premises, Mr. Fluxion," continued the professor, nettled at the obvious displeasure of the senior authority. "The scholastic department is under my direction in the absence of the junior vice-principal."

"That is admitted."

"But the captain, a mere boy, may send away one-half of the students, and then require the other half to be on duty all the time in the management of the vessel. In other words, he may practically abolish the scholastic department," added Mr. Primback triumphantly, for he believed he had made out a very strong case.

"And the head of the scholastic department takes pride in being so ignorant of nautical affairs as to be incapable of judging whether or not the captain is justified in sending away one-half of his ship's company, and requiring the other half to do duty on board of his own vessel," answered Mr. Fluxion, with some excitement in his manner.

"Then, as the acting principal, I may be carted all over the ocean at the pleasure of this boy!" exclaimed the professor. "I may not even protest when he chooses to depart from the course of any boyish enterprise that happens to excite his imagination."

"That is precisely the situation," replied the senior vice-principal, with a smile. "The boy will be held responsible for the management of the vessel; and, if he depart from the prescribed course without sufficient reason for doing so, he would be punished for it. If he took the vessel out upon such a boyish expedition as you describe, he would certainly lose his place as commander."

"But the boy is placed over the man: I am ignored, though I am old enough to be the boy's father," protested the professor.

"The boy has no authority over you, any more than you have over him, in nautical matters. The sailor is placed over the landsman. But you forget, Mr. Primback, that this is an exceptional case. The accidental absence of the vice-principal in charge caused all the difficulty. This is a thing that is not likely to happen again. A sudden squall rendered it impossible for him to return to his vessel."

"Am I to understand that you approve the conduct of this boy, sir?" demanded the professor.

"If he had obeyed your orders, he might have been compelled to abandon Mr. Frisbone and the two ladies to their fate, to say nothing of the duty of saving the steamer. I do approve the conduct of Capt. Wainwright; and I think he deserves nothing but praise and commendation for what he has done. I am sure the principal will take the same view of the matter," replied Mr. Fluxion.

"Then I am to be snubbed by this boy?"

"I understand you to say that he has been courteous and polite to you."

"I have no fault to find with his manner; only with his refusal to obey me."

"Then I think nothing more need be said about the matter. If you had confined yourself to your own duties, there would have been no trouble."

"I consider myself censured by your decision; and I desire to resign my position as an instructor in this institution," added Mr. Primback, with all the dignity he could assume.

"I have nothing to do with your resignation: that should go to the principal," replied Mr. Fluxion, who hoped to see a more reasonable person in his place, and one who knew a brace from a bobstay.

The professor disappeared in his state-room, and related his grievances to Dr. Crumples, who had no sympathy at all with him.

The more interesting question to be settled was the destination of the Ville d'Angers. The vice-principals talked it over for some time, without coming to a conclusion, and then decided to visit the steamer to confer with Mr. Frisbone. The Prince gave them a hearty greeting; but he had no opinion in regard to the disposal of the vessel. There was no law, so far as they were aware, that required the vessel to be taken to one port rather than another; and it was finally decided that the voyage to Madeira should be continued, the steamer accompanying the two schooners.

But Mr. Fluxion was not satisfied with the present arrangement in regard to the ship's company of the Ville d'Angers, since it was composed of one-half of the Tritonia's people, while the Josephine remained fully manned. He thought the burden of taking the steamer into port should be more equally divided between the two vessels. Mr. Pelham doubted whether it was expedient to mix the two crews; but his senior overruled his objection, and a new list was made out for the ship's company of the extra vessel. The names were shown to O'Hara by the vice-principals.

"I suppose you don't object," said Mr. Fluxion, with a rather sarcastic smile; for he was not much inclined to consult the wishes of the young gentlemen when he detailed them for duty outside of their own craft. "You will have more officers, and a larger crew for the steamer."

"Upon me sowl, I do object!" exclaimed O'Hara, with no little excitement in his manner, after he had looked at the list of officers.

"Well, what's the matter now?" demanded the senior vice-principal, with something like a frown on his bronzed face.

"I like the ship's company we have now a great dale better," replied O'Hara decidedly.

"It would be quite as respectful if you should pronounce the English language properly when you address your superior officers," added Mr. Fluxion, who was by far the severest disciplinarian in the squadron.

"I beg your pardon, sir," said O'Hara, touching his cap, and taking it off while he bowed low to the senior officer present. "I did not intend to be disrespectful."

"Very well, Mr. O'Hara: you have shown that you can speak English as well as French, Italian, and Irish," replied Mr. Fluxion, his face relaxing into a smile again. "What objection have you to the list in your hand?"

"I like the present detail better, sir."

"That is no answer to my question. What objection have you?"

"The first is, that this reduces Mr. Speers to the rank of second officer, when he has done all the hard work of putting the steamer into sailing-trim as first."

"If an officer from the Tritonia has the command, the Josephine should have the second place on board," added Mr. Fluxion.

"I think that is quite fair," interposed Mr. Pelham.

"I think so myself, if the Josephine is to take part in getting the vessel into port," continued O'Hara, who could not help recognizing the fairness of the senior's decision. "But my second objection is to mixing the two crews at all."

"I see no objection to that," said Mr. Fluxion.

"I'm afraid they won't agree together," suggested O'Hara, shaking his head.

"If there is any danger of a disagreement of this kind, it is time the two crews were mingled, so that they may learn a new lesson in discipline."

"There has always been a good deal of rivalry and some hard feeling among the different vessels of the squadron, sir," continued O'Hara; and it is probable that the boy knew more about this matter than the man, and the junior vice-principal, who had been a student in the institution, understood it better than the senior.

"I can conceive of no disagreement among officers and seamen while on duty. You are to be in command of the steamer, Mr. O'Hara; and if any one from the Josephine refuses to obey your orders, or makes trouble on board, you will promptly report it to me; and, if the offender is an officer, he shall take the lowest number in the ship," replied the stern disciplinarian, with the feeling, that, if there were any such insubordination in the vessel, he would like to get hold of it.

"But the vessels may be separated again, as they have been before," suggested O'Hara, who was certainly very much opposed to having any of the Josephine's officers under his command.

"We are not likely to be separated again: we have had one hard storm, and we are not in much danger of having another before we get to Madeira, which will be in three or four days at the most."

"I will do the best I can, sir," replied O'Hara, touching his cap to the senior.

"I don't like to have the students serve as firemen," continued Mr. Fluxion. "Possibly I may be able to find a crew of firemen for the steamer."

"How will it be possible for you to find a crew of firemen here in mid-ocean?" asked Mr. Pelham, smiling with incredulity.

"The Josephine has not been without an adventure any more than the Tritonia," replied Mr. Fluxion. "Yesterday morning at daylight we picked up a boat in which were six men. They are all Frenchmen and Italians; and say their steamer was sunk in a collision with another vessel in the night. Most of the crew and passengers got on board of the other vessel, and they took a boat to go to her; but it was upset in the heavy sea. They righted the boat, and all but one of them succeeded in getting into it again; but the other vessel was out of sight in the fog then, and they were unable to find her. This is the story they tell; and I have no doubt it is true. Very likely they belonged to the Ville d'Angers."

"If they did, how was it possible for you to have picked them up?" asked Mr. Pelham.

"The steamer could not have been a great way from either of us when you heard the guns, though the Tritonia, as we may see by comparing the reckoning, was considerably to the northward of the Josephine," added Mr. Fluxion.

"But where are these men? They have recognized the steamer by this time, if she was the one in which they were employed."

"Probably they have not seen her yet," replied Mr. Fluxion, laughing. "They slept all day yesterday; and, as I did not see them on deck when I left the schooner, I suppose they are sleeping off another day. They asked for wine, and insisted that they must have it; and they have slept all the time since I told them we had none on board."

The change was announced to the ship's company of the Ville d'Angers; and the half-dozen students who were required to return to the Tritonia were indignant and dissatisfied; but none of them dared say any thing in the presence of Mr. Fluxion. They were ordered into the Josephine's boat, and left on board of their own vessel. The cutter then proceeded to the Josephine, and both vice-principals boarded her. O'Hara went with them.

It was found that the men picked up in the boat were still asleep under the top-gallant forecastle, where quarters had been fixed up for them. Mr. Shakings, the adult boatswain of the Josephine, was directed to call them; and they soon presented themselves in the waist, where the vice-principals were waiting to examine them in regard to their vessel. They were a very hard-looking set of men; and it was evident enough that severe discipline would be required to keep them in order.

As soon as they came on deck, they discovered the Ville d'Angers, which lay astern of the Josephine. They threw up their hands in astonishment when they saw her, and uttered a great many wild exclamations.

"What was the name of your steamer?" asked Mr. Fluxion in French.

"The Ville d'Angers," replied one of them; and then they all indulged in another volley of exclamations.

"Is that the Ville d'Angers?" inquired the senior, pointing at the steamer.

"It is not possible!" shouted several of them at once. "She was sunk. A big hole was cut in her bow; and the water was pouring into her when we left her."

They all talked together, and it was almost impossible to understand them. Some spoke in French, and others in Italian; for it appeared that there was a scarcity of Frenchmen, so many of them had gone into the army. The most intelligent one was an Italian; and he was conducted to the quarter-deck, where O'Hara was instructed to question him. But all the information needed had been obtained from Mr. Frisbone.

This man said his name was Alfonzo. He was asked if he and his companions were willing to work as firemen of the steamer on the trip to Funchal, if they received good wages. Then the fellow put on a cunning look, and it was plain that he was disposed to drive a sharp bargain. He thought a moment; and the interpreter saw that he was studying up some hard terms, and was going to ask for something which he regarded as exorbitant.

"We worked on the Ville d'Angers six days for which we have received no pay," said Alfonzo, with a cunning leer on his face. "Pay us for this time, and we will work on the steamer."

"What were your wages on the steamer?" asked O'Hara.

The fellow hesitated a moment, and then said three francs a day. O'Hara reported the substance of Alfonzo's reply to the senior, at the same time expressing his belief that the Italian was lying, and that the firemen — for such they all were — had not been paid more than two francs, or at most not more than two and a half.

"Sixty cents a day is little enough for men who work in the fire-room of a ship at sea; and they shall have their own price," replied Mr. Fluxion.

O'Hara informed Alfonzo that his terms were acceded to, and he was told to settle the matter with his companions. He looked quite sad, instead of rejoicing that his terms had been accepted: he was sorry that he had not asked more. The others assented.

"This young gentleman is the captain of the steamer," said Mr. Fluxion, pointing to O'Hara.

The firemen all laughed as they surveyed him from head to foot; and possibly they thought they should have an easy time of it on board of the Ville d'Angers, if she was to be managed by boys like those of the Tritonia. They were ordered into the boat, and were put on board of the steamer.

"Mr. Speers particularly desires that the studies may be continued while we are on board of the steamer," said O'Hara, when the men had been sent away.

"Speers!" exclaimed the senior vice-principal, evidently astonished at the suggestion. "He is the young man who went from the steerage up to first master, and whose guardian is looking for him, I believe."

"The same, sir."

"He shall be gratified; and Capt. Fairfield, our extra instructor, who is the most versatile scholar in the squadron, shall be transferred to the Ville d'Angers," added Mr. Fluxion.

"Capt. Fairfield!" exclaimed O'Hara, afraid the instructor might be a sailor, and be placed over his head as an acting vice-principal; for, like most young men, he preferred to have the supreme command of the vessel.

"He is a West-Pointer, and knows no more about a ship than a marine; though he is perfect in the theory of navigation," Mr. Fluxion explained. "You will divide your authority with no one, Mr. O'Hara. I shall send boatswain Shakings of this vessel with you to look out for your rigging."

"What are my orders in case the vessels should be

separated?" asked the young commander of the Ville d'Angers, though he was a year older than a young man we knew who had the full command of a thousand-ton ship; or another who brought his bark safely into port through the worst storm of the season.

"I suppose you would prefer to have your steamer separated from the rest of the squadron," added Mr. Fluxion, laughing.

"I beg your pardon, sir; but I might have run for any port in the world when I had the steamer all to myself; but, instead of that, I went to look for the Tritonia," replied the captain, a little hurt by the remark of the senior.

"You did exceedingly well, Capt. O'Hara; and I may add that I have full confidence in you. I know of no officer in the squadron whom I should prefer for the service to which Capt. Wainwright first appointed you; and I commend him for the good judgment he exercised in his selection. I only wonder that he did not appoint Scott, who is a prime favorite of his."

"I thank you, sir," replied O'Hara, touching his cap. "But Mr. Scott is a good officer, sir."

"As good as any in the squadron, but not the best for an independent command," added the senior.

By this time the cutter had returned; and the Josephine's portion of the crew of the Ville d'Angers were sent on board. The Tritonia's part were already on duty. As soon as the boat was hoisted up at the davits, the two schooners filled away. A six-knot breeze was blowing, and they were soon at a considerable distance from the steamer; for O'Hara had been instructed to station his ship's company under the new arrangement before he got under way.

He immediately called all hands, now consisting of six officers and twenty-four seamen beside himself. As he had twelve hands in each watch, he divided each into quarter-watches. He appointed four quartermasters, who were to have charge of the wheel under the officer of the deck, and a few petty officers for other duties. The state-rooms were assigned to the students; and the regulations of the academy squadron declared to be in full force on board, so far as they were applicable.

"It is now four bells in the afternoon watch; and the second part of the starboard watch has the deck," said Capt. O'Hara, when all the arrangements had been completed. "The officers and seamen will take their stations."

Raymond was the officer of the second part of the watch indicated; and he repaired to the pilot-house to assume his duties. The quartermaster of the second part was there, with a seaman to assist at the wheel.

"I don't like this arrangement," said Gregory, the first officer, who had been fourth lieutenant of the Josephine, as he followed the captain forward.

"I am sorry you don't, Mr. Gregory," replied O'Hara, rather coldly.

"I don't think there is any need of quarter-watches in this steamer," added the first officer, with more emphasis than before.

"I don't think so either," chimed in Clinch, the third master of the Josephine.

"That shows that we differ in opinion a little taste," returned O'Hara with a smile. "You may start her now, Mr. Raymond," continued the captain, when he came to the pilot-house.

"Start her, sir," repeated Raymond. "One bell, quartermaster."

"One bell, sir," returned the quartermaster, as he pulled the handle on the wheel-frame.

The screw began to turn slowly, and the Ville d'Angers went ahead. A few minutes later the speed bell was rung, and the steamer increased her rate to something like ten knots an hour, though she was capable of making twelve or more. But a thick fog had settled down upon the ocean, and nothing could be seen of the rest of the little fleet. The captain ordered the regular fog-signal to be sounded at intervals, and a sharp lookout to be kept for the other vessels.

CHAPTER X.

SOMETHING ABOUT THE MADEIRA ISLANDS.

ON board of the Josephine and the Tritonia, the number sent away rendered it necessary to reorganize the watches. While the vice-principals were attending to this duty, the wind suddenly changed, so that the vessels could not lay their course; and it had headed them off till they were standing nearly to the southward. At the same time the fog shut out the Ville d'Angers from view. For a time after the course had been changed, the fog-signals of the steamer were heard; and then they ceased.

As the steamer was not disturbed by the change of wind, Mr. Fluxion feared she would run ahead of the little squadron, and lose sight of her associates. He directed the captain to tack after the Josephine had run some five miles to the southward, so as to keep somewhere on the track of the steamer. The fog was very deep and dense, and he wondered that the Ville had ceased to whistle. He was not prepared to believe that the captain of the steamer would wilfully run away from her consorts; and the situation puzzled him. The Tritonia was near enough to hear the signals of the other schooner; and there was little danger of losing sight of each other unless heavy weather came on, of which there were some indications.

The captains had consulted their barometers as soon as the watches had been re-arranged. Wainwright was astonished to observe a considerable fall of the instrument; and he immediately reported the fact to Mr. Pelham, and Capt. Vroome did the same to Mr. Fluxion. Every preparation was at once made for heavy weather; and they had it before dark.

While the fog was still hanging over the ocean, the wind began to come in heavy gusts, and all the light sails were hastily taken in. Just after dark the fog lifted, or was driven to seaward by the strong breeze. The vice-principals looked anxiously for the lights of the Ville d'Angers; but nothing could be seen of them in any direction. During the night the wind blew a fierce gale from the southward. At daylight the gale had moderated, but the fog settled down on the water again. Nothing was seen or heard of the steamer. For three days more, in all sorts of weather, though the wind was generally contrary, the schooners continued on their course, and then arrived safely at Funchal.

"There is the Prince at anchor off the Loo Rock!" exclaimed Mr. Pelham, as the Tritonia approached the town of Funchal.

"That's an odd-looking rock," added Scott, who heard the remark. "It looks like the head of the sea-serpent, with a fort built on the top of his cranium."

"That fort commands the harbor, if we can call this a harbor when it has no shelter from any storm from the east or south, where most of the tempests of this region come from," continued the vice-principal, who had been at these islands before. "The rock is seventy feet high; and the Portuguese have made it impossible to climb up its steep sides, except by the steps opposite the island. The top of it is three hundred feet long by a hundred wide; and this space is covered by a fort, mounting fourteen guns, which is always kept garrisoned, as a sort of regulator of the vessels in the roadstead. If they don't obey orders, and follow the rules of the port, a gun from that fort will remind them of the neglect; and any attempt to evade them will bring a shot."

"There is a mole, or something of that kind," added Scott, who was off duty, and was privileged to observe the wonders of the shore.

"That is the Pontinha. It is a sort of breakwater, though it affords no great protection to vessels, which are sometimes obliged to get up their anchors, and work out to sea, to avoid being cast upon the rocks. It is an embankment built out to a small island on which is the fort of San José. You see that the vessels behind the Loo Rock are moored in a line. They are made fast to heavy cables, secured by iron bolts to the rock at the bow, while a stern line is carried to the shore of the main island. The bottom is very rocky, and the holding ground is not good."

All hands were called to be ready to moor ship; but even this was not allowable until the health officers had visited the schooners, and a government boat had been alongside. When these formalities were all completed, the two vessels hauled in beside the American Prince, and were moored like the other craft.

As soon as the rules of the port would permit it, — for no vessel can communicate with the shore, or with another vessel, until the proper permits are obtained, — the vice-principals went on board of the Prince to report to the principal, who of course had no intimation of the stirring events which had transpired on the passage from Gibraltar. The boat's crew that pulled them to the steamer boarded the Prince; and the students told the story of the Ville d'Angers, though the Princes had nothing of interest to relate in return, for the ship had not sailed till the violence of the storm had abated, and had made a tolerably comfortable voyage.

The Princes thought the fellows in the picked-up steamer were having a jolly time of it; and most of them were willing to believe they had taken it into their heads to go off on a cruise by themselves, and would return when they got ready. Scott defended O'Hara from the implied charges against him, and was confident the Ville d'Angers would soon arrive.

"It will be a big lark for those fellows," insisted McLane, the fourth lieutenant of the Prince.

"It's no lark at all, Mack," replied Scott. "O'Hara is a countryman of yours, and you judge him by yourself."

"That's so!" exclaimed McLane. "If I had the command of a fine steamer like the Ville d'Angers, I don't think I should hurry to get into port with her."

"That will do for you, but not for O'Hara. When he gets out to sea he knows the way back," added Scott.

"You won't see that steamer for a week at the least," persisted McLane.

"I can't say that we shall; but, if we don't, it will not be for any fault of O'Hara."

"If it were my case, I would take the steamer to New York, stopping at the 'Isles of the Sea' on the way, making sure that I kept out of the way of the academy squadron all the time," continued the lieutenant of the Prince.

"It's easy enough for you to tell what you would do, Mack; but the principal knows you well enough not to trust you with a mud-scow, to say nothing of a fine steamer like the Ville d'Angers."

"Don't you think I could handle a steamer as well as O'Hara?" demanded the Prince, a little nettled by the raillery of the Tritonia.

"Perhaps you could; but you couldn't find your way to the port named in your orders, according to your own confession."

"Well, O'Hara hasn't done it yet."

"But he will do it, unless there is some good reason to prevent him from doing so."

This sort of banter continued till the vice-principals came out of the main cabin with Mr. Lowington. The principal of the squadron had listened with the deepest interest to the narration of the subordinate officials. When he was informed that thirty-one of the students were on board of the steamer, on their way to the Madeiras, or roaming at their own pleasure over the ocean, he looked very anxious and troubled. The fact that Mr. Frisbone was with them afforded him some relief.

"I am rather sorry that one of you had not gone with them," added he, fixing his gaze upon the cabin floor.

"Possibly one of us might, if our experience on the day we sailed from Gibraltar had not taught us better," replied Mr. Fluxion; who, as the senior vice-principal, was responsible for all that had been done after the Ville d'Angers overhauled the Josephine. "I thought Mr. Pelham was very indiscreet to leave his vessel, even to board mine on business, and I was not disposed to have the mistake repeated."

This statement brought in the earlier history of the eventful cruise, and the junior vice-principal delivered the letter from Judge Rodwood to the principal. He read it, and then listened to the account of Tom Speers's running away from the fortune in store for him.

"The judge can have Speers as soon as he wants him," added Mr. Lowington. "A student with three millions behind him, and a letter of credit for four thousand dollars in his pocket, is a nuisance."

"I think not, sir, in this case," interposed Mr. Pelham. "Speers is a very ambitious young man: he jumped from the steerage to first master of the Tritonia, and contrived to avoid going to London to meet Judge Rodwood because he was not willing to leave the vessel. He desires to finish his course; and there is not a better sailor or a more faithful student in the squadron."

"I am glad to hear you speak so well of him; but this letter contains a request that he be discharged from the academy, and be sent to London. I am asked to telegraph that he is on his way."

"It is **too late to do any thing** of that kind now," added Mr. Pelham. "Speers did **not open** the letter which enclosed this one till the Tritonia was at sea; and he did **not** open the telegraph despatch for the reason that he did not believe it was for him."

"He has managed it very well. This letter contains a request from his former and from his present guardian; but the young man is **not here, and** I cannot discharge him. Should **I do so, it is not** probable that he would find his **guardian in London** if I sent him there: I shall **therefore** do nothing till **I** receive further instructions," continued the principal. "But this is a matter of little consequence compared with the cruise **of** this French steamer."

Again the principal inquired into all the circumstances of the parting of the vessels in the fog. Both of the vice-principals assured him that the captain **of** the Ville d'Angers was an entirely reliable student in every respect, and **that he was too** high-toned **to** go off on an independent cruise.

"I supposed the steamer had **got in ahead of us** while we were standing to the southward, and that we should find her in Funchal on our arrival," explained Mr. Fluxion.

"If that were the case, she ought to have been here yesterday," replied the principal. "What do you suppose can have detained her?"

"**I can** imagine **a dozen circumstances** which may have **delayed her,** and **none of them may be the proper** explanation," answered the **senior** vice-principal. "There was a smart gale in the night, after we parted; **but I can** hardly conceive of such a thing as the Ville d'Angers, which was a nearly new vessel, and seaworthy in every respect, foundering in such a light storm. She may have broken her shaft, or deranged her machinery."

"That would compel her to come in under sail," suggested the principal.

"She is well found in every respect; for I directed Shakings to overhaul her, and report to me. But it may take her two or three days longer than it has the schooners to get here. The officers may have had trouble with the foreign firemen, for I think they were a desperate set of villains. But Mr. Frisbone, Shakings, Rimmer, the cook, and two stewards, make six full-grown men; and some of the students are about equal to able-bodied men: so that, if there has been a fight on board, I am confident our side has got the best of it," continued Mr. Fluxion, who was a muscular Christian, and rather enjoyed the idea of reducing the firemen to a proper state of subjection if they attempted to put on airs.

"Raymond, the fourth officer, is as brave a fellow as ever trod a deck; and I will match him against any two of those firemen," added Mr. Pelham, who also had some taste for a fight in a good cause.

"I sincerely hope that nothing of the kind has occurred on board of the steamer," said Mr. Lowington, who was thoroughly a man of peace, and justified no fighting that could possibly be avoided.

"I don't think any thing of the kind has occurred, and I mentioned it only as a possibility. It is more probable that some derangement of the machinery of the vessel had delayed her; and I shall expect her to come into port within two or three days," continued Mr. Fluxion. "In the mean time, the students on board are pursuing their studies, so that there will be no time lost."

The vice-principals returned to their respective vessels; but the principal could not help being very anxious for the safety of the thirty-one students on board of the Ville d'Angers. Possibly he was not so confident as his junior officers that the young men had not gone "on a lark" in the vessel. While this conversation was going on, the signal, "All hands attend lecture," had been displayed on board of the steamer. All the boats were in the water, and the students were soon assembled in the American Prince. As usual, there was a large map of the country to be described, hung where all the pupils could see it. In this instance it was a map of the Madeira Islands, drawn on a large scale by the professor himself. Mr. Mapps stood by it with a long pointer in his hand, when the students took their places.

"The Madeiras are a group of five islands," the professor began, flourishing the pointer over the map to attract the attention of his audience. "They are some six hundred miles from Lisbon, four hundred from the nearest part of the African coast, and five hundred from the nearest of the Azores. The principal island is called Madeira, from which Porto Santo, the only other island of any importance, is only thirty-five miles distant. The other three islands are called the Desertas: they are merely uninhabited rocks.

"Madeira and Porto Santo contain an area of three hundred and seventeen square miles, which is equal to about one-fourth of the State of Rhode Island; and contain a population of one hundred and sixteen thousand inhabitants, or about half that of the same State.

"Both of the inhabited islands are mountainous in their structure, and are mostly bordered by steep cliffs on the sea. Soundings are obtained by the ordinary deep-sea lead only close to the shore; and even there the water is over two hundred feet deep. Though the island is of volcanic origin, only one crater is to be found in the mountains. The greatest elevation is about six thousand feet.

"Funchal is the principal town, and has about twenty thousand inhabitants. Its principal business is in wine and fruit. In later years the vine has failed to a great extent, and the commerce of the island has been greatly reduced. Many of the inhabitants are in a state of destitution; and beggars are more common here than in most of the countries of Europe.

"These islands, as well as the Western, or Azores, are dependencies of the kingdom of Portugal. They are represented in the legislature of that country, and have, besides, a local government of their own. The currency of the islands is the same as that of Portugal; and you will find here most of the manners and customs of that country. Possibly some of you will think you have been here before. The city, like Messina in Sicily, which you will remember, is built on a small plain, watered by three little streams that rise in the interior of the island, or on the surrounding hills. Indeed, the island is very like Sicily.

"One of the great natural curiosities of Madeira is the Coural, or Curral, as different writers call it. It is an immense chasm, with perpendicular sides, thirteen hundred feet deep. It is near the middle of the island; and, if the time permits, I believe you will take a walk to it; for there are no carriages in the country, or any roads that are practicable for them. People who can not or will not walk have to be transported by manpower. In some parts they slide down the steep hills on sleds, as boys coast on the snow at home. The roads most travelled are paved with cobble-stones, or the heavy rains would wash them entirely away; and they are thus made the smoother for the sleds. A kind of sled, called a 'buey cart,' drawn by oxen, is also used to some extent. A hammock swung on a long pole, the ends of which are borne on the shoulders of two men, would seem to be the most natural conveyance for a sailor.

"You will have an opportunity to see the country and the city for yourselves, and I will not describe them to you. The people are very gentlemanly and polite, though I believe they are no more given to hard work than the natives of the mother country. The island is a great resort for invalids, especially those with pulmonary complaints; and the same is true of the Azores. The average temperature is sixty-four degrees. A hot south-west wind, which comes over from the great desert of Africa, sometimes carries the mercury up to eighty degrees, though the heat in summer rarely exceeds seventy. But the quality of the climate depends upon the uniformity of its temperature. There are no sudden changes; and one month will not differ from the one before more than two or three degrees. But Dr. Winstock, who spent a winter in the island, informs me that he has seen some very disagreeable weather here."

Professor Mapps finished his brief lecture, leaving much to be learned by the students in their walks about the city and the island. The boats of the Tritonia and Josephine returned; and what was left of the day was used by the officers and seamen in looking at the strange sights that might be seen from the decks of the vessels.

As the squadron was to remain some days at Funchal, study and recitations were not entirely suspended; but, as both watches could be engaged at the same time, the full routine was completed at one o'clock, and the rest of the day was improved on shore. Dr. Winstock took under his care for the excursion, Sheridan and Murray of the Prince, and Wainwright and Scott of the Tritonia.

"This is a rough harbor for a commercial town," said Capt. Sheridan, as he landed from the boat, and looked back to survey the beach, on which the sea was breaking with considerable force.

"It is a very poor harbor," replied the doctor. "Sometimes the sea is so high in the roadstead, that it is not safe for vessels to lie at anchor; and a government boat goes to them, and advises them to get to sea."

"What sort of a boat do you call that?" asked Scott, as he pointed to a very handsome barge near the shore. "The sailors have coalhods, with marline spikes sticking out of the tops."

"That is a government boat, as you may see by the uniform of the officers in it. The cap of the boatmen looks something like an inverted tunnel. But they have a nice time of it under that awning."

The doctor's party by his advice had decided to use their first half-day on shore in making a visit to the church of "Nossa Senhora do Monte," or "Our Lady of the Mountain," which is located on a hill nearly two thousand feet above the sea. The place affords a beautiful view of Funchal and its surroundings. It was an up-hill walk; but most of the ascent was gradual, though a portion of it was very steep. On the way they had an opportunity to see some of the modes of conveyance mentioned by the professor of geography and history.

"It don't seem to me that I should feel very comfortable to have men carrying me about the island," said Murray, as he stopped to see one of the hammocks, which was not unlike a palanquin. "I should feel as though I were a burden upon my own kind."

"They have very good horses here, though they are rather small, — about the size of those they use for the ascent of Mount Vesuvius."

At last the church was reached after a most fatiguing tramp, for the students had not got on their land legs. Most of the way, the road, paved with cobble-stones, was enclosed by a wall over which none of the party were tall enough to see; and this made the walk dismal at times, though they always had a view when looking behind them. But this wall was covered with vines; and, as it was spring-time, the air was laden with the perfume of flowers.

There is nothing about the church worth seeing; and the business of the day was concluded by ascending one of the two towers that crown the building, where the party remained till sunset. The church faces the sea; and from the elevated tower a panorama of a portion of the city and a great deal of magnificent scenery was spread out before the observers; and they returned to their vessels delighted with the excursion.

Mr. Lowington was pacing the quarter-deck of the Prince when the students returned; and it was observed that he cast frequent glances to seaward in search of the missing steamer, but she did not put in an appearance in the offing that night.

CHAPTER XI.

BUDDING VINES AND ORANGE-GROVES.

THE night passed away, and the morning, and the Ville d'Angers did not appear off the island. The principal had a long and anxious conference with Mr. Fluxion. There was only one thing it was possible to do, and that was to send the Prince in search of the missing steamer; but it was decided to wait a day or two longer before this was done.

The next afternoon the doctor and his little party landed in the city, and began to explore the place. After months of constant sight-seeing, they found little in the way of public buildings, squares, or streets, to engage their attention, and were more inclined to get out into the country among the budding flowers and orange-groves.

"That's one of the carts we read of," said Scott, laughing, as he stopped to view a sort of sled on which a yoke of small oxen were hauling a pipe of wine.

"It is one of the kind we see in Funchal, and elsewhere in the island," replied the doctor. "Wheels are not practicable among these hills; and I am not sure that this thing pulls any harder than the car with the revolving axle which we saw in Portugal."

"It certainly does not make any more music," added Murray, referring to the hideous screeching of the cart they had seen in Lisbon.

The sled was something like a "stone-drag" used in the New England States. It was a plank eight feet long and a foot and a half wide, hollowed in the middle so that a wine-cask will fit into it. It was four inches thick, and pointed off at the bow like a boat. Under it were two wooden runners. While the students were looking at it, and while the driver was still yelling with all his might at his diminutive cattle, a boy threw a sort of mop made of rope-yarns, which he had just dipped into a puddle of water, under the forward end of the sled. The runners passed over it, wetting the bottoms, thus making them run a little easier, and removing the danger of fire from friction.

"This is the Praca Constitucional, a very common name for a square in Spain and Portugal. It was formerly the 'Praca da Rainha,' or Queen Square; but the Constitution is more popular than the Queen."

From the square the party passed into the market-place adjoining it. Provisions, vegetables, fruit, provender for horses, and wood were the articles on sale. It was just such a sight as they had seen in Lisbon, and the venders were yelling their wares vigorously when any one that looked like a buyer came in sight. One man had a pole on his shoulder, on which were hung by the legs a dozen pairs of chickens, all alive, and kicking to the extent of their ability. Another had pigeons; but he had considerately killed them before he suspended them on the pole. The one who drove a single pig had about the same luck with him as any other attempting this difficult feat.

LIEUTENANT SCOTT'S ADVENTURE. Page 153

"Drive him the other way!" shouted Scott to the Portuguese, pointing behind the driver.

"He don't understand you," interposed the doctor, translating the remark into Portuguese.

The man laughed as though he had heard the joke before; but he did not adopt the suggestion.

"What's the use of that brush they have tied up in bundles?" asked Sheridan, as they paused before a vender of this sort of merchandise.

"The bakers and others use it to heat their ovens," replied Dr. Winstock. "Wood is a very scarce article in Madeira, though the name of the island in Portuguese means 'wood.' There is little or no need of fuel here, except for cooking purposes. Those bundles of little sticks are not much better than the fagots. All the coal has to be brought from other countries; and that makes it very expensive. The wealthier people and the boarding-houses use it."

"Boarding the invalids that come here must be a great business among the people," said Wainwright, as they passed a group of pale consumptives, seated in the sun on the Praca.

"It is a very important item of the business of the island."

"Do you think it does them any good to come here?" asked Scott.

"Undoubtedly it does; though, if you visit the cemeteries, you will find a great many English and American names on the gravestones. The great difficulty is that those troubled with pulmonary diseases come when it is too late for the climate to benefit them."

The party passed into the principal street of the

town, which was not more than twenty-five feet wide, and it was a broad thoroughfare for Funchal.

"Every gentleman seems to be acquainted with every lady he meets," said Sheridan, as they made their way through the crowded street.

"That remark applies only to the native gentlemen; and it is the custom for them to lift their hats to every lady they meet," replied the surgeon.

"I suppose that is done to make business for the hatters," added Scott.

"No: the Portuguese are even more polite than the French, so far as these outward expressions are concerned; but I doubt whether either would do as much for a lady who really needed assistance as Americans or Englishmen," continued the doctor. "I can't say that I like to see gentlemen bowing to ladies who are entire strangers to them. It is making themselves altogether too familiar, though the custom of the country may justify almost any thing."

"This looks like Spain," said Wainwright, pointing to a lot of men from the country, who were driving three or four donkeys each, loaded with skins filled with wine. "They leave the legs of the goats on for handles."

"Those sacks look something like a goat," added Murray. "I wonder how they can sew them up tight enough to prevent them from leaking."

"They can roll the edges of the skins together a little when they join them, and sew through four thicknesses of the skin," replied the doctor.

"Is that Madeira wine in those sacks?" inquired Murray.

"Probably not; for that is a scarce article, even in this island, at the present time. Porto Santo, or Holy Port, was the first island discovered and settled. Columbus lived there for a time; and his house is still shown. He married his wife there. The discovery and settlement of Madeira followed soon after; and two years later the Portuguese brought from Candia or Crete a vine which proved to be admirably adapted to the climate. The wine made from it became celebrated all over the civilized world. Like port and sherry, it obtained its peculiar flavor from the kind of grape of which it was made. Ten years ago, owing to the failure of the vine-crop, there were only four hundred pipes of it remaining in the island, while twenty-five thousand pipes had once been the average quantity manufactured in a year. The disease attacked the vine nearly twenty years ago; but the people are doing their best to replace it, and doubtless the commerce and reputation of the island will be fully restored. Probably the greater portion of all the wine sold for Madeira is not such; and not a little of it is manufactured in the shops where it is sold, in England and America."

The party passed through the town, and went out into the country on the west side; and, following the road up the hill, they reached the summit of the "Pico de Sao Joao," on which was a fort. From this high point they obtained another view of the city and its suburbs. Beyond the town the shore of the island was composed of sheer precipices, hundreds of feet in height. Near them was a "quinta," or country-house, of some wealthy islander, to which a beautiful garden was attached. As they passed the main gate of the grounds, a gentleman attending a very pretty young lady came out. Dr. Winstock raised his cap to him, and the young officers followed his example.

The owner of the "quinta" politely returned the salutation, and spoke to the surgeon in English; for many of the educated people of the island speak this language, and most of the foreign commerce is carried on with England. Two saddle-horses were standing at the gate, in charge of as many servants; but the gentleman and his daughter — for such was the relation between them — seemed to be in no haste to mount their puny steeds.

"You are English people, I see," said he, with a pleasant smile. "My house and grounds are at your service. This is the quinta da Sao Joao."

"I thank you heartily for your courteous invitation; but perhaps you may be disposed to withdraw it when I add that we are not English, but Americans," replied Dr. Winstock.

"By no means!" exclaimed the gentleman, whom they afterwards heard addressed as Don Roderigue. "I repeat it with even more earnestness than before."

"Thank you, sir; and we shall be very happy to avail ourselves of your permission to visit your gardens."

"You are all officers, I see," continued Don Roderigue, who evidently had some Yankee curiosity.

"In one sense we are: we are all connected with the academy squadron, now moored in the port of Funchal."

The Portuguese had never heard of it; and the surgeon briefly explained it, and invited Don Roderigue to visit the ships of the squadron. He promised to do so, and he and the young lady proceeded to mount their horses. The father was safely seated on his little steed, and the groom was assisting the daughter to the saddle, when the little brute suddenly whirled about like a top, and started off at a dead run. Dona Maria's foot had not been fairly placed in the stirrup, nor had she taken the reins into her hands; so that she was almost helpless.

The two grooms started after the little horse; but, the faster they ran, the more intent the brute became to get away from them. The father uttered an exclamation of anguish, and galloped his horse in the direction the lady's steed had taken. The students were almost paralyzed with fear for the safety of the beautiful girl. The runaway pony turned a corner at the end of the garden; and, at this moment, Scott darted across the grounds, leaped over a high wall, and came into a road in the rear of the estate, the geography of which he had been studying from the top of the Pico de Sao Joao. He came into the road just ahead of the horse; and he was a long distance in advance of the grooms and the lady's father. Dona Maria had evidently lost her footing in the stirrup; for she had slipped partly off the saddle, and was clinging with both hands to the pommel.

Scott had thrown off his uniform coat as he ran across the garden, so that he might be free to act when he tackled the horse; and he felt strong enough just then to throw him over the high wall if he could get hold of him. He sprang into the middle of the road; and it was nothing more than a narrow lane, leading to the stables of the estate, which the pony seemed to prefer to an excursion in the delightful air of the afternoon. The vicious little brute saw him, and attempted to pass at one side of him; but Scott was quick enough to catch him by the bridle-rein. Then came the tug of war; for the pony was not disposed to be so easily captured, and began to rear and plunge to disengage himself from his captor. But Scott was used to horses, and held on. In a moment he had brought the horse down sufficiently to enable him to put his arm around the waist of the maiden, and lift her to the ground.

She was out of breath, so that she could not speak, though she gasped out some sentences in her native tongue, which Scott could not understand. She was too weak to stand; and the gallant lieutenant was compelled to hold her with one arm, and the horse with the other, till assistance came. Don Roderigue was the first to arrive upon the spot. He leaped from his horse, and seized his daughter in his arms.

"Was she thrown from the horse?" he asked.

"No, sir: I don't think she can be much hurt," replied Scott; and he described her position at the moment he had stopped the pony.

By this time Dona Maria was able to speak for herself; and Scott thought she had a very musical voice, though, as she spoke in Portuguese, he could not understand a word she said. The gallop in that uncomfortable position must have jarred her frame considerably. The grooms came up, and took charge of the horses.

"Young gentleman, I owe you very great thanks for

the service you have rendered to my daughter and to me," said Don Roderigue, extending his hand to the lieutenant.

"Don't mention it, sir," exclaimed Scott, laughing at the earnestness of the grateful father. "We were on the top of that pico, and I saw this road leading down to the stable. When the horse started, I thought it likely, as he turned the first corner, that he would make for the place where he got his oats; and I took a short cut over here. I happened to be just in the nick of time for business."

Scott jabbered this off as fast as he could, while he blushed like a red rose, apparently to interrupt the flow of grateful expressions to which the gentleman was disposed to give utterance. When he had finished his explanation of the manner in which he had happened to save the young lady from a greater disaster, she walked up to him, with a sweet smile on her face, and extended her hand to him. He could not do less than take it, though he felt and looked very sheepish about it. Almost any of the officers of the squadron who had passed the age of sixteen would have been delighted to take such a little hand as that; but there was not one in the whole crowd who was so little of a lady's man as Scott. When he took the pretty hand, Maria spoke to him in Portuguese, and shook his great paw.

"Those are my sentiments exactly; and I couldn't have said it half as well myself," he replied, with a broad grin on his face.

"Speak to him in English, Maria: he does not understand you," interposed Don Roderigue.

"I shall thank you very much for what you have did for me," said she laughing, perhaps because Scott did, or perhaps at the quality of her own English.

Scott bowed, touched his cap, and turned red again. He was very anxious to have the subject changed, and insisted that Madeira was a fine country.

"I say I shall tank you ver much for what you have did for me," repeated she, evidently a little vexed.

"Don't mention it. This is a delightful climate you have here in Madeira," stammered Scott.

"He don't understand my English," pouted the little beauty, shaking her shoulders; but, as she spoke in her own language, Scott could not understand her.

"Maria says she thanks you very much for what you have done for her; and she is very sorry she cannot make herself understood in English," said Don Roderigue.

"I understood her perfectly," replied Scott.

"But you told her not to mention it; and I am sure that would be very ungrateful in her."

"I only meant that what I did was not worth the trouble of mentioning it."

"Now say it to him again, Maria, and he will understand you," continued her father.

"I shall thank you very much for what you have did for me," added Maria, turning to Scott, with a mischievous twinkle in her bright eyes.

"I understand you as well as though you had been my next-door neighbor in the United States of America all your lifetime," replied Scott, with his broad grin.

"Oh! now you spokes too much, and I can't understand what you speaks," chattered the maiden.

"I am happy to please you," said Scott, measuring off the words one at a time.

"She has begun to learn English, and she speaks very little yet," added her father.

"I am much glad," shouted Maria, dancing with delight when she realized that her English had been understood. "I shall forget you never."

"Beautiful country!" added Scott, flourishing his right hand around him.

"Ver beaut'ful," cried Maria. "My horse," and then she pointed at the pony, and made her hands fly up and down in imitation of the feet of the animal.

"Ran away," replied Scott, completing the sentence when she broke down.

"My horse ran away!" she shouted, with childish vim, though she was not less than sixteen. "You stop my horse. I thank you ver much for what you have did."

"May I ride your horse?" asked Scott.

"You? ride horse?"

The young officer then indicated what he wanted in pantomime. Don Roderigue declared that the pony had always been very gentle, and had never behaved so badly before since he was a colt. He added that Scott might ride him if he wished to do so. The joker leaped upon his back as lightly as a cat; but the little beast began to rear and plunge and dive in the most extraordinary manner. Scott was a good horseman, and the pony could not throw him.

"I am confident something ails this horse," said he, dismounting.

He then unbuckled the girth, and Don Roderigue

ordered the groom to assist in the operation. The saddle was removed, and a large spot of blood was found on the skin of the horse. Scott looked at it, and found a wound, made by the sharp point of a nail which had been driven through the wooden part of the saddle-frame.

"I don't blame the horse for making a row," said Scott, as he pointed out the wound. "Any horse would make a fuss with that nail sticking into him;" and as he spoke he took his knife, and dug out the offensive iron.

Maria laughed and danced about all the time; and when the cause of the pony's misconduct was discovered, and shown to her, she began to pet the animal in the most loving manner. She was glad to find that her steed had a good excuse for his bad behavior. The saddle was restored to his back, and Scott mounted him again. This time he acted as well as any pony could.

"You ride?" asked Scott.

"Yes: I ride.".

Her father did not object, and the lieutenant lifted her into the saddle. She cantered off as briskly as though nothing had happened. Don Roderigue insisted that Scott should mount his horse, and ride back to the garden gate, where he had left the rest of the party. In a moment he overtook the lady. She chatted and laughed all the way, and Scott felt more as though he had fallen into a sugar-bowl than ever before in his life.

Don Roderigue decided to postpone his ride, and to entertain the party. Maria seemed not to be sorry for the change of programme; and Scott presented her to all his brother officers and to the surgeon. They spent a delightful afternoon among the budding flowers and orange-groves of the magnificent estate of their host. He was an exceedingly hospitable man, and the supper prepared for them was an elaborate banquet. He was very much surprised that all his guests should refuse to partake of the old and rare wines he set before them; but the doctor was able to give him a satisfactory explanation of their refusal, so that he did not feel hurt.

When they were ready to depart, they found two of the sleds of the country ready at the door, in which they were to descend the long hill to the city. They took their seats; and a man placed himself on each side of the sled, holding a rope from the forward end of the runner to guide and control the vehicle. They made the descent very rapidly; and the students declared it was almost as good as coasting on the snow.

The next day Don Roderigue, his wife and daughter, visited the vessels of the squadron, and were treated with the distinguished consideration to which their social standing entitled them. The Portuguese gentleman was delighted with the order and the nautical evolutions of the young sailors. In return for the courtesy extended to him and his family, Don Roderigue invited all hands to spend a day at the "Quinta da Son Joao;" and he insisted that all should come. They all went; and the officers and seamen had the gayest lark of the year.

Quite a number of Portuguese, English, and French young ladies were also invited; and the dancing in the great hall of the mansion was kept up till midnight.

Two days later the liberal host invited the party he had first met to visit the *Curral*, and ascend the Pico Ruivo. He provided horses, guides, and servants for the excursion, and entertained them royally till their return to the vessels.

The *Curral* is the greatest natural curiosity in Madeira. It is a vast ravine, and may once have formed a deep lake. It is surrounded by lofty mountains, which add greatly to the grandeur of the scenery. It reminded the students of the " Dry Dock," as they called it, in the Saxon Switzerland.

The *Curral* is about thirteen hundred feet deep, and the greater portion of its sides are perpendicular rock. Every thing in the vicinity is very picturesque, and the students were delighted with the excursion.

CHAPTER XII.

CONCERNING THE MISSING STEAMER.

"THERE is a steamer coming into port!" shouted one of the idlers in the foretop of the American Prince, one morning after the squadron had been a week at Funchal.

A dozen glasses were brought to bear upon the approaching steamer, which was coming in from the north-east. She was not a large vessel, and was square-rigged forward, like the Ville d'Angers; but it could not yet be determined whether she had two or three masts, as she was headed directly towards the Loo Rock. The picked-up steamer was barkentine rigged; and, so far as could be judged at that distance, the new-comer was about her size.

The American Prince had been out on a three-days' cruise in search of the Ville d'Angers. She had spoken several vessels without obtaining any intelligence of the missing steamer. She had just returned to Funchal. Mr. Lowington was very much depressed at the ill success of the expedition; but Mr. Fluxion insisted that the Ville d'Angers was all right. She had plenty of coal, plenty of provisions, and she was a good, strongly-built vessel: he had examined her in detail, and he did not believe that the students could have foundered her if they had tried to do so. The worst he could conceive that had happened to her was, that she had broken some of her machinery, and had drifted away to leeward before the south-east winds which had been prevailing for a week.

"But you say her sails were in good order and condition," replied the principal. "I presume her commander knew enough to get sail upon her if her engine was disabled."

"If he did, he has had a head-wind all the time, and will have to beat his vessel all the way. It is very likely the steamer is not in good sailing-trim, for such craft as she is don't work well under sail alone," continued Mr. Fluxion.

"But that vessel coming into this port is using steam," said Mr. Lowington, as he directed his glass towards her again.

"Of course I can't tell what has happened to the Ville d'Angers, but I feel quite confident that she is all right. We have had no very bad weather since we parted company, and not a great deal of fog near the islands," persisted Mr. Fluxion, who felt it "in his bones" that the steamer and her crew were safe, though he could give no good reason for his belief.

"I think that is not the steamer you have described," said Mr. Lowington, in heavy tones; for he was very sad at heart.

"I don't think it is, myself," added the vice-principal. "This one has only two masts, if I mistake not. She is a very fast sailer though."

For half an hour longer all hands watched the approaching steamer, which left a long line of dense black smoke for miles astern of her. It was settled that it was not the Ville d'Angers, for she was rigged as a topsail schooner. She was a very jaunty-looking craft, with raking masts, and smoke-stack; and she cut her way through the water like a fish, creating hardly any commotion in the waves around her. Outside she was painted a shining black, while inboard she was milk-white. Her rigging was hauled taut, and every thing about her was as neat and ship-shape as on board a man-of-war.

"That is not the Ville d'Angers; but, as she comes down from the north-east, she may have seen her," said Mr. Lowington, putting away his glass, which was no longer needed to observe the approaching craft.

"She is so trim and taut, I think she must be a man-of-war," added Mr. Fluxion. "She looks like one of our smaller gunboats. I see she has the American flag at her peak."

"She carries a private signal at her foremast head," continued the principal, taking his glass from the brackets on the companion-way. "Can you make it out, Mr. Fluxion?"

"It blows out straight from us, so that I cannot see the letters upon it."

"Young gentlemen, can you make out the letters on the private signal of that steamer?" asked the principal; turning to the students, who were as much interested in the new-comer as the faculty were.

"I have it, sir," replied one of the sharp-eyed students, who had been studying this signal for some time. "It is an arrow, with the word 'Marian' above, and an 'R' below it."

"Then it is not the Ville d'Angers, nor a man-of-war," said Mr. Lowington very sadly. "I hoped it might be the latter, at least; for she would have been more likely to be able to give us some information in regard to the missing vessel."

"On board the Prince!" shouted Mr. Pelham from the deck of the Tritonia, which was moored next to the steamer.

"On board of the Tritonia!" returned Carson, the first lieutenant of the ship.

"That steamer is the Marian, Judge Rodwood's yacht," replied Mr. Pelham.

Carson communicated this information to the principal, for neither he nor Mr. Fluxion knew the name of the judge's steam-yacht; or they did not recognize it if they had heard it mentioned. By this time the Marian had stopped her screw off the Loo Rock; and the government boat was pulling out to her. As she had a clean bill of health from her last port, she was subjected to no detention; and the government officers assigned her a place to moor near the Josephine. As she passed under the stern of the Prince, two gentlemen were seen on her rail, who seemed to regard the Prince with great interest. One of them was a tall man, with a white beard and white hair; he pointed to the name on the stern, and became quite excited.

"That must be Judge Rodwood," said Mr. Fluxion. "He has come to look for his runaway ward."

"And I wish we had his runaway ward for him," added the principal. "However, I do not feel that any one is to blame for what has transpired."

"Certainly not," replied Mr. Fluxion. "We could

not bring in the steamer without the young gentlemen; and that was just the kind of experience they needed to fit them for the business of life."

"I have sent the young men away in charge of one of the vessels of the squadron several times, and this is the first time any of them has failed to report where he was ordered," continued the principal. "Wainwright brought the Tritonia from the Baltic up the Mediterranean alone, when the vice-principal on board was worse than useless, and anchored her safely in the Golden Horn."

"Yes, sir; and you may depend upon it that O'Hara will do as well on the present occasion as Wainwright did," replied the vice-principal cheerfully.

"I hope he will; but I would give a thousand dollars at this moment to know that he and his shipmates are safe and well."

"Possibly this steam-yacht will be able to afford us some information," suggested Mr. Fluxion.

"There is a remote chance that she may have seen her. The judge telegraphed to his ward at Gibraltar from London: as he got no answer to his letter or despatch, possibly he went to Gibraltar on his way to Funchal. If O'Hara could not make his way against the head wind, after he broke his machinery, he may have headed his vessel for the nearest port, which is Lisbon or Cadiz. The Marian may have seen the Ville d'Angers," reasoned Mr. Lowington.

"But that steamer has not had time to go to Gibraltar, and then come down to Madeira, since we sailed from that port. I don't believe she has been to Gib."

"We shall soon know; for here comes a boat from

the steam-yacht," added Mr. Lowington, as a dashing barge, with crimson velvet cushions in her stern sheets, pulled up to the accommodation steps.

The six seamen who were at the oars were dressed in uniform, and had the word "Marian" in gold letters on their hats. Every thing about the boat was very stylish, as it was about the yacht itself. The tall gentleman with the white hair and beard, who wore the uniform of the New York Yacht Club, led the way up the stairs, and was the first to come upon the deck of the Prince. He was followed by the captain of the yacht and a gentleman in civilian's dress. Mr. Lowington was at the gangway to receive the visitors. The judge touched his cap, and so did the principal.

"Are you the captain of this steamer?" asked the judge.

"No, sir; but I am principal of the academy squadron, of which this is the chief vessel; and I am really, though not nominally, the commander of the ship," replied Mr. Lowington, who usually allowed the captain to answer such questions, in order to give him the needed experience in all affairs relating to the vessel.

"Then you are the gentleman I wish to see," continued Judge Rodwood, introducing himself, and then presenting Capt. Goodwin, the commander of the Marian.

"Capt. Goodwin!" exclaimed the principal, as he glanced at the person named. "I ought to know him, for he was formerly one of my pupils," and he grasped the hand of the captain.

"I am very glad indeed to meet you again, Mr. Lowington," replied Capt. Goodwin. "You see that

I am making use of the practical knowledge I obtained in the Young America; and I was very sorry to hear that the old ship had gone to the bottom."

"Capt. Goodwin has told me all about your academy; and he always speaks of you with the highest respect and regard," interposed Judge Rodwood. "But have you a young man among your students by the name of Thomas Speers?"

"We have such a name on our books; but I regret to say that he is away just now, and we are not a little anxious about him and his companions," answered Mr. Lowington very seriously.

The principal then detailed all the circumstances connected with the absence of Tom Speers. Mr. Pelham was sent for; and he was very glad to meet Goodwin, who had been a pupil with him when the Young America first crossed the Atlantic. He explained more particularly why the despatch and the letter had not been opened sooner.

"Then the young rascal has purposely kept away from me," said Judge Rodwood. "His uncle has left him three millions of dollars; and he makes me chase him all over the world to put him in possession of his fortune. As Tom is nearly twenty-one, I thought I should be doing him a good turn if I took him out of school. The Marian really belonged to Tom's uncle; and, as the boy is fond of the sea, I thought I would give him the benefit of it. I used to keep the best state-room on board for Mr. Speers; and I still reserve it for his heir."

"I should have discharged the young man if I had received your letter in season to do so before we sailed from Gibraltar, and sent him on to London," added Mr. Lowington.

"But it seems that he does not wish to be sent off; and in that case I am willing that he should remain in your academy," observed Judge Rodwood. "If he had telegraphed to me that he did not wish to leave his vessel, I should have been perfectly satisfied, and permitted him to remain. In fact, I am not legally his guardian yet, for the young man has a voice in the business himself."

"Do you hail from Gibraltar now, sir?" asked the principal.

"No, sir: I have not been anywhere near Gibraltar. When I received no reply to my despatch or letter, I telegraphed to a correspondent of our banking-house, and learned that your squadron had sailed for Funchal, and that young Speers had undoubtedly gone in the vessel to which he belonged. I am off on a cruise; and I was rather pleased with the idea of going to Madeira in search of my ward."

"Then you are direct from England?"

"I am: the Marian is six days from Southampton. As I was anxious to find young Speers before you left these islands, I required the captain to hurry her; and I think we made fifteen knots an hour a good part of the voyage."

"I am very anxious indeed about the safety of Speers and his shipmates," continued Mr. Lowington; "and I hoped, when I saw your steamer, that you would be able to give us some information in regard to the steamer picked up by the Tritonia."

"We haven't seen her; have we, Capt. Goodwin?"

asked the judge, turning to the commander of the Marian.

"Think not: indeed, we have seen but one steamer during the trip, at least after we got off into blue water," replied Capt. Goodwin.

"We saw a steamer towing a dismasted vessel, you remember," interposed Dr. Phelps, the other gentleman of the party from the Marian, who was making the voyage for his health with his friend the judge.

"True: I did not think of her. The other was a P. and O. steamer, bound into Southampton," added Goodwin. "What sort of a vessel was it the Tritonia picked up?"

"She is a screw steamer of about six hundred tons, three masts, square rigged forward," replied Mr. Pelham. "She is painted black; and her cabin is under a poop-deck. She is long, and very narrow for her length. Her name is the Ville d'Angers, and she has a French register. She was abandoned by her ship's company, for she had a hole stove in her starboard bow by a collision with another vessel; but her damages had been thoroughly repaired."

"The steamer that was towing the dismasted vessel corresponds to the description you give of the Ville d'Angers," said Capt. Goodwin. "But I suppose half the steamers that ply between the ports of England and the Continent would fill the bill as well."

"I was looking through the glass at that steamer for half an hour," interposed Dr. Phelps. "I was sitting on deck with nothing else to do; and I was trying to ascertain the condition of things on board of the dismasted vessel."

"Did you notice any thing particular about her?" asked Capt. Goodwin. "But we didn't go within two miles of her; though I noted in my log the fact that we passed a steamer towing a dismasted vessel."

"The glass was a very powerful one; and I tried to make out the people on board of the wreck and of the steamer, but I could not."

"Did the steamer sit low in the water, or was she well up?" asked Mr. Pelham.

"I am not a nautical man, and I am not a competent judge; but I should say she was more out of the water than the Marian," replied the doctor.

"Could you tell what color she was painted?"

"Black, while the vessel she was towing was green; and I noticed this fact particularly, for it was an odd color for a vessel, as I understood the matter. I was going to say, in regard to the steamer, that she was not black the whole length of her, on the side next to me."

"On which hand did you leave the steamer and her tow, Goodwin?" asked Mr. Pelham, beginning to be a little excited over the matter.

"This was off Ushant; and we were on the shore hand of her."

"You left her on the starboard hand; and the steamer was headed which way?"

"She was going a little east of north; and I concluded that she intended to make either Plymouth or Southampton. She may have gone more to the eastward when she was well up with the cape," added Capt. Goodwin.

"Then it was the starboard side of the steamer that was seen by Dr. Phelps?"

"Certainly it was: she was on our starboard, headed to the northward," replied Goodwin.

"You said the steamer was not black the whole length of her, Dr. Phelps?" continued the vice-principal of the Tritonia, warming up still more as the investigation proceeded.

"I said so; but, if you give me any nautical conundrums, I can't guess them," answered the passenger, laughing.

"What color was the part of the steamer that was not black, if you please, Dr. Phelps?" asked Mr. Pelham.

"It was a kind of straw-color; possibly yellow. It was a sort of an irregular patch at the forward part of the vessel. If it had been on the roof of an old barn in the country, I should say that it had a lot of new shingles laid among the old ones," answered the doctor.

"Precisely so! and that part of the steamer's side near the forward part of her — and that was on her starboard bow — was the new planking of the Ville d'Angers," exclaimed Mr. Pelham excitedly. "I would not give any one ten cents to insure my statement that the steamer towing the dismasted vessel was the Ville d'Angers!"

"It may be," replied the principal, musing.

"I am confident I am right."

"I think you are, Pelham," added Mr. Fluxion, who was particularly pleased to have his hopeful theory substantiated.

"But the Ville d'Angers must have made good time, towing a wreck, to have been off Ushant when you saw her there," suggested the principal. "It is hardly possible it was she."

"It took us three days to make Funchal after we lost sight of the Ville d'Angers," said Mr. Fluxion, figuring with a pencil on the back of a letter. "When did you see this steamer, Capt. Goodwin?"

"In the first part of our second day out," replied the captain of the Marian.

"Then the Ville d'Angers had five days to make Ushant; and she could easily do it in that time: she had the wind with her all the way."

"And she had all her sails set; and it was blowing fresh when we saw her. They had a jury-mast on the wreck, with some sail on it," added Capt. Goodwin.

"It blew a gale in the Bay of Biscay the next day, and I have no doubt it extended up to the coast of England," said Judge Rodwood. "Do I understand you, Mr. Lowington, that you send these boys off on such expeditions as this one?"

"Some of these boys, as you call them, judge, are older than I was when I had the command of a full-rigged ship for a time. No, I do not send them off on such expeditions when I can avoid it. I have told you that our friend Mr. Frisbone was on board of the steamer; and my young gentlemen had the alternative of leaving him and his ladies on board, or taking possession of her. I think they acted wisely, though I cannot explain the conduct of the present commander of the Ville d'Angers in towing this wreck to England."

"In my judgment he had a good reason for doing so," added Mr. Fluxion. "O'Hara is twenty years old; Gregory, his first officer, is nineteen; Speers is the second officer, and he is nearly twenty-one. The other two officers are about the same age. There isn't a fellow among them that is not fit to take that steamer to any port in the world; and no officers, even in the navy, have been so thoroughly trained in the discharge of their duties."

Mr. Fluxion got just a little excited in the defence of the policy of the principal. He had been an instructor in the institution since it was organized, and he knew the nature of the training the students had received; and any one who was fit to be an officer had been obliged to work his way up to the position.

"You think the steamer was bound to Southampton, do you, Capt. Goodwin?" asked Mr. Pelham.

"I have not the least idea for what port she was bound; but she was going east of north when I saw her last, so that she could not have been bound for Liverpool, or any port up the west coast," replied Capt. Goodwin. "I should judge that she would be most likely to go into Southampton; for she would find the least difficulty in the navigation in making that her destination."

"Then she probably got into Southampton four days ago," added Mr. Pelham. "Very likely she put about immediately, and sailed for Funchal. She may be here by to-morrow or next day."

"Unless the agents or the owners happen to see her, and put in a claim upon her," suggested Mr. Fluxion: "her case has to be settled in the courts yet."

"Southampton will be a good place for the business," said the principal; "but that will leave her ship's company in England without a vessel."

"Leave that to O'Hara; and Tom Speers has money

enough to pay the passage of all his shipmates to Madeira in the next steamer," said the judge, laughing. "But Frisbone is with them; and I am sure he will see them through all right. It is hardly worth while to worry about them. I desire to see young Speers very much indeed; and, if he prefers to retain his place in the Tritonia as first master, I shall make no objection. If I thought I should find him at Southampton, I would return there at once. Can you advise me what to do, Mr. Lowington?"

"The chances are, as Mr. Pelham suggests, that the Ville d'Angers will return to Funchal at once; and you had better remain here a few days at least. If the steamer does not appear in three days, I am inclined to think I shall run over to Lisbon, or some other port, where I shall be likely to obtain some intelligence of the missing vessel. If we could get at the ship-news for the last week, we should know whether this steamer had gone into Southampton or not."

"Then I will remain here a short time," said the judge. "The African mail-steamer is due here in a few days; and she will bring the latest ship-news."

"We have almost taken it for granted that the steamer towing the dismasted vessel was the Ville d'Angers; but we may be mistaken, after all. Any other vessel may have had her side planked up; and it is not a very unusual thing for a steamer to have her bow stove in," added the principal. But he was hopeful that the vessel described would prove to be the missing steamer; and it removed in a measure a heavy load from his mind.

After breakfast the principal and some of the young

officers visited the Marian by invitation. In the afternoon Scott and his party visited the quinta of Don Roderigue; and the second lieutenant of the Tritonia felt sufficiently at home there to invite the judge and the doctor to accompany them, for he had been assured that any of his friends would be welcome there.

Three days passed away in the enjoyment of the scenery and the hospitalities of Madeira; but the Ville d'Angers did not arrive.

CHAPTER XIII.

A MUTINY IN THE FIRE-ROOM.

AS no one could see the Ville D'Angers and the two schooners in the dense fog that settled down upon them after the crew of the steamer had been re-organized, it would be difficult to determine precisely in what manner they were separated. Capt. O'Hara did not start the screw of the steamer until he had stationed his ship's company in accordance with his instructions given by the senior vice-principal. If there was any fault anywhere, it was in the instructions.

Observations had been taken on board of all the vessels at noon, and the course for the Madeira Islands was ascertained to be south-west, half-west; and the two schooners went off in this direction, with the wind from the southward, but veering to the west. O'Hara used up about two hours in stationing his crew, arranging the quarters of the officers and seamen, and in giving his instructions. By this time the Tritonia and the Josephine were a dozen miles on their way, and they looked like white specks on the ocean to the naked eye. The young captain believed that the Ville d'Angers, from what she had done, would sail twelve knots an hour; and at this rate he could overhaul the rest of the fleet in a couple of hours. But the Ville d'Angers was hardly under way before the fog settled down upon her, and shut out the schooners from view.

The heavy whistle of the steamer could be heard for a long distance; but the bell and fog-horn of the other vessels could not be distinguished by the lookout of the Ville d'Angers. Then the wind hauled to the westward, heading off the sailing-vessels. O'Hara was watching the weather and the vessels very closely all the time; and, though the direction of the wind did not greatly affect the steamer, he saw that the Josephine and Tritonia could no longer lay their course.

He continued the steamer on the course given out for two hours, without seeing or hearing any thing of his consorts. The captain began to be a little worried; for he would as soon have thought of drowning himself as of disobeying the orders of the senior vice-principal, and going off on an independent cruise. It was evident enough to him, that the schooners had tacked, or had been crowded off their course by the changing wind; he could not tell whether they had gone to the westward or southward. He wished Mr. Fluxion had told him what he should do under such circumstances as the present, which might have been easily foreseen.

"Upon my sowl, I am afraid we shall part company with the rest of the fleet," said the captain to Tom Speers, who was on the deck.

"It seems to me we have done it already," replied the second officer.

"That's a fact! Now the wind has changed, and it bothers me to know whether the schooners have tacked and stood to the southward, or kept as close to the wind as they could, and gone off to the westward."

"It isn't possible to tell what they have done."

"That's true for you!" added the captain, musing. "Now let us think it over seriously. We ought to have overhauled the Josephine and Tritonia just where we are at this moment," and he glanced at the clock that hung in the pilot-house. "But there is no sight nor sound of them here. — Blow the whistle, Mr. Raymond, if you please."

"We have whistled every five minutes since the fog settled down upon us," replied the fourth officer, as he sounded it again.

It was time to heave the log, and the officer of the quarter-watch left the pilot-house to attend to this duty. In a few moments he reported the steamer as going only eight knots an hour. O'Hara was vexed at this low rate of speed; for he was persuaded that the steamer was good for at least twelve knots. He went to the engine-room to inquire into the matter. Richards was in charge of the engine; and he was seated on his cushioned bench, reading a novel.

"What the blazes are you doing in here?" shouted the captain, abating no little of his natural politeness. "Sure, the steamer is making only eight knots an hour by the last log; and the schooners will bate us out at this rate."

"We are making but thirty-eight revolutions a minute; and eight miles is all that can be expected," replied the assistant engineer.

"Well, what's the matter with her?" demanded O'Hara, not a little excited.

"I can't get steam enough to do any better," replied Richards rather doggedly, for he did not like the manner in which the captain had spoken to him.

"Can't you get all the steam you want?" asked O'Hara, in a more moderate tone; for he began to see that his manner was a little too arbitrary.

"I have called down into the fire-room twenty times for more steam, and I have been down myself; but I don't seem to make myself understood," replied Richards in a more affable tone, corresponding to that of the captain.

"Those blackguards of firemen are not doing their duty!" exclaimed O'Hara, rushing down to the fire-room, believing the difficulty was altogether in the matter of language.

He spoke to the Italian in his own language; and the fellow shrugged his shoulders, and looked insolent, though he said nothing to which exception could be taken.

"Fill up your furnaces!" shouted the captain, repeating the words in French for the benefit of the ones who did not understand Italian. "We are making but eight knots an hour; and we shall lose the rest of the fleet at this rate!"

The men heaved in a few shovels of coal; and O'Hara, believing he had said and done all that was necessary, left the fire-room. He went upon the poop-deck, where he found Tom Speers; and both of them gazed out into the dense fog, and listened for any sounds that might indicate the situation of the rest of the fleet.

"Do you make out any thing, Speers, darlint?" asked the captain.

"Nothing at all," replied Tom. "In my opinion we have seen the last we shall of the schooners till we get to Funchal."

"Don't say that, Tom: I would rather lose my command than part company with the rest of the fleet."

"I don't see why you need mourn about the matter. We know where we are bound, and we can get there without any help from the schooners," added Tom.

"If we lose them they will say we did it on purpose."

"They can't say that; for our log will show just how it happened, after we compare it with those of the other vessels."

The young captain was very impatient; and, after waiting half an hour, he ordered the officer of the watch to heave the log again. It was done, and the report was only seven knots.

"Faix, it seemed to me she was going at a snail's pace," said O'Hara, now thoroughly roused by the tardy movement of the vessel.

"I don't understand it," added Tom.

At this moment one of the crew who had been detailed to act as an oiler, because he had a taste for working on machinery, came upon the upper deck.

"Mr. Richards directs me to report to the captain that the engine is making but thirty revolutions a minute, and that the firemen won't do any better," said the oiler.

"That's what the matter! Bad luck to those same blackguards of firemen! We should have done better with some of the fellows in the fire-room!" exclaimed O'Hara, as he hastened down to the main deck.

He had hardly reached the foot of the ladder before Mr. Frisbone hailed him, coming out of the cabin.

"What's the trouble, Capt. O'Hara?" shouted the Prince, in his usual loud tone, though the captain was not six feet from him. "I've been taking a nap; and, when I waked up, I thought the steamer had stopped; but I found she was moving a little. Is any thing out of kilter?"

"We are making but six knots an hour, sir; and the rascals of firemen won't work," replied O'Hara.

"Won't work? What's got into them?"

"I don't know, sir: I am going down into the fire-room to see what the trouble is."

"All right: that's the way to do business; and I'll go down with you," added the Prince.

They stopped in the engine-room to hear what the engineer had to say about it. Richards had been down, and had called in French a dozen times for more steam; but the firemen would not do any better. He had found the furnace-doors open; and he concluded that the Italians and Frenchmen had concluded to strike for higher wages, though they had received their own price for their services.

"We will soon see about that!" exclaimed O'Hara, as he began to descend the iron steps into the fire-room.

"I guess we can straighten them out," added the Prince, as he followed the captain.

They found the firemen — not only the watch on duty, but all of them — seated in the airiest part of the room, smoking their pipes and cigars as coolly as though every thing was going well on board. The doors of the furnaces were fastened wide open, and the steam was rapidly diminishing in pressure.

"What are you about?" demanded O'Hara, very indignant at the state of things he found in the fire-room.

Mr. Frisbone went to the furnaces at the same time, for it was of no avail for him to say any thing to these men who did not understand his language. He closed the doors of the furnaces, which were tolerably well supplied with coal, and opened the draughts. As he did so, one of the Frenchmen came up to him, followed by two more.

"*Non! Non!*" shouted one of them, as he closed the draught, and threw open the doors again.

He proceeded to make a rather violent speech in his own language, which was not understood by the Prince. But the latter could understand the man's actions if not his words; and they meant rebellion as plainly as though it had been formally declared in the English tongue. He was not a man to be set aside by anybody; and he pushed the Frenchman away, and opened the doors and draughts again. He had scarcely completed the task before one of the men struck him a violent blow on the head, which felled him to the floor. But he was not badly hurt, and leaped to his feet on the instant. In the twinkling of an eye he had knocked over two of his assailants; and the third was on the point of hitting him on the back of the head with an iron bar, when O'Hara, seeing his danger, rushed upon the Frenchman, and, seizing the man by the neck, jammed his knees into the small of his back so as to throw him over backwards.

Richards stood in the engine-room at the head of the steps, watching the progress of events. When the Frenchman knocked the Prince over, the engineer called Shakings and Rimmer, both of whom tumbled down the steps in season to defend the captain from a violent assault on the part of the Italians, who were disposed to make common cause with their fellow-laborers. Raymond, hearing the noise in the fire-room, hastened below, followed by Tom Speers. These ample re-enforcements caused the firemen to fall back, and place themselves on the defensive.

"I am ready to fight if need be, though I am a man of peace," said the Prince, puffing with his exertions. "But I should like to know what I am fighting for. What's the matter? What has caused this row?"

"The men won't work," replied O'Hara.

"What's the reason they won't work?" demanded Mr. Frisbone, who was sufficiently familiar with labor difficulties to be competent to meet any emergency of this kind. "Aren't they satisfied with their wages?"

"They want a portion of wine served out to each man while they are at work," replied O'Hara, to whom Alfonzo had explained the desire of the men, and the reason why they had stopped work.

"Wine!" exclaimed the Prince, in utter disgust.

Mr. Frisbone, as shown in a preceding volume of this series, was a very fierce temperance man, and did not believe that intoxicating drinks of any kind, not even wine and beer of the mildest type, were proper for use under any circumstances. He did not tolerate the drinking customs of any nation he visited. He never tasted the cup in any form himself, never gave it to his neighbor, or permitted it to be given to him if he had the power to prevent it.

"Alfonzo says they asked for wine on board of the Josephine, and were told there was none on board. He did not believe a statement so absurd as this one seemed to him; and he and his associates considered the reply as a refusal to grant their reasonable request. He thought it was no use to ask for wine again; and they have struck for it as the only way they are likely to get it," explained the captain.

"Struck for wine, have they?" demanded the Prince, gazing with contempt at the firemen. "But, while we are settling this question, the fires are going out; and soon we shall have no steam at all."

The Prince closed one of the furnace-doors, and Shakings another. All the draughts were adjusted so that the fires began to roar.

Alfonzo spoke a few sharp words to his companions; and they began to arm themselves with such weapons as were at hand, — pokers, shovels, hammers, iron bars. Shakings wanted the party to "clean them out" without any delay. While things were in this attitude, the cook and one of the stewards came down into the fire-room, and intimated that they were ready to do duty as the occasion might require.

"No clubs," added Shakings, when he saw the steward pick up a coal-breaker. "We don't want any weapons. We can bring them to their senses quicker without breaking any of their bones; and we want to use them, not kill them."

The Prince liked this argument, and warmly seconded it. The boatswain of the Josephine was the self-constituted leader of the party, possibly because there was more fight in him than in any other. He made a spring at Alfonzo, who was armed with a hammer used in breaking coal. He clinched with the fellow, to whom the weapon in his hand was rather an incumbrance than otherwise. As he raised it to strike his assailant, Shakings seized him by the arm. A sharp struggle ensued; but the stalwart tar was too much for his opponent, and in a moment he had thrown him to the floor, and put his foot upon him.

The Prince pitched into the Frenchman who had struck him before. He wrenched a shovel out of his hands, and then threw him down. Observing how the boatswain handled his man, he followed his example, holding the rascal down with his foot, while he menaced him with the shovel if he attempted to use his hands. Rimmer was slower and clumsier than the boatswain, but he succeeded in taking down one of the smallest of the Italians. Raymond did not scruple to tackle another; and so quick were his movements, that his man was down almost as soon as the leader of the firemen. All the others went for the remaining two of the foreigners; and they were soon *hors de combat*. The prestige seemed to be with the Americans from the beginning.

It was a very striking spectacle, even after all the hitting had been done, to see six men held down on the floor. Tom Speers had fought like a tiger with a Frenchman he had tackled alone in the beginning of the affray; and, though O'Hara came to his aid, it was not till he had nearly overcome his foe.

"What shall we do with them?" asked the Prince, as soon as he could obtain breath enough to speak.

"Who hasn't his hands full?" demanded the boatswain.

"I haven't," replied the captain.

"Then have rope enough sent down to tie these fellows hand and foot, if you please, captain," added Shakings.

But all the watch except the quartermaster and the seaman at the wheel had heard the noise of the conflict, and had secured positions where they could see what was going on in the hold. As soon as they heard the call of Shakings, they gathered up all the spare line they could find about the deck and in the lockers, and threw it down into the fire-room. O'Hara passed them to the victors in the conflict, and each secured his own man. The battle was ended, and the victory won.

"Do you want wine now, you villains?" said the Prince when the conquest was completed.

"But we are pretty much out of firemen," added the captain, as he looked at the mutineers, made fast to the stanchions and other parts of the vessel.

"I am willing to take my turn at the shovels," replied the Prince.

By this time the fires in the furnaces were burning in the most satisfactory manner; and the Prince declared that the steamer was increasing her speed. The captain directed that several of the students who had done duty in the fire-room before the foreigners came on board should be detailed to serve again. Four of them appeared in answer to the summons; and, as the novelty of the occupation had not worn off, they were glad to be employed in this capacity again. All hands except the firemen, the boatswain, and the carpenter, left the fire-room.

The Italians and Frenchmen were fully convinced that they had made a mistake in refusing to work: they began to talk among themselves; and some of the amateurs understood enough of what was said by the actual firemen, to comprehend that they were ready to resume their work. But the students said nothing about what they had heard. In the course of an hour the foreigners were tired of their confined position, and begged to be released from durance, promising to do their duty faithfully.

When the captain came down to see them a little later, they plead with him; and he consulted with Mr. Frisbone and the boatswain.

"Let 'em loose, and set 'em to work; but don't give 'em any wine, or liquor of any sort," said the Prince.

"I don't know whether there is any wine on board," replied O'Hara. "If there were I wouldn't give it to those fellows after they have behaved so badly. But I don't think they will give us any more trouble after the pounding they have had."

Shakings was directed to release the firemen; and, when he did so, he blustered and handled them so roughly, that they seemed to be inspired with a wholesome terror of his fists. He cuffed and kicked them more liberally than Capt. O'Hara thought was necessary; and the latter suggested the propriety of treating a fallen and submissive foe with a little more magnanimity.

"Bless your heart, captain, it isn't of any use to treat such fellows gently. They aren't used to it. If you treat them well they will turn upon you, and bite," replied Shakings, as he released the last man; but, in deference to the captain, he failed to kick him as he had the rest of them.

The three who were on watch sprang to the shovels, and were disposed to waste the coal in their zeal to do their duty. The Italians, who were off duty, went to their quarters under the forecastle. O'Hara did not like the way they behaved, and he directed Shakings to keep a close watch over them.

"Have you heard any thing of the rest of the fleet, Speers?" asked the captain, as he joined the second officer on the poop-deck.

"I have not; and the fog is thicker than ever," replied Speers. "Have you looked at the barometer lately? It feels like bad weather to me. The sea seems to have an ugly look, what we can see of it."

"I looked at it just as I came up; and it indicates a little more wind than we have been having the last twelve hours; but I don't think it is any thing very bad that's coming."

"What was that?" said Tom Speers, suddenly looking to the northward.

"Well, what was it? I didn't hear any thing," replied O'Hara, gazing in the direction indicated.

"I don't know what it was; but it sounded like a gun, or the stroke of a bell," added Speers.

"Gun on the starboard quarter, the lookout forward reports," said Raymond, hailing the captain from the main deck.

"All right: we heard it here," replied O'Hara. "Is it a gun, or a bell? Report if you hear it again, Mr. Raymond."

"If it was a bell, it may be the other vessels of the

fleet. If it was a gun, it was not fired by the Josephine or the Tritonia, for the reason that neither of them has a gun to fire."

"I hear it again; and I am sure it is a bell," exclaimed Tom Speers.

"Whisht! Wait till you hear another; for the two schooners are together, and when one rings the other will, you may be sure," added the captain, not a little excited.

But no other stroke of a bell was heard for a little time.

"I know the sound of the Tritonia's bell; and it isn't she," said O'Hara. "It is a much heavier bell we hear."

All hands listened again.

CHAPTER XIV.

THE WRECK OF THE CASTLE WILLIAM.

THE sound of the bell was heard again in a few minutes. It had a heavy and dull tone, unlike that of the bells of the schooners. All hands on the Ville d'Angers listened attentively to the sound.

"I think it must be the bell of one of the consorts," said Capt. O'Hara, when he had heard the bell at least a dozen times.

"It don't sound like the bell of the Tritonia," replied Tom Speers, after he had heard it once more. "And all the sounds are from the same bell. If the two schooners were off in that direction, we should hear the bells of both of them."

"I'll tell you what it is: the fog makes the difference in the sound from what we are accustomed to hear. We never heard the bell except when we were on the deck where it was rung. It stands to reason that it would be another thing when heard at a distance, and in a thick fog," continued the captain, who wished the sound might come from the consorts, and was influenced by his desire.

The sound seemed to be a long way off; and the captain said it bothered him to know how they happened to hear it when it was so far off. He called Mr. Shakings and Capt. Fairfield, and asked them to give their opinion in regard to the tones of the bell. They did not think it was the bell of the Josephine, to which they were more accustomed to listen on board; but it might be, for bells sounded different under varying circumstances. At last O'Hara decided to run for the sound of the bell, and directed the officer of the deck to change the course to north, for this was the direction from which the sound came.

Capt. O'Hara could not reconcile himself to the sound of the bell; but he thought, as had been suggested, that the condition of the atmosphere might alter the tone of the Tritonia's bell. He concluded that the schooners had fallen off their course as the wind veered, and the Ville d'Angers had run ahead of them. This was the only explanation he could give; and, in the absence of a better one, it satisfied him for the time. The firemen did their duty now, though Shakings showed himself to them once in a while so that they need not forget him.

Every thing seemed to be going well on board, and a sharp lookout was kept for the rest of the fleet ahead. The bell to the northward sounded more and more distinctly as the steamer advanced; and the nearer she came to it, the louder it sounded.

"That can't be the bell of the Tritonia," said Tom Speers, as he met the captain on the poop-deck.

"Begorra, I don't believe it is!" exclaimed O'Hara, in whose mind the question had been raised anew. "Upon my sowl, it is big enough for a church-bell; and we have come nearer to it than we were when we first heard it."

"It must be some other vessel," added Speers. "It isn't a steamer, or she would whistle in such a fog as this."

"No: sure it's not a steamer; and what the blazes is it?" queried the captain, very much puzzled. "I hope we shall not miss the rest of the fleet."

"I hope not; but, if the schooners stood down to the southward, we have very little chance of seeing them again, unless this fog lifts soon," replied Speers.

"Have you seen Gregory and Clinch since the ship's company was stationed?" asked O'Hara, suddenly changing the topic of the conversation, though he did not cease to peer into the dense fog ahead.

"Neither of them has been on deck since the second part of the starboard watch took the deck," answered Speers.

"Where are they?"

"I don't know. They went into the cabin, and I suppose they are there now. They have a state-room together."

"I don't quite like the conduct of Gregory, who is the first officer," added O'Hara, in a low tone. "He took the trouble to tell me he did not approve the arrangement of the watches as I had made it."

"I dare say he will assent to it," added Tom. "I don't know him at all, and never served in the same vessel with him."

"He used to be a mighty hard boy at the time he was in the steerage of the Young America; but when he got into the Josephine, he reformed; and Mr. Fluxion believes he has made a man of him. Perhaps he has: I don't know. If he has, there has been a big change in him."

"Let us hope he will be a good officer while he is on board of the steamer."

"Certainly we will hope so; but it was a bad beginning for him to object to the arrangement of the watches before he had been on board two hours."

"What does he object to?" asked Tom Speers; and he was willing to believe there might be something wrong about the arrangement, for it would not be at all strange if a mistake had been made.

Tom thought it might be possible that his friend the captain had been just a little "airy" in his dealings with the two officers from the Josephine, though he had never noticed any thing of the kind in O'Hara while they had been together in the steamer. Such an exhibition would not be very remarkable in a young man, placed in command of a steamer with the arbitrary control of thirty of his companions. He was determined to caution his friend in regard to the manifestation of any thing that could be construed into an overbearing or domineering spirit. He knew very well from experience, that such an appearance would excite opposition, if there was none in the beginning.

"What does he object to?" repeated O'Hara. "He says he objects to the arrangement of the watches."

"What did you say to him?" asked Tom curiously, if not anxiously.

"I only told him I was sorry he didn't like it," replied the captain, smiling, as though he thought he had answered the complaint very properly.

"Did he say any thing more?"

"Yes, he did: he added that he didn't think there was any need of quarter-watches," chuckled O'Hara;

"and Clinch took the trouble to say he didn't think so either: as if he considered it important that I should know the first and third officer were of the same mind on the subject."

O'Hara talked and chuckled and laughed like one who felt that he occupied a strong position. He was quite happy over it; for, if there was to be any trouble on board, he was altogether in the right, and the other party all in the wrong.

"What did you say then?" inquired Tom Speers, desiring to know whether or not there was any foundation for his fears and suspicion.

"I told them that showed we differed in opinion a little taste; and I smiled as swately as though I was spaking to Miss Louise in the cabin below. And that reminds me to say I think the girl is a little swate on you, Tom, my boy, since you pulled her out of the say," said the captain, getting excited as he proceeded, and relapsing into his Irish brogue.

"Never mind the girl," added Tom impatiently, though he blushed a little as he turned away to wipe off the dampness that had gathered on his face from the fog. "I am not one of your romantic pups who think a girl ought to be his wife because he has rendered her some little service."

"Faix, it was no little service you rendered her; for she was sure to be drowned if you hadn't got to her with the life-buoy as soon as you did."

"Never mind that now, Capt. O'Hara," interposed the young hero.

"Oh! you are not on duty now; and you needn't measure off your words into lengths with me just now," said O'Hara, with a laugh.

"Do you think Gregory is discontented?" asked Tom.

"If his words come from his heart, he is; but that is his fault," replied the captain very lightly. "If he don't like the arrangement of the watches, he can't help himself; for I am the commander of this ship."

"Excuse me, O'Hara, as I am not on duty just now, if I speak to you as a friend."

"Certainly, my boy: blaze away! I won't put you in irons for any thing you may say now," added O'Hara curiously; for he had not the least idea that he had done any thing wrong, or even out of taste.

"Don't you think it would have been better if you had answered Gregory and Clinch in a little different way?"

"What do you mane? Wasn't I civil to them? Didn't I smile as sweetly upon them as though they hadn't raised a ghost of an objection to the watches?"

"Of course you are the captain, and you were not obliged to make any explanations; but don't you think it would have been better if you had been a little more conciliatory toward Gregory and Clinch, even if they were a little wrong?" asked Tom.

"Faix, I don't know: I didn't think of that," repeated O'Hara thoughtfully. "They supposed it was my arrangement they were objecting to all the time, when it was the orders of the senior vice-principal himself."

"So much the worse, if they thought the plan was your own," added Tom.

"Well, now, I thought it was so much the better!" exclaimed the captain.

"So much the better for you, but so much the worse

for Gregory and Clinch," continued Tom. "Possibly the first officer thought you ought to have consulted with him about the arrangement of the watches. All I mean to say is, that it would have been more magnanimous to have told Gregory, when he objected, that you were only carrying out the orders of the vice-principal."

"Perhaps you are right, Tom, my darling," added O'Hara, musing.

"It was not in the midst of an emergency, O'Hara; and he did not refuse to obey orders. If he had, and you had knocked him down, it would have been all right. It is only fair to let the first and third officers know, if they object to any thing, that they are kicking against the senior vice-principal, and not against you," continued Tom, as sagely as though he was a fit judge to settle a case between his captain and an officer above himself.

"That's all very well; and I think you are right this time, Tom, if you never were before," answered O'Hara. "But am I to make a distinction between the enforcement of my own orders and those of the powers above me? If I tell the officer of the deck, and it happens to be Gregory or Clinch, to stop the engine, am I to explain that this is the order of the senior vice-principal, and not my own? or, if it should be my own, to argue that it is all right?"

"Certainly not; nothing of the kind! I said in the beginning that this was a matter of magnanimity, and not of right. Your orders are to be obeyed without a question on the part of any one on board; not even Capt. Fairfield or Mr. Shakings having the right to object."

"I see: I understand you perfectly, Tom, my darlint; and I am much obliged to you for the trouble you have taken to say all this. Give me your flipper! I like you betther than ever, if you are a millionnaire; for it's a good friend that will point out another's faults."

"I don't point out your faults, O'Hara. I am afraid, if I were the commander of this steamer, I should be a little 'airy;' and I was dreading lest you might be, though, upon my honor, I haven't seen any thing of the kind in you."

"It's moighty aisy y'are on me, Tom; and I believe I have been airy; but, upon my sowl, I'll never do it again! I like you better than if you had given me the half of your three millions; and I wish you were the captain of the steamer, instead of myself."

"Nonsense, captain! You are ten times as fit to command her as I am; and I am glad it is as it is."

"Whisht!"

"Vessel dead ahead!" shouted the lookout, on the jib-boom of the steamer, where the officer of the deck had sent him when the bell began to be heard very distinctly on the forecastle of the steamer.

The officer of the deck hastily repeated the cry, and ordered the quartermaster to put the helm hard down. At the same time he rushed into the pilot-house, and rang the speed-bell for the engine to "slow down."

"Can you make her out?" said the captain, gazing into the dense fog ahead.

"I don't see any thing; but we are more than a hundred feet farther from the vessel than the man on the forecastle."

"I will go forward, then," added O'Hara, suiting the action to the words.

Tom Speers saw Gregory and Clinch come out of the cabin, and follow the captain forward, and he concluded to remain where he was; for he was off duty, and he did not care to have the other officers of the steamer regard him as the adviser of the captain, if the commander asked him any questions.

The Ville d'Angers slowed down in obedience to the will of the assistant engineer in charge. If the lookout had been less vigilant, the steamer would have struck the vessel ahead square on the broadside, and that would have been the end of her. But Raymond, as the officer of the deck, was always exceedingly careful; and he had spent most of his time at the heel of the bowsprit since the position of the craft was clearly indicated by the sound of the bell. The whistle had been sounded on the steamer at short intervals; and, as it came nearer, the bell was rung more vigorously, so that each vessel had a clear idea of the position of the other.

Gregory and Clinch went forward behind the captain, and they could not help being considerably excited over the prospect of some sort of an adventure. But they said nothing to O'Hara; and it was evident from their actions that they were a little "disgruntled."

"I believe O'Hara has lost his wits," said Gregory, in a prudently low tone. "It beats me to know what he is chasing this vessel for, running some miles off the course."

"I suppose he thought that bell belonged to one of the schooners," added Clinch.

"It sounds more like one of the bells of the churches of Paris than it does like the Josephine's; and he might have known that it did not belong to one of the schooners," growled the first officer.

The captain had certainly allowed the Ville d'Angers to continue on her course to the northward after he and Tom Speers were reasonably confident that the bell did not indicate the presence of the other vessels of the fleet. Possibly O'Hara's curiosity had been excited, and he wished to see the vessel that rang the heavy bell; but it is more likely, that, in the conversation which ensued, he had forgotten for the moment that the vessel ahead could not be either of those for which he was in search. He desired to satisfy himself, after he had gone so far to the north, — only a few miles, however, — that the bell was not on either of the vessels, and that they had not run off in this direction. By sweeping off a little to the westward, on his return, he might fall into hearing distance of their bells or horns.

"Do you make her out, Mr. Raymond?" asked O'Hara, as he ascended to the top-gallant forecastle.

"Distinctly, sir," replied the officer of the deck.

"What is she?"

"It seems to be a wreck, with a number of persons on board of her. All her masts have been carried away; she has a square sail rigged on a jury-mast, and is running before the wind," added Raymond, as he made out the details he mentioned.

"I see her now," continued O'Hara, as he traced the outline of the vessel through the dense mass of fog which covered the sea.

"We are running by her, sir," said Raymond. "Shall I stop her?"

"Stop and back her," replied the captain.

"Ring one bell!" shouted the officer of the deck.

"One bell!" responded the quartermaster in the pilot-house; and he rang it.

"Ring two bells!" added Raymond.

"Two bells!" repeated the man in charge of the wheel; and, when he rang them, the screw began to turn backwards.

"Stop her!" said O'Hara, when he judged that her headway was overcome.

"Ring one bell!" added Raymond.

"One bell, sir!" echoed the quartermaster; and the engine stopped.

While this was done on board of the steamer, the hands on the wreck let go the halyard of the square sail, and it came down on the deck. The hulk was moving so slowly that it forged only a little ahead of the Ville d'Angers, leaving her on the weather quarter of the deck. From the top-gallant forecastle of the steamer, the officers had a tolerably clear view of the dismasted vessel, which might have been a ship or a barque, for the stumps of her three masts could be distinctly seen. She was painted green, and looked like a very old vessel, for her bow was as stunt-built as the craft of a hundred years ago.

"Hail her, Mr. Raymond, and let us ascertain what we can of her," said Capt. O'Hara.

"Ship ahoy!" shouted the officer of the deck, through the speaking-trumpet which had been supplied by Mr. Fluxion; for this instrument meant twice as much to him as to any other officer in the squadron.

"On board the steamer!" replied a man on the deck of the hulk.

"What vessel is that?"

"The ship Castle William, from Calcutta to Portsmouth, with invalid troops!" yelled the man on the deck of the wreck; and there seemed to be not more than three men on duty there.

"Tell him we will send a boat on board," said the captain; and Raymond repeated the words.

"Don't do it!" shouted the man earnestly. "We have small-pox and typhoid-fever on board."

"Phew! here's a nice kettle of fish!" exclaimed O'Hara.

"Keep to windward, and come a little nearer!" called the spokesman of the wreck.

The captain gave the necessary orders to back the Ville d'Angers, and run up a little nearer to the wreck. Taking the suggestion of the man on the hulk, he thought there would not be any danger in going to windward of her.

"Do you hear that, Clinch?" said Gregory, with no little excitement in his manner. "There is small-pox and typhoid-fever on board of that wreck; and O'Hara is going to get nearer to her."

"I don't like the idea," added Clinch.

"Capt. O'Hara, I protest against going any nearer to that vessel!" said Gregory, walking up to the captain, and touching his cap as he spoke. "She has contagious diseases on board of her; and we shall all take them."

"There is no danger, I think, while we keep well to windward of her. The breeze is pretty fresh, and I don't believe the disease can travel up against it," replied O'Hara, mindful of what had passed between Tom Speers and himself, though he was at first inclined to make no reply to the protest.

"I don't think it is safe: I protest, and insist that the steamer be put on her course to the Madeiras!" added Gregory, in a very offensive manner.

"Shall we abandon this wreck, without even ascertaining whether or not she needs any assistance?" demanded O'Hara, with some indignation in his tones.

"You need not go any nearer to her, at any rate," replied Gregory, somewhat shaken by this argument; for all the students had been thoroughly schooled in the lesson of humanity, that every sailor was bound to assist every other sailor in distress.

The captain made no further reply to the first officer. Possibly he did not run the steamer as near to the wreck, for he directed the course, as he might have done if Gregory had said nothing.

The Ville d'Angers was stopped on the quarter of the wreck, and at about half a cable's length from it.

"How many have you on board?" asked O'Hara, taking the trumpet from the officer of the deck.

"Thirty-two," replied the spokesman of the wreck.

"Are you the captain?"

"No; he is down with fever: I am the mate."

"How many sick have you?"

"All but three men,—myself and two seamen. Five of the crew have died, and eight are sick."

It appeared from the answers of the mate, that the

Castle William had left Calcutta with a crew of sixteen, including the officers. She had in her steerage twenty-one disabled soldiers, among whom the typhoid-fever had broken out after she left St. Helena, where she had put in for supplies. At this place she had received a sailor to work his passage; and, when the ship had been out a week, he was taken down with the small-pox. They had made a place for him in the head; but five of the crew had already died with this disease and the fever. Six more were sick with the fever, and two with the small-pox.

Certainly it was a terrible state of things on board of the wreck, which had been short-handed, and was thrown on her beam-ends in the recent gale, or hurricane the mate called it. The three men had cut away the masts, and this had righted her.

CHAPTER XV.

A CHANGE OF DESTINATION.

MR. FRISBONE had gone down into the fire-room as soon as the order was given to slow down, in order to see that the firemen did not do any mischief to the boilers or engine by too much firing while the steam was not used. But the men seemed to be very well disposed, and had opened the furnace-doors when the engineer on duty gave the order. The spare steam was blowing off at the same time. As the Prince was thus engaged in preventing a catastrophe in the engine or fire room, he did not learn the condition of things on board of the Castle William till the captain sent for him and for all the adult officers on board of the Ville d'Angers. It was a desperate case which the young officers were called upon to settle; and O'Hara was disposed to take the advice of all that were older and wiser than himself.

"Do you need assistance?" asked O'Hara, after he had sent for the adult portion of the ship's company. But it seemed like a foolish question to ask; for here was a dismasted hulk, on board of which were thirty-two human beings, all but three of whom were disabled. There were not well ones enough to take care of the sick, to say nothing of handling the vessel. If left to themselves, they must all miserably perish in a few days, for the storms of the Bay of Biscay would soon make an end of the unmanageable hulk. Of course she needed assistance; and it would be inhuman in the last degree to refuse it.

"We need assistance very badly," replied the mate of the Castle William. "We must all die of disease or go to the bottom, without it."

"Do you need provisions and stores?" inquired O'Hara.

"We have provisions enough, but we want fresh vegetables and stores for the sick."

"We will send you what we have," replied the young captain. "What else do you want?"

"We can never get into port on this wreck. She has a very valuable cargo in the hold."

"Do you wish for more seamen?"

"If we had a hundred men, they could hardly save the ship if it came on heavy weather. Will you tow the wreck into port?" asked the mate; and this last request was evidently what he had desired to reach from the beginning.

"We will consider it," replied Capt. O'Hara, not a little startled at the request.

"Our sick people are well provided for; and this is the best thing you can do for us. You will make a good thing by it."

By this time the Prince, Capt. Fairfield, and the adult forward officers, had gathered in the pilot-house for consultation. O'Hara stated the situation of the wreck and the people on board of it. He laid before the council all the information he had obtained from the mate of the Castle William; but he expressed no opinion or desire on his own part. He wished to hear the opinion of his elders before he gave his own.

Mr. Frisbone listened very attentively to the statement of the captain; and he did not speak a word till O'Hara had said all he had to say.

"I want your advice," continued the captain. "Of course it was not supposed, when I was placed in command of the Ville d'Angers, that I should be called upon to settle such big questions as this one."

"But I have faith to believe that you would settle it right," added the Prince. "There is only one thing to be done in a case like this; and all the lawyers and doctors of divinity in the world couldn't make our duty any plainer to us; and that is, to relieve the distressed, and at any cost of labor and trouble."

"That's the talk!" shouted the impulsive and warm-hearted Shakings, bringing his fist down upon the wheel with force enough to break his bones or split the wood. "Your honor is a sailor at heart, if you never did come in at the hawse-hole, and feel your way to the quarter-deck!"

So said Rimmer in his slower and more heavy tones.

"But there will be great risk in exposing the young gentlemen to small-pox and ship-fever," suggested Capt. Fairfield: not that he intended to object to the performance of a humane duty, but because he desired to have both sides of the question considered; and there were thirty-one young lives to be cared for, as well as thirty-two older ones.

"I think we ought to save a fellow-creetur from

death when the risk of losing our own lives is no greater than the chance of saving them that's in danger," replied the Prince emphatically. "That's my doctrine!"

"Your honor was cut out for a sailor; and you missed your calling, that you are not now in command of the finest ship afloat!" exclaimed Shakings, with enthusiasm.

"That's all gammon, Mr. What's-your-name," said the Prince.

"My name is Shakings."

"I should think it might be; but do you suppose all the good feeling and humanity in the world belong to sailors?" demanded the Prince. "That's only the shakings of a bad logic."

"Your honor proves that the sailors haven't all the good feeling in the world."

"If you are an American citizen, don't call any man 'your honor,' unless it is the judge on the bench. You are getting things mixed up with them lords and dooks on this side of the ocean," continued the Prince reproachfully. "I call myself an American Prince; and I don't eat dirt before any man, and I don't like to see other princes do it."

"It is the first duty of an American sailor to be respectful to his betters; and I use the lingo I learned, because I am in the habit of doing so when I see a man do a handsome thing, as your honor always does," said Shakings with a laugh.

"This is neither here nor there; only I don't like to see any flunkying at any time. We are called upon to give some advice to the captain; though, in my opinion, he don't need any."

"I believe we are giving it; and I suppose he understands what we all think about it by this time," continued Shakings.

"If I comprehend the views of Capt. Fairfield, he objects to rendering assistance in the present instance, as it would expose our ship's company to these contagious diseases," added the captain, turning to the instructor of the Ville d'Angers.

"By no means!" protested Capt. Fairfield warmly. "I should feel guilty to the end of my life if we should leave these poor people to perish without giving them all the aid in our power."

Shakings thought the instructor had spoken like a "sodger" before; and his present speech was more like that of a sailor.

"Then there appears to be no disagreement among you, gentlemen," added Capt. O'Hara. "I agree with you that the people on the wreck ought to be relieved."

"Spoken like a true sailor!" ejaculated Shakings.

"Or like a true soldier!" exclaimed the Prince.

"Thank you, Mr. Frisbone; and I won't stop to tell you what soldiers have done a thousand times for those in distress," added Capt. Fairfield.

"We are to assist the people on the wreck," interposed the captain. "How, and to what extent, is the next question.— Mr. Raymond, keep the whistle going every five minutes."

"We are doing so, sir," replied the officer of the deck, who was planking the forecastle.

O'Hara stated that the sufferers on the wreck needed no provisions, only fresh vegetables and comforts for the sick. As the steamer was abundantly provided with the former, it was promptly decided to send all that could be spared of them. As to comforts for the sick, which they understood to include medicines, the Prince declared that he would consult his wife, who was one of the best nurses in the world, and had saved his life when the doctors gave him up, by her intelligent care. The benevolent gentleman was on the point of starting for the cabin, when the captain interposed.

"We have not settled the worst and hardest question of the whole, Mr. Frisbone," said O'Hara. "I have an opinion on the subject; but I wish for your advice."

"What on airth comes now?" demanded the Prince, closing the door he had opened.

Since his wife had become Mrs. Frisbone, and they had crossed the ocean, she had been doing her best to improve the grammar and pronunciation of the Prince; and she had succeeded wonderfully well, considering the hard subject she had to deal with. He talked tolerably well under ordinary circumstances; but when he was dealing with a great question, or became very much excited, it was observable that he relapsed into nearly all his old barbarisms of speech.

"The mate of the Castle William wishes the steamer to tow the wreck into port," added O'Hara.

"Into port!" exclaimed the Prince.

"He does not say what port; but the ship was bound to Portsmouth, England."

"Where is that?" asked the Prince, whose geography was sometimes at fault.

"It is close by Southampton."

"That's not the nearest port?"

"By no means. We are not more than three hundred nautical miles from Lisbon; and about the same from Cadiz."

"I expect, with those diseases on board, that the Spaniards, the Portuguese, or even the English at Gibraltar, would keep the people on the wreck in quarantine for about forty days; and the chances are that most of them would never see England again," said Mr. Rimmer.

"How far is it to Southampton?" asked the Prince.

O'Hara went to the chart-room, measured off the distance, and returned to the pilot-house.

"I make it about twelve hundred miles," he said, as he joined the circle.

"I don't believe in taking this steamer into a French or Spanish port," added the Prince. "I think that as much as one-half of her belongs to the academy squadron, as salvage; and a port in England is the best place to have the business properly fixed up."

"The mate of the Castle William says she has a valuable cargo in her hold; and I suppose we shall be entitled to salvage in her," suggested the captain.

"Of course you will; and I don't think Mr. Lowington will lose any thing if we should take the wreck to — that place you mentioned."

"Portsmouth."

No one objected to this business view of the situation; and it was in council agreed, that it would be expedient to tow the wreck to Portsmouth in preference to any port on the Spanish peninsula.

"I am confident that if Mr. Lowington or Mr. Fluxion were here, he would send the steamer to England with the wreck," said Mr. Shakings.

"But I desire to do all I can to find the consorts before we do any thing," interposed O'Hara. "When that is done, I am willing to act on my own responsibility, with your advice."

"There is no let-up in the fog," added Mr. Rimmer, as he took a long look on all sides of the steamer.

It was decided to wait till it could be ascertained whether or not the Josephine and the Tritonia were anywhere in the vicinity. The boatswain and the carpenter were instructed to fire the gun, which the Prince had used so effectually on the night of the collision, every thirty minutes during the rest of the day, or until the fog cleared off. The first gun was discharged immediately. At the moment of the report, the quartermaster struck eight bells in the pilot-house; and it was repeated on the great bell forward.

"All the port watch on deck!" shouted the acting boatswain's mate, as he piped the call through the ship.

It was the first dog-watch; and the first part of the port-watch had the deck for one hour. It was in charge of Gregory; and Raymond gave him the orders he had received, and handed him the trumpet as the indication of his authority. But there was nothing to do on board, except to keep a sharp lookout, and to give the fog-signals.

The stewards had been directed to get out the vegetables to be sent to the wreck; and they were attending to this duty. About a dozen boxes of onions, turnips, and potatoes, and a smaller variety of other vegetables, were now in readiness at the gangway to be conveyed to the Castle William. In the mean time the American Prince had gone into the cabin to consult his wife in regard to the needs of the sick on board of the vessel.

Mrs. Frisbone had been seasick for several days; but she had now completely recovered. The motion of the steamer, even while she was hove to, was quite easy; and the lady was sitting at the table in the after-cabin, as the part in the stern which was separated from the rest by the curtain was called. Miss Rodwood was at her side; and both of them listened with the deepest interest to the story of the Prince.

"I want you to see about getting together some things to send to these poor people," said the Prince, when he had finished his narrative. "Perhaps you can tell what medicines they need, and get them out of the chist."

"I will get them out of the chest"—

"Out of the chest, and not out of the chist," added Mr. Frisbone, with a laugh. "I suppose we ought to let 'em all die while we make the chist into a chest."

"Not so bad as that; but chist is particularly bad pronunciation. I cannot tell what the sick sailors and soldiers need in the way of medicines without seeing them," protested the lady.

"But they are all sick with contagious diseases!" exclaimed the Prince.

"I have had the small-pox, and I am not afraid of that. I have taken care of many people who were sick with the typhoid-fever, of which ship-fever is only another form. I will go on board of the ship, and do all I can for the poor creatures," replied Mrs. Frisbone earnestly.

"You, my dear?"

"I never yet shrunk from doing my duty, and I shall not now," added the lady.

"I will go with you, sister!" exclaimed Miss Rodwood.

"You will not expose her to these diseases?" demanded Mr. Frisbone, not a little alarmed at the proposition.

"I cannot prevent her from doing a duty which is as binding upon her as it is upon me," replied Mrs. Frisbone, with a sort of solemnity that greatly impressed her husband.

"Very well; and I shall go with you," continued the benevolent American noble. "If it is your duty, — and I don't dispute that it is, — it is as much mine, and I shall share it with you. But we must not expose any of these boys to the contagion. I wouldn't have one of them catch the small-pox or the ship-fever for a million dollars. I haven't any thing in particular to do on board of this vessel; and I can just as well be on board of the other, doing what I can to make the sick comfortable."

The adults and the officers were astonished when the decision of the Frisbone party was announced. Capt. Fairfield and O'Hara did their best to reason them out of the purpose; but that was useless. Mrs. Frisbone declared that God had given her this duty to perform, and she should be recreant to her trust if she failed to do it. This was her opportunity to do the will of Heaven; and she could no more neglect it than she could refuse her daily bread.

"If I take any disease, and die, I shall die at the post of duty; and I should be afraid to die anywhere else," said the heroic woman; "and I shall not have lived in vain. Louise can do as she pleases. I do not ask her or my husband to go with me."

"But Miss Rodwood has been an invalid, and it will be a pretty severe experience for her to act as a nurse on board of a mere hulk, taking care of soldiers and sailors," said Capt. Fairfield.

"Perhaps it is just the experience my sister needs; and it may prove to be a blessing to her," replied Mrs. Frisbone. "If she can put her whole mind to this humane task, I am sure it will be a benefit to her."

The lady evidently had views of her own on this subject; and, as it appeared that her sister's mind was somewhat affected, it was possible that she understood the case better than any other person.

The next thing was to get the devoted party on board of the wreck without exposing any of the students to the danger of infection. O'Hara studied the case, and talked it over with the carpenter and boatswain. It was not prudent to board the Castle William on the weather side, for the sea would be likely to stave the boat against her sides. If it went to leeward, the crew of the boat would be exposed to the peril of the pestilential air from the ship. At last it was decided that none of the students should go in the boat that conveyed the passengers and stores. The Prince, the adult forward officers, and one of the stewards, were to act as oarsmen. The stores were sent first; and they were hoisted by the three well men on board of the ship. The ladies who had been so unwilling to be lowered in a boat when the object was to save their own lives were let down into the cutter in a sling; and they were safely hoisted on board of the Castle William. The boat returned with all its crew except the Prince.

The Ville d'Angers then ran off a considerable distance from the wreck, as far as she could and not lose sight of it. It was very quiet on deck and in the cabin. The vessel was rolling in the sea, and there was nothing to be done but to wait for the fog to lift. Gregory, the officer of the deck, was like a monarch without a kingdom; and when Clinch came in his way, he insisted that it was dull music.

The steamer had been turned head to the sea, and the screw was revolved just enough to keep the vessel from drifting upon the Castle William. When she was in danger of losing sight of the wreck, the engine was stopped for a time. But the quartermaster attended to all this business, and to the sounding of the whistle.

"I wish I was back in the Josephine again," said Gregory when he met Clinch.

"Why so? This isn't a bad craft to be on board of," replied the third officer.

"This steamer is officered by about all the Tritonia's fellows," growled Gregory. "Those that came from the Josephine are mere ciphers. O'Hara hasn't spoken a word to me since we made out that wreck; and I am the first officer of the steamer."

Clinch did not say any thing; but he thought the captain had not much encouragement to consult his first officer, who had done nothing but object and protest when he did any thing.

"I suppose he had made up his plan; but he hasn't said any thing to me about it," continued Gregory.

"He has put the Frisbones on board of the wreck, and sent off all the vegetables we had on board. We may get the scurvy for the want of them. Now we are as fast here as though we were aground."

"What are we waiting for?" asked Clinch.

"I don't know. Don't I keep saying the captain don't tell me what is going on?" snarled Gregory, as though he were anxious to find a sufficient cause for getting up a mutiny.

And so the day wore away. In the evening the fog lifted; but nothing could be seen of the two schooners, for they were far on their way to Madeira. But O'Hara was not quite satisfied to undertake such an enterprise as had been agreed upon, until it was no longer possible to confer with the vice-principals of the squadron. As the night was clear, he decided to run for three hours to the south-west, and return if he found nothing of the rest of the fleet. At midnight, when the steamer was over forty miles from the Castle William, nothing could be seen of the lights of the Josephine and Tritonia; and, very unwillingly, he ordered the Ville d'Angers to be headed to the north-east. After a run of less than three hours, the wreck was readily found, for lights were exhibited on board as before she lost her masts. Raymond, who was in charge of the deck of the Ville d'Angers, hailed the wreck, and was answered by Mr. Frisbone. The wind was freshening, but the sea was tolerably smooth.

O'Hara was still up, though he had taken a little nap, and directed the steamer to be run as close as possible to the hulk; and a small line was heaved to her deck by Shakings. With this the heavy hawser of the ship was drawn over the stern of the steamer, where it was made fast. While the boatswain was attending to the securing of the hawser, O'Hara and the Prince had some talk about the condition of the sick. They were all comfortable; and Mrs. Frisbone had worked out a revolution in the state of things between decks. The captain laughed when the Prince said he had been at work whitewashing since he came on board.

When the hawser was ready, O'Hara gave the order to go ahead; and the steamer started on her voyage to England.

CHAPTER XVI.

THE WINE-ROOM OF THE VILLE D'ANGERS.

THE VILLE D'ANGERS had been under way hardly an hour when the quartermaster in the pilot-house struck eight bells; and the first part of the port-watch was called to relieve the second part of the starboard. Gregory was the officer of this division, as Raymond had been of the last.

"North, half east," said Raymond, giving the course to his successor in charge of the vessel.

"North, half east!" exclaimed Gregory; and though it was his duty to repeat the course as it was given to him, in order to prevent any mistake, it was not necessary for him to say it with such a tone of disgust.

"That's the course we have been running for the last hour," replied Raymond quietly. "The officer of the deck will keep a sharp lookout for the tow."

"For the tow?" queried Gregory, as the fourth officer repeated the orders which were required to be given to his successor in charge of the deck. "What do you mean by the tow?"

"Of course you are aware that the steamer is towing the hulk of the Castle William?"

"I was not aware of it," answered Gregory. "When

I turned in at four bells last night, the steamer was headed to the southward and westward."

"We returned to the wreck before three, after an unsuccessful search for the rest of the fleet. We took the Castle William in tow; and now we are bound for Portsmouth, England. If you were not informed in regard to the movements of the steamer, I think you were the only officer on board who was in the dark."

Gregory and Clinch were jealous of the officers of the Tritonia. They had begun to object in the first of the cruise, and even before the steamer was under way. They had kept out of sight of the other officers, and had avoided the captain as far as they could. Gregory had been in charge when the steamer started for the south, after the fog lifted. O'Hara had tried to talk with him; but he was so stiff and distant that the captain gave it up, and allowed him to live within his own shell. He had been relieved by Clinch at ten in the evening; and the third officer was no more inclined to be sociable than the first.

At midnight Speers had been called; and, as soon as he took the trumpet, the course of the steamer had been changed to the northward again. In the last half of this watch, when Raymond had the deck, the wreck had been taken in tow. The captain remained on deck long enough to ascertain that the Ville d'Angers was making ten knots an hour, with the ship in tow; and he hoped in the morning to do even better than this. Thus it turned out that Gregory and Clinch knew nothing of the destination of the steamer.

Possibly Gregory was as much astonished as he pretended to be, when Raymond told him the vessel was bound to England. He had certainly been ugly ever since he came on board. It seemed to him in the beginning, that O'Hara ignored him in re-organizing the watches, and especially in not speaking to him about the quarter-watches. But then, he was looking for a cause of offence; and those who look for it are sure to find it.

"Though I am the first officer of the steamer, I have not been consulted about any thing," replied Gregory, in answer to Raymond's remark.

"I do not know that any of the officers have been consulted," added Raymond, who did not like the attitude of Gregory.

"I suppose I was ignored because I came from the Josephine. The Tritonia's officers seem to be in the ascendant on board of this vessel," continued Gregory, in the most forbidding of tones.

"I don't think it can make any difference what vessel the officers came from."

"Tell that to the marines! isn't the captain hand and glove with Speers, the second officer? Are they not together all the time they can be?" demanded the irate watch officer.

"I think Speers has been consulted no more than you or I have," replied Raymond, moving away from the pilot-house; for he saw that it was of no use to argue the point with one so unreasonable as Gregory showed himself to be.

"Hold on a minute, Mr. Raymond," interposed the discontented officer. "Do you think it is right for the captain to disregard his orders, and take the steamer to England?"

"The captain can answer that question for himself, and I cannot answer it for him," replied Raymond. "All I have to do is to obey my orders."

"Suppose he should take it into his head to run for the South Sea Islands on a pleasure-excursion: should you feel it to be your duty to obey orders without a protest, and go with him?" demanded Gregory.

"The captain is not doing any thing of that sort, and there is no need of answering conundrums," replied Raymond warmly. "This is a case of life and death with thirty-two people on board of the wreck; and it has been decided by the captain, after consultation with all the adults on board, to tow the hulk to Portsmouth."

"But it is a thousand miles to England."

"It is more than that; but, if it were three thousand, I should obey orders all the same."

"I don't think we are justified in obeying orders under such circumstances," continued Gregory. "I think Mr. Fluxion will blame you and me if we assist in sailing the steamer off on this long voyage, when the orders were to take the vessel to the Madeiras."

"Of course you have a right to your own opinion, Mr. Gregory," added Raymond coldly. "Good-morning."

The fourth officer left the pilot-house, where the conversation had been carried on in the presence of the quartermaster and the seaman who were steering the steamer. He was sorry he had listened so long to the malecontent; and, as he walked aft, he debated with himself whether or not he ought to wake the captain, and inform him of the mutinous sentiments uttered by the first officer. But Gregory had taken the trumpet, and had not yet declined to obey the orders of the captain as transmitted to him by his predecessor in charge; and he concluded to say nothing that might place him in the position of a tale-bearer. He turned in; but, as he had had his full six hours of sleep, he lay awake thinking of what Gregory had said to him.

Gregory wanted to do something; and, by diligent thinking, he had fully persuaded himself that the course taken by Capt. O'Hara was all wrong. In the first place, he was exposing the ship's company to the perils of contagion; and, in the second, he was disregarding his orders to take the steamer to Madeira in the event that she should part company with the schooners. He concluded that these were the orders, though he had not heard the senior vice-principal give the instructions to the commander of the steamer.

"I think you are quite right, Mr. Gregory," said the quartermaster at the wheel, after Raymond had gone. "If the truth were known, Capt. Fairfield is of the same mind. I know the fellows from the Josephine don't like the idea of breathing the air from that floating hospital for the next week or ten days; nor of going off on a' cruise two or three weeks, wherever Mr. O'Hara or the Tritonia chooses to take them."

Gregory listened to this long speech without saying a word. The sentiments were his own; but they were mutinous in their nature, and he ought to have reproved the quartermaster for speaking to his superior officer in such terms of the captain.

"How were we going when the log was heaved

last?" asked the first officer, taking no notice of the speech of the man at the wheel.

"Ten and a half, sir," replied **Stokes**.

Gregory went aft, calling for the watch on the forecastle to follow him, and heaved the log. To his astonishment, the Ville d'Angers was making eleven knots. The firemen were evidently doing their best. He had heard Mr. Frisbone say that the steamer would make fifteen knots under favorable circumstances, and that she had done it most of the time before the collision. At this rate she would be in Portsmouth in five days. He looked at the hulk astern, and saw that she carried the square sail she had rigged on the jury-mast, and the wind was fresh enough to help her along a knot or two an hour.

Gregory examined the tow-line, as he had been instructed to do, and found it all right so far as he was able to judge. When he had complied so far with the routine of the vessel and with his orders, he went forward to the engine-room. Alexander was on duty there; and he was the only one of the Tritonia's ship's company on the watch in charge of the steamer. Mr. Fluxion and Mr. Pelham had agreed that officers and seamen from each vessel should be in the same watch, so far as it was practicable; and this arrangement would remove any possible danger of quarrelling and disagreement among the students from the different craft. This had been done; but the rule could not be applied to the engineers, for both of them belonged to the Tritonia. But the "greasers," one from each quarter, belonged to the regular watch.

"Good-morning, Mr. Gregory," said the chief engineer, with a yawn, as the first officer stepped into the engine-room.

"Good-morning, Mr. Alexander," replied Gregory coldly, as he invariably spoke to all the officers of the Tritonia. "You have on a big head of steam."

"The firemen have done very well since I came on watch," answered the engineer, with another yawn.

He had not been careful to improve all his opportunities for sleep, as a sailor should, and as the students had learned to do when on regular duty, and had not turned in till after ten o'clock in the evening; and he had been called at twelve. In the force of engineers the steamer was short-handed; and the watch was changed at six and twelve, night and day; and this bill had been adopted at the request of the engineers themselves, so that they could find no fault with it.

"We are making eleven knots; and that's high speed for a steamer towing a six-hundred-ton ship," added Gregory, who was really sorry to find the engine doing so well.

"So much the sooner this voyage will be over," answered Alexander; and then he yawned again, for he had not slept more than those two hours out of the last twenty-four.

"Why, don't you like it?" asked Gregory, not a little astonished to hear a Tritonian express even a hint of being dissatisfied.

"I can't say I do," replied Alexander, with a heavy gape; "at least, I have had about enough of it, as the thing is going now. A fellow can't stand it without his sleep. I have to keep my eye on that gauge all the time; and it is with the utmost difficulty that I can keep my peepers open."

Alexander gaped again, and Gregory seated himself by his side.

"It is rather rough on you to serve these six-hour watches," added the first officer.

"I shouldn't have minded it for a short cruise; but I didn't ship as an engineer for a trip to England and back."

"I suppose Richards likes it, don't he?" Gregory proceeded, anxious to obtain more information in regard to the sentiments of the engineers.

"He is more discontented than I am. He is growling all the time; and he was downright mad when he learned that the recitations were to be carried on to-morrow, just as they are in all the vessels of the squadron. I shall be in a pretty condition to study my lessons, after this watch is finished. I shall turn in as soon as I get my breakfast, and sleep till noon, when I have to take my place in the engine-room again. How am I to keep up with the class, and run this machine twelve hours a day?"

"You can't do it, of course."

"No more can Richards. He came within one of slipping out of the cabin on the first of the month, when Speers came in from the steerage; and he wants to make his election sure next time."

"It is a hard case for both of you. But I suppose you volunteered for this duty?"

"Richards and I were the only fellows who knew any thing about an engine, and we were really forced to volunteer," yawned Alexander. "I wish we were on our way to Madeira, instead of on a trip to England."

"What is the matter with these fellows down in the

fire-room?" asked Gregory, whose attention had been attracted several times during the conversation, by the singing and laughing of the men at the fires.

"They seem to be very jolly to-night for some reason or other," replied the engineer, gaping fearfully as his drowsiness gained upon him.

The first officer wondered why the men were so jolly at that early hour in the morning; and to satisfy himself he went down into the fire-room. After he had taken a few steps upon the iron stairs, he saw one of the Frenchmen strike off the neck of a bottle with a bar of iron. He poured the contents of the bottle into several tin cups, and passed them to his companions, retaining one for himself. The liquid was very red; and the officer had no doubt it was claret wine, such as is usually furnished to the passengers on board of French steamers.

The men drank off the contents of the tin cups, and then began to sing with renewed energy. It was the quantity of wine they had drank, which made the men so jolly. He was confident that it had not been furnished by the officers or the stewards; and it was plain enough that the foreigners had found it in the hold of the vessel.

Gregory spoke French well enough to do his part in carrying on an ordinary conversation in that language; and, descending into the fire-room, he asked the Frenchmen where they had obtained the wine. The men had drank too much to be disturbed by any common event; and they all laughed heartily at the question. The three Frenchmen were on duty, and Pierre spoke for them.

"You are not the captain?" said he, looking the first officer over from head to foot.

"No: I am the officer of the deck," replied Gregory.

"Plenty of wine in this vessel," said Pierre, laughing again as though he was the happiest mortal in existence.

The other two men threw open the furnace-doors, and began to shovel in the coal at a furious rate. But the officer observed that they kept an eye on the draughts, and used all the precautions against fire or injury to the boilers, doubtless doing so from the sheer force of habit.

"Where did you get the wine?" repeated Gregory, as the fellow did not answer him.

"Very good wine!" exclaimed Pierre, taking another bottle from one of the coal-bunkers, and breaking off the neck as he had done before. "Try some of it;" and he handed the bottle to the officer.

The first officer of the Ville d'Angers, though he had been a good seaman and a good scholar for a considerable time, was not one of the "chaplain's lambs," as the good boys were called by the bad ones. He had no conscientious or other scruples against drinking a glass of wine, or even a bottle, as he had done when the eyes of the professors were not upon him.

Gregory took the bottle; but he was not inclined to drink out of the dirty tin cup of the firemen, or to cut his lips with the glass of the broken bottle. The fireman saw his difficulty, and then disappeared for a moment, returning with a clean tumbler, which he had evidently taken from the mess-room forward of the engine on deck. He handed it to the officer with the greatest show of deference and politeness. Gregory filled the glass, and drank it off, though it was a heavy dram for a young man of his years.

"Where did you get it?" asked the officer.

Instead of answering the question, Pierre took a lantern which hung at the entrance of the port bunker, and led the way along the machinery of the engine to a small door which opened into the after-hold. On each side of the engine was a store-room; and Pierre took a key from his pocket, and opened one of them. Gregory saw that it was the wine-room of the steamer. Upon skids on the floor were several casks; and above them were bins filled with bottles containing "vin ordinaire," or common claret. On the other side were more bins, filled with other kinds of wine.

"Plenty of wine," said Pierre, as he pointed with entire satisfaction to the display of bottles. "This is the best;" and he took one from the bin he pointed at.

Gregory read the label on the bottle, and understood the matter well enough to realize that it was a kind of Burgundy, much stronger than claret. He took a couple of the bottles from the bin, and put them in the pockets of his pea-jacket.

"Give me that key, Pierre," said Gregory.

"No! no! no!" protested the Frenchman, with the greatest earnestness.

Certainly Pierre had given his confidence to the officer without any reserve; but he had done so only after he had partaken of the wine offered him. Whether Pierre had any Arabian notions about hospitality, and believed that Gregory could not betray him after drinking out of the same bottle; or whether he thought that the officer could not misuse his secret after he had shared in the guilt by partaking of the stolen fruit, or the juice of it, — or not, — cannot be imagined; but he seemed to be as free with his officer as though he had been one of his companions in the fire-room.

But Pierre had an opinion of his own in regard to the key; and he positively refused to give it up. Gregory began to feel the effects of the strong Burgundy in his head, for he could not carry off a whole tumbler of it without being fearfully shaken in his upper works. He felt the need of fresh air; for the hold was hot from the furnaces. He tottered back by the way he had come, followed by Pierre, who was evidently assured that he had made a friend of the first officer of the steamer, and that was almost as good as securing an alliance with the captain. The Frenchman assisted the officer of the deck out of the hold, for his steps were becoming more and more unsteady as the fumes of the wine rose in his head.

"What is the row down in the fire-room?" asked Alexander, as the tipsy officer appeared in the engine-room.

"Nothing particular," replied Gregory, trying to stiffen the tones of his voice, which he could not help realizing were very shaky. "The Frenchmen feel good, and that makes them sing and talk loud; but they are so far from the cabin that they can't be heard, and won't disturb any one. Do you know whether there is any wine on board?" asked Gregory.

"I don't think there is; but I wish there were some,

for I think a little of it would wake me up," replied Alexander.

"Wait a minute, then," added the first officer as he stepped out of the engine-room, and went to the mess-room, where a lunch was kept on the table for the benefit of the officers and seamen of the watch. Drawing the cork of one of the bottles, and taking a tumbler from the table, he hastened back to the engine-room as fast as his shaky legs would permit, and poured out a glass of the rich Burgundy, and offered it to the chief engineer.

"What's this?" asked Alexander, taking the glass.

"You said you wished there was some wine on board, and that a little of it would wake you up," added Gregory. "Here it is;" and he spilled a part of it on the floor as the steamer gave a smart roll.

Alexander took the glass, though he had some serious doubts about drinking it. He had very rarely drank wine; he very rarely had a chance to drink it; but if it would wake the firemen, as the noise indicated that it did, — for he was not so stupid as not to understand what produced the unusual hilarity when Gregory came out of the fire-room, and offered him a glass of wine, — it would have the same effect on him. Still he hesitated till one of his longest gapes had nearly choked him; and then he drank off the contents of the glass.

"Now we are in for it together!" exclaimed Gregory, when the engineer had tipped off the red draught.

"What do you mean by that?" demanded Alexander, who did not exactly like the words, or the chuckle that accompanied them.

"Give us your hand, Mr. Alexander! we are friends

now, if you do belong to the Tritonia," said the malecontent, with a laugh, for the liquor was beginning to make him a little excitable.

The engineer could not well refuse his hand, and he gave it to the jolly officer of the deck. Gregory left the engine-room, and went to the mess-room. It was lighted, and he found a hiding-place for the two bottles of wine. He walked about the deck in the fresh air of the night; and he felt happy and contented for the time, and not at all inclined to foment a mutiny. When four bells were struck, and Clinch reported to him to relieve the deck, he let him into the secret, and gave him a tumbler of the Burgundy. He took another at the same time, and turned in without waiting to observe the effect upon the third officer.

CHAPTER XVII.

STRIKING WHILE THE IRON IS HOT.

BURGUNDY is bad stuff for anybody, and especially bad for boys. Clinch found it necessary to keep at a respectful distance from the seamen of his quarter-watch, for he was conscious of being quite unsteady on his feet; of being shaky to a degree that could not be accounted for by the motion of the steamer. But he knew what he was about all the time; and, when he attended to the heaving of the log, he kept up a constant shouting to the hands at the line, to stimulate their interest in their work, and thus prevent them from observing him. But the very thickness of his tones as he spoke was enough to betray him, if there had been any one present who was accustomed to this phase of intoxication.

Alexander had found it more difficult to keep awake after he had loaded himself with Burgundy than it was before. If he kept his seat, he was sure to fall asleep; and several times he "lost himself." He knew that the captain had a habit of prowling about the deck at all hours of the night, as well as of the day; and for this reason he felt obliged to keep on his feet during the remainder of his watch, for it would have ruined him to have the commander find him asleep at his post. He did not consider the Burgundy experiment a success.

Gregory slept like a log in his state-room till eight o'clock, when all hands were called. He got out of his berth with an aching head, and was as cross as a spoiled child. He went to breakfast; but the strong wine had destroyed his appetite so that he could not taste food, and he only drank a cup of coffee. When the meal was finished, Capt. Fairfield, who had prepared the forward part of the cabin for a schoolroom, summoned the starboard watch to attend to their recitations. The lessons had been assigned the day before; and the port-watch, composed of the officers and seamen from the Tritonia, had faithfully studied them. Richards had done so while on duty in the engine-room, for he had not work enough to keep him employed half of the time. He was so accustomed to watching the gauge and the motion of the machinery, that he could do it mechanically, as one writes with a pen without thinking that he is writing. The chief engineer had also studied his lessons when he ought to have been asleep.

Gregory heard the summons to the recitation. He had not studied his lessons, and the call was an unpleasant one to him. The after-effect of the heavy drams of Burgundy he had taken was not only to make him cross, like a wilful child, but as ugly as a hungry wild beast. He looked at the Josephines of the starboard-watch, as they passed into the cabin; and they appeared to him like lambs going to the slaughter. Not that they all, or even many of them, objected to the recitations; but he judged them by himself, and interpreted their feelings by his own. He was utterly opposed to the quarter-watch arrangement, which seemed to be connected with the study scheme, inasmuch as it afforded every student his needed recreation without interfering with his lessons in ordinary weather. He wanted the four hours' leisure when his watch was off duty.

Before the students had all seated themselves at the tables arranged for study purposes, Clinch came to the main door of the cabin, at which Gregory was standing. They had been cronies since they came into the Josephine, and each understood the other perfectly. Like many others, they had both been sent to the academy squadron after being expelled from other literary institutions. They would have passed for bad boys before; but the novel discipline of the nautical school had at least produced a temporary reform. They had not been made over in their minds and hearts, as many had; but they had been transformed into obedient sailors and diligent scholars. This was not enough; but it was better than nothing. Gregory was fourth lieutenant, and Clinch third master, of the Josephine; and no doubt they had fairly won these positions by their attention and zeal.

"Bob Clinch," called Gregory, as the third officer was passing into the cabin.

"What do you want, Dave?" demanded Clinch.

"I want to see you."

"What for?"

"Come out here, and I will tell you."

Gregory led the way to the port side of the deck,

and hauled his friend into a corner where he could speak to him without interruption. But suddenly he seemed to change his mind, and conducted him to the mess-room, which was not occupied at this time. Taking from its hiding-place in the bottom of a locker one of the bottles of Burgundy, he filled a couple of glasses from it; and the cronies tossed them off quite as a matter of course, as though it were a part of the regular routine of the vessel. Neither of them spoke a word, for each understood the other without any speeches.

"I object to the present order of things on board," said Gregory, when he had restored the bottle to its hiding-place, and rinsed the glasses so that no telltale odor should betray him. "I am not going in to the recitations."

"Then there will be a row," added Clinch lightly, as though it were of no particular consequence if there should be a tempest on board.

"I don't care if there is: in fact, I should rather like a little excitement," added Gregory. "I don't feel at home on board of this craft. I have been snubbed half a dozen times by O'Hara since I came into the steamer."

"Well, what are you going to do about it?"

"I am not going into the cabin to the recitations, in the first place."

"But you will have to fight that out with Capt. Fairfield, and not with O'Hara," suggested Clinch. "He is the schoolmaster of the ship."

"I don't care whom I fight it out with. I feel that I have been a good boy about as long as it will pay. It looks to me just as though we had come to the end of our service in the Josephine."

"But we shall return to her."

"I have my doubts about that. When we get to England, if we go there, this vessel will be seized, attached, taken possession of, or something or other of that sort, and we shall all be afloat at loose ends; and how shall we get back to the squadron among the Isles of the Sea? The Prince is not going to wait for us; and we have lost the Madeiras, which I wanted to see more than all the rest of the islands."

"I heard our vice-principal say that passengers are entitled to salvage if they save a vessel after she has been abandoned, or if they help take her into port after she has been partially disabled; and I suppose Mr. Frisbone will attend to the business, so far as the steamer is concerned."

"No matter for that: if we get to England, we shall have no vessel to chase the squadron in; and I don't believe we shall ever find it. I think the cruise of the fleet is ended, as I said."

"What is the use of beating about the bush all day, Dave? if you have any thing to say, why don't you say it. What do you mean to do?" demanded Clinch, a little impatiently.

"Are you going in to the recitations, Bob?" asked Gregory, as though this would settle the whole matter.

"No, not if you don't: I shall follow your lead."

"That's all I want to know," replied Gregory, opening the door of the mess-room, and passing out on the main deck.

"But that isn't all I want to know," added Clinch,

following him. "If there is going to be a row, I want to know my way into it, and my way out of it."

"I don't know that there will be any row," answered Gregory.

"If you refuse to attend recitations there will be, without any doubt."

"Capt. Fairfield wishes to see Mr. Gregory and Mr. Clinch in the cabin," said one of the quartermasters of the starboard watch, touching his cap to the conspirators at this moment.

"Tell Mr. Fairfield, that, with entire respect for him, we have decided not to attend recitations to-day," replied Gregory promptly.

Stokes was the quartermaster who had delivered the message; and he started back with astonishment at the reply of the first officer.

"Shall I say that to him?" he asked, thinking that perhaps Gregory was joking.

"Say that to him," added Gregory decidedly.

By this time the fumes of the wine were well up into his head, and he had a courage not his own; and Clinch was affected in the same way.

"Very well, Mr. Gregory," replied Stokes; but he did not seem inclined to deliver the message.

"Why don't you go back to the cabin with the answer I gave you?" demanded the first officer; but his manner was strange to the quartermaster,—rather silly and simpering.

"If the officers of the ship do not attend recitations, I don't know why the seamen should," added Stokes, encouraged to make the remark by the light tone of his superior.

"They can do as they please," answered Gregory, with a snuff and a chuckle. "But go and deliver the message to the instructor."

"I should like to ask if the rest of the starboard watch may decide not to attend recitations," continued Stokes, who was very anxious to learn something more in regard to the position of the officers before him.

"Come into the mess-room, Stokes," said Gregory, leading the way. "The rest of the watch can do just as they please."

The young tippler — he was nineteen — took the bottle from the locker, and, knowing the quartermaster very well, he gave him a glass of the wine. Possibly he thought the dose would stimulate his ideas, and enable him to reach the conclusion to which his superiors had arrived. Stokes was willing enough to imbibe, and he drank off the contents of the glass.

"I should like to know what's up," said the messenger from the cabin.

"In a word, then, we don't like the way things are managed on board. The captain has disregarded his instructions; and that absolves us all from obeying his orders," replied Gregory, as he drank another dram.

"Is that the idea?" asked Stokes.

"That's just it. The captain has divided us into quarter-watches, and it is by his royal mandate that we are to study our lessons and recite them."

"The captain's? If that is so, how does Capt. Fairfield happen to be on board?" inquired Stokes, who could not help seeing the flaw in the first officer's argument.

"I suppose he was sent on board to look after us a little."

"But all hands were required to take their books and exercise-papers with them."

"That was so that any might study who were inclined. I am not inclined."

"No more am I," added Stokes, laughing, as the Burgundy began to operate in his upper story.

"As a matter of duty, I don't know as we ought to let this thing go any farther; for, as the case stands now, O'Hara is actually running away with the vessel," continued Gregory, whose speech was beginning to be a little thick. "When a lot of fellows ran away with the Tritonia, and were going on an independent cruise in her, the ones that took possession of her and brought her back were treated like lords by the faculty, and praised up to the skies for what they had done."

"Come in, Lawring!" called Clinch, as he saw the other quartermaster of the starboard watch at the door of the mess-room.

"Capt. Fairfield sent me to see what had become of Stokes," said Lawring, as he came into the mess-room.

"Well, you see, don't you?" leered Gregory, whose head was buzzing as though it contained a circular saw in motion. "Here, Lawring, you are a good fellow."

The first officer took the second bottle of Burgundy from the locker (for the first was empty by this time), and filled the glass on the table. Clinch looked out of the window on the deck to warn his companion of the approach of any one who might interfere with their pastime. But no one disturbed them.

"Drink this, Lawring," said Gregory, when he had filled the glass.

"What is it?" inquired the quartermaster, as he looked from one to another in the apartment, wondering what could be going on.

"It's the best wine on board of the Ville d'Angers, and as good as you can find anywhere," replied Gregory in maudlin tones. "Take it, Lawring: it will do you good."

"Thank you, Mr. Gregory: I never drink wine," answered the quartermaster, as he looked over the three former occupants of the mess-room; and he was fully satisfied that all of them had been partaking of the wine.

If the first officer of the steamer was not tipsy, he had never seen a person in that condition.

"If you never drank any wine, it is time for you to begin," chuckled Gregory.

"Thank you, Mr. Gregory: I don't wish for any," returned Lawring decidedly.

"I tell you to drink it; and I am the first officer of this craft."

"Excuse me: I signed the pledge before I left home; and I intend never to drink any thing as long as I live."

"But I am your superior officer!" persisted Gregory, in broken speech. "You must obey me!"

The tippler began to be angry, and stormed at the quartermaster in his incoherent speech.

"I will not drink wine in obedience to any body's orders," replied Lawring firmly.

"You won't! then I'll make you drink it!"

"Dry up, Dave!" interposed Clinch.

"What reply shall I take to Capt. Fairfield, Stokes?" asked Lawring, as he opened the door behind him.

"Tell Capt. Fairfield, that, with entire respect for him, we have decided not to attend any recitations," answered Stokes, sending the reply which Gregory had given him.

"Don't let him go till I bust in his head!" exclaimed the first officer, staggering towards the door to intercept the departing quartermaster.

"No, no; don't get up a fight here," said Clinch, taking his crony by the collar, and detaining him.

Lawring did not wait for any thing more; but hastened back to the cabin, where the rest of the watch were engaged in their recitations.

"Stokes says, that, with entire respect for you, Capt. Fairfield, he has decided not to attend any recitations," said Lawring, reporting to the instructor.

"Indeed! and did you see Gregory and Clinch?" inquired the astonished teacher.

"They were all in the mess-room forward, sir."

"What does this mean? did they assign any reason for their conduct?"

"No, sir; but I think that all three of them have been drinking wine; and Mr. Gregory is intoxicated," added the quartermaster.

"Intoxicated!" exclaimed Capt. Fairfield. "I think you must be mistaken, Lawring."

"No, sir, I am not. They had a bottle of red wine, and Mr. Gregory asked me to drink a glass of it."

Capt. Fairfield was bewildered at this intelligence. Three of the students who ought to be at their studies were drinking wine in the mess-room. Certainly this was all wrong. The students were not allowed to drink wine, to say nothing of refusing to attend to the lessons. But the instructor was a prudent man; and he paused to consider his own powers in the premises. He had been sent on board to instruct the ship's company; and he concluded that his authority was the same as that of any other professor in the absence of the principal or a vice-principal. He had the entire control of the students during study hours, unless they were ordered to do ship's duty by the captain. He could not interfere with the navigation of the vessel; but he could compel the attendance of the pupils at the proper hours in the cabin.

Leaving the cabin, he went on the poop-deck, where O'Hara was, and stated the case to him. The young captain was very much disconcerted by the intelligence that some of the students were insubordinate, but especially so that the first and third officers were in a state of intoxication and rebellion. It was clear enough that the tipplers had found a way to get into the wine-room in the hold. Mr. Frisbone had taken the key to this room; and it was a mystery how the students had got into it.

O'Hara told Capt. Fairfield that he had full powers to compel the attendance of the members of the starboard-watch in the cabin, and advised him to call upon the boatswain and carpenter if he needed any assistance. While the instructor went to attend to this duty, O'Hara called for the stewards, and visited the hold with them. They knew nothing about the wine or the wine-room. The door was locked, and all appeared to be right about it. But, while they were investigating the matter, the captain saw Alfonzo come out of the fire-room, and creep under the engine to the door leading into the after-hold. He went below again, and the fireman unlocked the door of the wine-room. When he had gone in, the captain crept up to the door, and took out the key. Calling the two stewards, they drove Alonzo out, and locked the door.

"Keep this key," said O'Hara to the man who acted as chief steward, "and search the ship all over. If you find any wine or liquors, lock them up."

It so happened that the firemen had exhausted the supply they had in the fire-room, and had sent Alfonso for another stock. He had found the key in the fire-room. The stewards found that which Gregory had concealed in the locker, and it was secured. No wine was to be had except in the wine-room. As a further precaution, the captain ordered the carpenter to transfer two heavy bars of iron from another door to this one. As each bar was secured by a large lock, it was not likely the room would be broken into.

Capt. Fairfield went to the mess-room after he left the captain. The students there were respectful to him at first; but, when he spoke of enforcing his authority, Gregory was impudent; and the others, whose heads were full of wine, followed his example.

But the instructor was a rigid disciplinarian; and, calling in Shakings, they dragged the first and third officers and the quartermaster into the cabin. But they were all too much intoxicated to study or recite; and Capt. Fairfield locked them into a couple of spare state-rooms.

By noon they had all slept off the effects of the wine. O'Hara had been thinking all the morning about the case of discipline on hand, and confidently expected trouble as soon as the time came to change the watch. He had made up his mind what to do; but his action must be governed by the circumstances. Only three of the students from the Josephine had thus far been insubordinate; but all the rest might join them. But he apprehended no difficulty, for the officers and seamen from the Tritonia were enough to handle the steamer.

Gregory had been let out of the state-room, completely sobered, at half-past eleven, so that he could dine with his watch in season to take the deck at noon. He was even more cross and ugly than he had been in the morning.

"All the starboard-watch on deck!" shouted the acting boatswain, piping the call.

Gregory did not move from the seat he had taken at the cabin-door. O'Hara trembled as he saw that the first officer was intent upon making trouble.

"The deck is yours, Mr. Gregory," said Raymond, tendering to him the trumpet, in the usual form.

"I don't want it," growled the first officer. "I shall not do duty any more."

Raymond reported the answer to the captain.

"Call all hands!" said O'Hara promptly.

The call was immediately piped. As on board the vessels of the squadron, every officer and seaman had his station, and was required to repair to it instantly, whether the call came by day or night.

Every one went to his station except the three who had refused to attend the recitations. Possibly the conspirators could have induced others of their shipmates in the Josephine to join them; but they had had no time to work the case up.

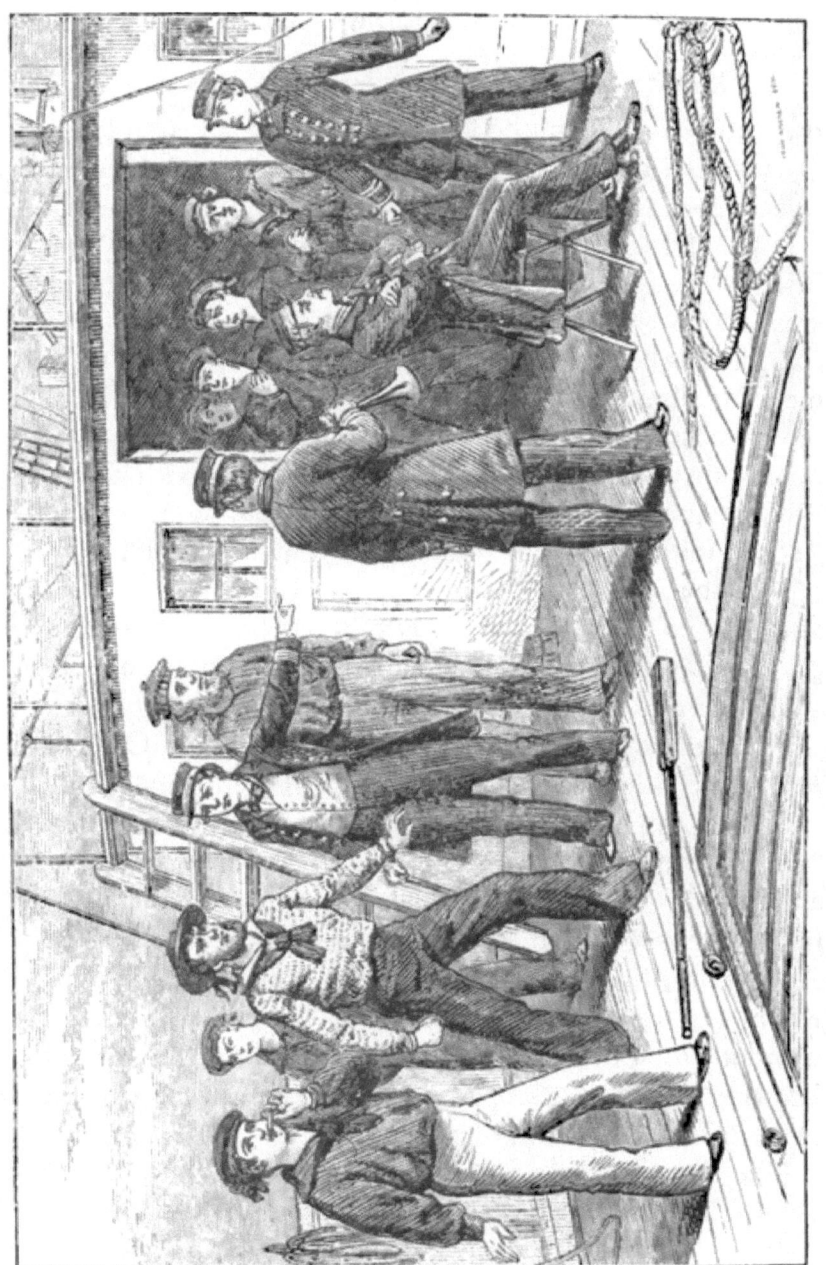

Mr. Shakings takes Charge of the First Officer. Page 249.

"Here, Winchell!" shouted Gregory to one of his own watch. "Don't go! We are going to stand out. O'Hara is running away with the steamer, and we need not obey orders."

"Mr. Shakings, you will take charge of the first officer," said the young captain. "Lock him into his state-room, and keep him there."

Clinch followed the lead of his crony, and Mr. Rimmer was directed to serve him in the same way. Both of them were disposed to show fight; but the stout boatswain and carpenter made quick work with them. Stokes concluded, at this particular moment, not to "stand out," and went to his station at the wheel.

No doubt Gregory was astonished to find himself and his conspiracy so easily overcome. He was a prisoner by himself, and likely to remain so for a considerable time.

As soon as the mutineers were disposed of, O'Hara called the ship's company together. He did not allude to the event which had just transpired, except to state the fact that there were two vacancies in the officers' cabin; and it was necessary that they should be immediately filled, for two quarter-watches were without officers. After consulting with Speers and Raymond, both of whom insisted that the vacant places should be filled without promoting either of them, the captain appointed Lawring first officer in place of Gregory, and Taylor in place of Clinch; both of them from the Josephine.

The firemen made a new demand for wine; but they obtained none, and they did not deem it prudent to "strike" again. In five days more the Ville d'Angers arrived at Portsmouth, with the Castle William in tow.

CHAPTER XVIII.

A TRIP TO THE CANARY ISLANDS.

"ARRIVED at Portsmouth, steamer Ville d'Angers, having in tow the hulk of the ship Castle William, dismasted in the violent gale of April 8," read Mr. Pelham, from a newspaper which had just been received by the African steamer.

He had hastened on board of the Prince with the paper as soon as he obtained it. The news was certainly very important, for it assured the principal that the missing steamer was safe; and, in the absence of any additional intelligence, it was presumed that her crew were all well.

Mr. Fluxion took the paper, and looked it over. He was especially happy because his confident prediction that the Ville d'Angers was all right, had been fully verified. Mr. Lowington was delighted in the safety of the students on board of her. The Marian was still in port; for Judge Rodwood enjoyed the climate of the island and the frequent hospitality of Don Roderigue so much, that he was in no haste to pursue his truant ward.

A boat was immediately sent to the Marian to inform the judge that his ward had been heard from, and was believed to be all right. He was glad to hear it, though he seemed to be in no hurry to leave the beautiful islands.

"Ah, here is more news!" exclaimed Mr. Fluxion, who was still looking over the paper.

"About the steamer?" asked Mr. Lowington.

"Yes, sir: here is a tolerably full account of the voyage of the Ville d'Angers, and of the state of things on board of the Castle William," continued the senior vice-principal, as he seated himself under the awning on the quarter-deck of the American Prince.

"Let us hear it," added the principal eagerly.

It was a Southampton paper; and the editor reminded his readers of the visit of the academy squadron to the waters of the Solent and Spithead, and the race around the Isle of Wight, about six years before. Then followed an account of the picking-up of the French steamer, and the subsequent falling-in with the wreck of the Castle William.

"A very wealthy American gentleman," the article continued, "who was the patron of the academy squadron, and had presented to its distinguished principal an elegant and costly steam-yacht of twelve hundred tons burden, happened to be a passenger, with his family, in the Ville d'Angers from Havre to Malaga. When the condition of things on board of the unfortunate Castle William was ascertained, this noble-hearted gentleman, with his wife and her sister, went on board of the hulk where pestilence and death were raging, and tenderly nursed the sick. Mr. Frisbone, who is jocosely called the 'American Prince,'— and he is one of Nature's most royal princes,— immediately resorted to various sanitary measures, and with his own hands whitewashed the space between decks of the fever-stricken vessel. The medicines and supplies put on board of the ship by the steamer were so well used that the sick immediately began to improve; and now all are doing well. They have all been removed to the quarantine hospital, where the small-pox patients are convalescent.

"Undoubtedly the careful nursing of the sick by this self-sacrificing gentleman and the ladies saved the lives of many, if not all, of the sick. Certainly the heroic exertions of the young gentlemen of the school-ship saved the vessel and her freight of human beings; and they deserve the highest praise. Mr. Frisbone, as the agent of the principal of the academy squadron, has libelled the Castle William for salvage; and we learn that negotiations for an amicable adjustment of the amount are in progress. The owners of the steamer, by their attorney, have already put in their claim for the Ville d'Angers, subject to reasonable salvage.

"We regret to add that there has been some trouble about the discipline among the young officers of the steamer. The first and third officers of the steamer, appointed by the senior vice-principal in charge of one of the vessels of the academy squadron, were mutinous, and refused to do duty, attempting to incite others of the crew to follow their example. Possibly it was a boyish frolic; but the young captain promptly caused the arrest of the two offenders, and has kept them prisoners in their state-rooms up to the present time. But all the rest of the ship's company yield a willing obedience to the authority of the captain.

"We regard Capt. O'Hara, for such is his name, as a rather remarkable young gentleman. Mr. Frisbone assures our informant that he is a thorough seaman, having served before the mast, and worked his way up to fourth lieutenant of the vessel to which he is attached. He was born in Italy, of an Irish father formerly in the English consular service, and an Italian mother. He is twenty years of age, and speaks Italian and French as fluently as he does English. Though there is an instructor, as well as two adult forward officers, attached to the ship, she is under the entire management of her youthful commander."

This was the principal portion of the article which Mr. Fluxion read, to which the party gave the most undivided attention. Of course it was gratifying to the professional pride of the principal; and both of the vice-principals congratulated themselves upon their own discretion in appointing O'Hara to the command of the steamer, though it was not foreseen that he would make such an extended cruise in her.

"I am sorry to learn that there has been trouble on board of the steamer," said Mr. Lowington, when the account of the voyage had been partly digested.

"But O'Hara seems to have made an end of the mutiny at once," replied Mr. Fluxion.

"He is a very decided fellow," added Mr. Pelham. "He is a peaceable and well-disposed young man; but he would fight his way through any thing if the occasion required."

"This paper says the first and third officers were insubordinate," continued the principal anxiously. "Who were these officers?"

"Gregory was the first, and Clinch was the third officer," replied Mr. Fluxion, not a little disconcerted, as the heavy frown on his brow indicated. "I am sorry to say that both of them were from the Josephine."

"They used to be bad boys," said Mr. Lowington.

"For the last year there have been no better officers or students in the vessel than Gregory and Clinch. I don't understand it," replied Mr. Fluxion, musing. "Possibly O'Hara has been a little airy, and provoked them: it would not be strange if any young fellow should feel good, in command of a steamer of six hundred tons."

"It is not at all like O'Hara to put on airs," interposed Mr. Pelham.

"Even if he did, that is no excuse for Gregory," added Mr. Fluxion.

"I suppose we shall not understand the matter till we see the students, and get their account of the affair," said Mr. Lowington.

"The name of my ward is not mentioned in connection with this business," remarked the judge.

"He is not mentioned as a mutineer; and so far it is perfectly satisfactory," added Dr. Phelps.

"I have no doubt he has done his duty faithfully," said Mr. Pelham.

"But when shall we have these young fellows back here?" asked Judge Rodwood.

"That is more than I can tell: they are out of my reach, and I cannot instruct them what to do," replied the principal. "But Mr. Frisbone is happily with them; and I have entire confidence in his good judgment and discretion."

"What will he do with them? He has no authority over them; and I fancy, if they once get ashore, Capt. O'Hara will not be as powerful as he seems to have been on board. What will they do?"

"I have no doubt Mr. Frisbone will send them to these islands in the next steamer, and come himself, if he is not wholly disgusted with his experience at sea."

"The steamer which arrived to-day is an extra one," said Mr. Pelham. "The next steamer will not leave Southampton till the 24th of the month, and will arrive on the 30th."

"And this is only the 21st," added the judge. "Shall we remain here nine or ten days longer?"

"We will consider that matter," replied Mr. Lowington, rising from his deck-chair.

The conference was ended, and all returned to their own vessels. The principal went forward to the chart-room, on the table of which was spread out the chart of the North Atlantic. He looked it over, applied the parallel ruler and the dividers. In less than half an hour orders were sent to the Josephine and the Tritonia to sail at four o'clock in the afternoon for Santa Cruz, Teneriffe, one of the Canary Islands. Notice of this intention was sent to Judge Rodwood, who immediately hastened on board of the Prince to ascertain more definitely the intentions of the principal.

"You seem to have come to a sudden conclusion," said the judge, when he met the principal on the deck of the Prince.

"My absent students cannot get to Funchal under ten days; and I cannot afford to lose so much time," replied Mr. Lowington. "It is only a day's run for the steamer to the Canaries; and we can spend a week at Santa Cruz, or in cruising about the islands, and return in season to take them on board."

"Excellent!" exclaimed the judge. "I shall go with you; and this excursion will afford me an opportunity to reciprocate the hospitality of our friend Don Roderigue; for I shall invite him and his family to take passage in the Marian."

"I was just thinking of offering them state-rooms on board of the American Prince; but I have no doubt you can accommodate them more elegantly than I can; and I will yield the privilege to you, judge."

"Thank you, Mr. Principal."

Judge Rodwood hastened on shore to extend the invitation to Don Roderigue; and great was the delight of the young officers when they saw Dona Maria go on board of the Marian just before the hour appointed for the sailing of the squadron. They lustily cheered the party. Don Roderigue raised his hat, and bowed his thanks, while his daughter vigorously waved her handkerchief.

Promptly at the hour set, the two steamers and the two schooners got under way, and stood out of the Bay of Funchal. The wind was quite fresh from the west, veering a little to the north, so that the sailing-vessels had all the breeze they wanted. It had been agreed that the vessels of the fleet should keep together, and the steamers were worked at about two-thirds of their ordinary speed to accommodate them. The course was true south till seven o'clock in the morning, when the Salvages, a group of islands with very rocky and dangerous surroundings, bore to the eastward; and then the fleet was headed to the east south-east. The islands looked barren and forbidding.

"Land, sharp on the weather-bow!" shouted the lookout on the top-gallant forecastle of the Tritonia.

"Land!" exclaimed Scott, who had the deck. "There is no land within a hundred miles in that direction. The lookout has a gravel-stone in his eye, and thinks it is an island."

"Don't be too sure of that, Scott," added the vice-principal, leaping on the rail at the weather side, and looking out in the direction indicated by the lookout. "I see it."

The lieutenant sprang into the weather rigging, and strained his eyes to the utmost; but he could see nothing that looked like land.

"I think I am getting blind, sir," added Scott, with a laugh.

"Where are you looking? Up here!" and Mr. Pelham pointed a considerable distance above the horizon.

"Up there! I shouldn't think of looking up there for land, unless I expected to find it in the moon," replied Scott. "The Mountains of the Moon are away over on the other side of Africa. Are you looking for them?"

"Don't you see that mountain?" continued Mr. Pelham, pointing again.

"I see it now," answered Scott, as he made out a mazy mass, high above the horizon. "What in the world is that?"

"It is the peak of Teneriffe."

"I have heard enough about it to know it without an introduction."

"It must be nearly a hundred miles off."

"And we are in no immediate danger of getting aground on that land."

This mountain was the point of attraction for the day, as it gradually displayed its outline more clearly to the students. At three o'clock in the afternoon, the squadron rounded Point Anaga, the north-eastern cape of Teneriffe. It was only nine miles farther to the chief town of the island; and by five, the squadron was at anchor, and all the formalities of the government had been complied with.

At eight the next morning all hands were assembled in the grand saloon of the Prince, to hear what Mr. Mapps had to say about the Canary Islands in general, and Teneriffe in particular.

"The *Islas Canarias*, as the Spaniards have it, or the Canaries, or Canary Islands, as we have it, lie between thirteen and eighteen degrees of west longitude, and between twenty-seven and a half and twenty-nine and a half degrees of north latitude. They have an aggregate area of thirty-two hundred square miles, and a population of two hundred and twenty-seven thousand. There are seven principal islands, the most important of which are Teneriffe, Grand Canary, and Palma. These islands are all very mountainous, volcanic, and rocky. The peak of Teneriffe, which we have had in sight since yesterday morning, is over twelve thousand feet high.

"The two most western islands are Hierro, or Ferro, and Palma, both of which contain peaks from five to over seven thousand feet high. The meridian which passes through **Ferro** was the one formerly selected as the first, from which longitude was measured; and for this reason it has been adopted as the dividing-line between the Eastern and Western Hemispheres. Gomera is fourteen miles south-west of **Teneriffe**. The water between these islands is very deep; and there are no dangers, except within a few hundred feet of the shore.

"Teneriffe is forty-five miles long, and twenty-two wide. The natives call the summit of the mountain which stands in the middle of the island, the 'Pico de Teyde.' We saw it yesterday morning when we were nearly a hundred miles from it; and the people say it can be seen a hundred and sixty miles, but this is vanity on their part. There are generally more or less clouds hanging about it. Santa Cruz, or 'Holy Cross,' is the most driving city of all the islands of the Atlantic. It has twenty thousand inhabitants. The mole which you see is of recent construction, and was very much needed to protect the shipping from the strong winds coming from north-east to south-east. There is some British naval history connected with this city. In 1657 Admiral Blake destroyed a Spanish fleet, anchored under the batteries of the town; and, favored by a sudden change of wind, got his ships out of the harbor with but little loss. Nelson lost an arm here in 1797, and was badly beaten in his battle with Fort San Miguel, which is still in existence. British flags are so scarce with the Spaniards, that those captured in this engagement are still on exhibition in the principal church of the city. In the middle of the summer the heat in the town is very oppressive; and the wealthy inhabitants flee from it to Laguna, a place among the hills, five miles inland.

"On the north-west side of Teneriffe is the port and city of Orotava, which is probably the best health station in the world for invalids troubled with throat and lung diseases. It is located in an amphitheatre of hills, two or three miles from the sea. It is even superior to Madeira in the uniformity of its temperature. The region around it is a perfect garden, and the thermometer never falls below fifty degrees, or rises more than a degree or two above eighty; and these extremes are of very rare occurrence. The average temperature is about sixty-eight degrees. One month hardly varies more than a couple of degrees from the one next to it. Invalids here may remain out of doors all the time, and keep their windows open night and day. But it has not yet become to any great extent a health resort; and there is a lack of accommodations for visitors and temporary residents.

"The Grand Canary is about fifty miles to the southeast of Teneriffe. It is a beautiful island, fertile and populous; and until recently the seat of government, which has been transferred to Teneriffe. It has a range of mountains, some peaks of which are over six thousand feet high. Many streams flow from these hills, which in the rainy season become raging torrents. Las Palmas, or the Palms, is a city of twenty thousand inhabitants, formerly the capital of the islands; but Santa Cruz de Teneriffe, as it is called to distinguish it from another Santa Cruz in the island of Palma, has wrested from it this distinction; and there is a strong rivalry between the two places. It is still the Church capital of the Canaries. It is overlooked by two high mountains; and through the city runs the Guiniguada River, which is crossed by a bridge with immense arches, built two hundred years ago. It has some fine buildings, and several educational institutions. The harbor is very bad, for a heavy surf rolls in most of the time; but it has a sheltered port two miles to the eastward of it.

"Fuerteventura lies east of Teneriffe, and is fifty-two miles long. It has the appearance of being a barren island, but has very fertile spots in it. The mountains are not so high as in Grand Canary, and it has no good harbors. Lanzarote lies to the north-east, and is thirty-one miles long. Alegranza is a small island, and the most northerly of the group; but it is celebrated as being the home from which first came the beautiful songster we call the canary-bird. There are other small islands. Fuerteventura is only about sixty miles from the coast of Africa.

"These islands form a province of Spain, and are represented in the Cortes of the mother country. Mail-vessels ply between the different islands, and there is frequent communication by steamer with Spain and England. The people are Spaniards, a little darker of complexion than those you meet in Spain. The islands are generally very fertile, and the productions of both the torrid and the temperate zone are raised here. The vine has been an important item, and forty thousand pipes of wine were the average manufacture until 1853, when the grape disease destroyed the vines; but, like Madeira, these islands are rapidly recovering from this disaster.

"The Canaries are believed to have been known to the ancients, and to have been mentioned by Pliny the Elder, and others, as the Fortunate Islands. The ruins of some stone temples in Gomera indicate that they were known to the Carthaginians. Like the Madeiras, they were discovered in modern days by a vessel driven off its course by heavy weather, in 1334. They were conquered — and the original inhabitants fought well for their country — by Jean de Bethencourt, a Norman baron in the service of Spain, in 1402. They were claimed by the Portuguese, and the natives were troublesome for a long period; but Spain eventually obtained full possession."

The professor finished his remarks, after he had spoken for some time about the manners and customs of the aborigines of the islands, as indicated by the implements and ruins found in them; and then the students of the Tritonia and Josephine returned to their vessels.

CHAPTER XIX.

WALKS AND TALKS ABOUT THE CANARY ISLANDS.

AS soon as the lecture of Mr. Mapps was ended, all hands were allowed to go on shore. The elegant barge of the Marian had gone directly from the American Prince to the landing-place, having on board Don Roderigue and his daughter. The boat was pulled by four seamen with a coxswain in the stern, all attired in holiday uniforms; and the barge was fitted up as gayly as a festive gondola in the Grand Canal of Venice, for the young lady and her father.

"Here we are!" exclaimed Lieut. Scott, as he stepped on the shore with Capt. Wainwright. "I had an idea we should hear immense flocks of canary-birds whistling in the island, and be in canary-seed up to our knees."

"Of course you did not expect to see canary-birds in the streets of a city, unless you saw them in cages," added the captain. "Didn't the professor just tell you these birds came from the island of Alegranza?"

"I supposed he only said that to get off that jaw-breaker. I couldn't tell the names of more than two of these islands after he had given them all."

"That was because you had not looked them up beforehand. Most of them are given on the chart of the North Atlantic."

"I am not so much of a bookworm as some of the fellows."

"Here comes Dr. Winstock," continued Wainwright, as the captain's barge of the Prince came up to the landing.

"I suppose he will convoy us here, as he has before," added Scott. "I wonder if there is a place on the face of the earth where he has not been."

"He was a surgeon in the navy for a good many years; and I suppose our men-of-war have visited all these islands."

"Are you willing to take us in tow, doctor?" asked Scott, as the surgeon, attended by Capt. Sheridan and Lieut. Murray, approached them.

"I shall be very happy to do so if you won't labor too hard with those tremendous jokes of yours," replied the doctor, laughing.

"I don't think I labor very hard at them. I try to be as solemn as an owl; but somehow I don't get along worth a cent," pleaded Scott.

"I should be sorry to have you break your back by struggling in the other direction; and I have not the slightest objection to your jokes; only labor not to be funny."

"I strive not to do so; and I have rejected some of the best things ever thought of, because I found I had been studying upon them."

"Doubtless you did wisely. But we will commence our walk," added Dr. Winstock, as he led the way from the shore. "I suppose you noticed the appearance of the island from the ships?"

"I noticed it during the whole of my watch yesterday," replied Scott; "and I thought it looked more like a busted volcano than any thing I ever saw before."

"At a distance the mountain near the centre seems to be the whole island; and some of the pictures of the peak make it rise directly from the sea."

"The whole thing looked like a cinder just raked out of a blacksmith's forge. It don't look so now."

"It reminds me of Greece, where the hills are red and barren. There appears to be no room for the cultivation of any thing on this island, as you look at it from the sea; for we cannot see any thing of its beautiful valleys and plains enclosed by mountains. But the appearance is not very far from the fact, for not more than one-seventh of the whole surface of the island can be cultivated; but the arable land is immensely productive."

"What do they raise here?" asked Murray.

"Grapes, which they manufacture into wine and brandy; mulberry-trees, with which they feed the silkworm, and silk is one of the exports; potatoes, wheat, Indian corn, oranges, almonds; and the bees produce honey and wax for shipment. Cochineal is a very important article of commerce."

"What is cochineal?" asked Scott. "I heard some one say it was made of bugs, and was used to color candy and things."

"Some one told you correctly. Cochineal is a very valuable dye-stuff. It consists of the bodies of the *cocus cacti*, a little bug about the size of a grain of barley, but more in the shape of a dried pea. It belongs to the *cocidæ*, which are the most injurious of insects about plants, as in hot-houses. The orange-trees of the Azores were well-nigh destroyed by them in 1843; and Fayal, which usually exports twelve thousand boxes of this fruit, did not send off a single one that year."

The party had paused on the street near the beach to hear the account; and the doctor pointed out a package of the cochineal, as an illustration of his subject.

"The *cocus cacti* is so called because it feeds on a certain kind of cactus, which has to be cultivated as the food of the insect. The production of cochineal was carried on in Mexico, which is the country of the cactus, long before it was known to Cortes or any other European. Only the female insect is used in the manufacture of the color. The male has wings, but the female has none."

"That's so that they cannot go gadding about," added Scott.

"Very likely; for the female fastens herself to a plant; and this branch is cut off with the creature upon it. The laborer forms a sort of soft nest on the cochineal plant; and, when the mother has been placed on it, she lays her eggs. The young when hatched spread themselves over the plant, feeding upon it, till they are in condition for use. As the insect produces several crops of eggs in a year, the young are soon ready to lay eggs; but they must be killed before they are in condition to do this, or it would injure the quality of the cochineal. The branch on which the insects are gathered is cut, and plunged into boiling water, in order to kill them. They are then collected and dried; and in this condition it takes seventy thousand of them to make a pound of cochineal."

"Then it is the corpses of these bugs that is used to put the red streak into a stick of peppermint candy," added Scott.

"Such is the fact; and it may cure you of the tendency to eat candy."

"I think not, sir; for I can stand it if the corpses can," answered Scott.

"We will walk up into the town," continued the doctor, leading the way.

"The houses are very pretty," said Sheridan, as he noticed the extreme whiteness of all the buildings.

"They are built of stone, and whitewashed."

"Just as they serve erring office-holders at home."

"They can't make them white as these houses are."

"Creation! there is a woman that looks like a squaw of a band of travelling Indians!—stove-pipe hat and all!" exclaimed Scott. "There is another with a load on her head."

"The women are the principal beasts of burden in Teneriffe. They walk twenty miles in from the country, with a load of market-stuff on their heads," added the doctor.

There was nothing very peculiar about the costume of the woman, except the hat, and a sort of cloth thrown over the head, and worn under the hat, which dropped over the arms and shoulders, like a shawl. The lower class of men wore short trousers, the front covered with goat-skin, a short jacket, and gaiters over their shoes. Many carried a staff as tall as the arm-pits. There were a few beggars about the streets, as there are in all Spanish towns; and their costume is as miscellaneous as those in Spain wear, except that the cloak is not endurable in this warm climate.

"This is the *Plaza de la Constitucion*," said the doctor, as they entered a handsome square, bordered by a broad street, and liberally provided with street-lamps.

"I knew it was before you said a word!" exclaimed Scott.

"How did you know it?".

"Because the Spaniards all live on the constitution; and they have a square in every town that is big enough to hold one, with that name to it," replied the joker, laughing. "I think they will use the constitution up one of these days, and have to fall back on the by-laws."

"But this is a very pretty square; and the whole town is as neat as any thing we have seen," added Sheridan. "These buildings are very fine; and I am sure I had no idea of finding any such a town among the Isles of the Sea."

"The Spaniards here think a great deal of their city; and they have been liberal in the matter of public improvements," replied the surgeon. "This piece of sculpture, which looks something like a monument when seen at a distance," he continued, pointing to the object at one end of the enclosure of the square, "is a statue of the Virgin of Candelaria, representing her appearance to the *Guanches*, as the original inhabitants were called, and thus converting them to Christianity."

The colossal statue is on the summit of the monument, which has four other figures at the base. At the other end of the plaza is a very handsome marble cross, which symbolizes the sanctity of the city name.

"This is the house in which was born the Marshal O'Donnel, Duke of Tetuan," said the doctor, as he pointed to the building, a small and modest structure.

"He is a brave general in the French army. I was reading about him the other day. He was taken prisoner at Sedan last summer while we were in the north of Europe," said Scott.

"Now, that is not a creditable joke," added the surgeon. "You ought to know better."

"But I don't know any better."

"You are thinking of Marshal McMahon. This is O'Donnel, another man entirely," interposed the doctor.

"It was not a joke, but a blunder," said Scott, blushing. "They have Irish names; and both of them seem to be out of their element in France and Spain. But who is O'Donnel, anyhow?"

"He isn't McMahon, anyhow, — nor Gen. Howe. His ancestors were Irish refugees, who came here after the battle of the Boyne. He went into the Spanish army, and was a colonel at the age of twenty-five. He distinguished himself as a soldier, and for his services in Morocco was made Duke of Tetuan, which is a division of that country. He has had great influence as a statesman, having been minister of war, and president of the council. He had his ups and downs, as all Spanish statesmen have. He has headed an insurrection, and has been banished. He died in 1867. You must have heard of him when you were in Spain."

"I think I did, sir; but I have heard about so many men, that I get them a little mixed."

"Like the *plaza* and the *alameda* in all Spanish

towns, this square is the great resort of the people in the evening. The band plays here, and the scene is quite lively," continued Dr. Winstock. "When I was a young man I used to see a deal of flirting on this square; but since I have grown older I don't notice such things. I was stationed on the coast of Africa, in a sloop-of-war, looking out for slavers; and the ship came up here to recruit the health of the men. One of our officers was smitten with a Santa Cruz beauty; and he adopted the custom of the country. He followed her about the streets, dogged her steps, in a manner that would have amounted to an outrage at home. At last he obtained an introduction to her; but this was hardly necessary, though his prejudices required it of him. But he only saw her in the plaza, and in the Prince Royal Square; and she evidently liked him as well as he did her. Not till they were engaged was he permitted by the custom of the islands to enter her father's house, or hotel it was in this instance; for she was a *Canarienne*, and only a temporary resident."

"Did the officer marry her?" asked Murray, with deep interest.

"Of course you would not be satisfied to have me omit the *denoûment* of the novel," added the surgeon, laughing. "He did marry her; and I think she is a dignified matron in the city of Philadelphia at this time."

The party walked about the city till they had exhausted its sights, which was soon done. The doctor introduced his charge to the delicious chocolate to be had at the cafés on the plaza; but some of them declared that it was too thick, and preferred the ice-cream made from the snows of the peak of Teneriffe. The cicerone then proposed a long walk, which would occupy the rest of the day.

"I am ready, for one; but what do you call a long walk, doctor? Some folks think three miles is a long walk; but I don't apply the phrase to any thing less than fifty miles," replied Scott.

"I propose to go to Laguna, the ancient city of this island. It is five miles distant; and, as the town is two thousand feet above the sea, it will be up-hill all the way. If you are too tired to walk back, you can return in the *dilijencia*."

The party gladly assented to the plan; and they started out of the city. In a short time they left the well-paved streets of the great road, which is fully equal to the royal highways of Spain.

"Laguna is a summer resort for the wealthy people of Santa Cruz; and the heat on the seashore, when the wind comes from the coast of Africa, is intense," said the doctor, as the party trudged on their way. "But it is not the most desirable place on the island, for it is subject to heavy rains. Orotava, concerning which I gave Mr. Mapps some information for his lecture, is a much more desirable place; and one of these days, when a railroad is built to it, the citizens will live there in the summer, and do business in the city. We shall have an opportunity to visit the place."

"What in the world is that growing in that field?" asked Scott, as he looked over the walls that bounded the road.

"What do you suppose?"

"I haven't the least idea; but the plants must be sick, for they seem to be tied up in rags."

"Those plants are cacti; and I think I have told you something about them to-day," added the doctor. "The rags are tied about them to protect the insects, for they are full of them. It takes about three months for them to attain their growth, and be ready to lay eggs. They furnish the principal occupation of the laboring-classes since the failure of the vine. When I first came along here, this road was bordered with extensive and beautiful vineyards; but they have given place for the present to this not very handsome plant, which was brought here from Mexico."

"Those are funny-looking houses!" exclaimed Murray, as they came upon a little collection of dwellings of the peasants.

"They are very comfortable houses for poor people," replied the doctor; "a great deal better than many of the laboring-people of Spain occupy."

Some of them were built of stone; others were evidently composed of poles set in the ground; and in the latter case the walls, as well as the roofs, were thatched.

"All the poor people do not have houses as good as these, but, like the gypsies of Granada, have to burrow into the rocks to make caves for dwellings. But this is a very soft climate, and the house is not of so much consequence as in Russia or Norway."

"There is a woman with a load on her head! it looks like garden-sauce. There is another with a pile of wood on her crown," cried Scott.

"Domestic animals are not very plenty in these islands; and the women seem to have a monopoly of the carrying-trade," continued the surgeon.

"Hi! Hi!" shouted Scott, as they turned a bend in the winding road. "There are your beasts of burden!"

"What are they?" asked Sheridan.

"Camels; don't you know them?"

"I never saw one before in my life, replied the captain of the Prince.

"Here is a train of them, each with his bell. We are not far from the Great Desert, where these animals do all the carrying; and a considerable number of them have been brought to these islands."

After a while the novelty of the scenes along the road wore off; and some of them declared that the country was not much different from Madeira. About two o'clock in the afternoon they reached Laguna, and spent a couple of hours in seeing its sights. A very fine organ in the cathedral was shown to them; and in another church there was a miraculous picture in which the subject wept on proper occasions. They were much interested in the museum, where they saw specimens of the implements used by the aborigines, who had no knowledge of the use of iron. Knives were made of pieces of lava; and horns were used for ploughs. The people embalmed the bodies of their dead after the manner of the Egyptians; and mummies enclosed in goat-skin were on exhibition.

About four the excursionists started on their return; and all of them walked, for, if any were tired enough to ride, they were too proud to say so. When they had gone about half of the distance, the stage passed them; but it immediately stopped, and Dona Maria and her father stepped out of it.

"Maria insists upon walking with the young gentlemen," said Don Roderigue apologetically.

"I am dead of that stage!" protested the maiden.

She placed herself at the side of Scott, and walked along as briskly as any of the party. She wanted to talk English; and she was very proud of the progress she had made since the students had first come to her father's *quinta*. Of course there was no such thing as fatigue after the fair girl joined the party. The officers were inclined to rally Scott a good deal on account of his relations with the fair Portuguese: but he did not appear to be smitten; and, as she did not understand English well enough to appreciate his humor, she was not the company he liked best.

The next day another excursion was made into the country in another direction; but it was about the same thing as before. The students wanted to make the ascent of the peak of Teneriffe; but the undertaking was too difficult, if not too dangerous, for the principal to sanction it. On the third day after the arrival of the squadron, it sailed again for Las Palmas. A couple of days were spent there; and the vessels proceeded to the north side of the island of Teneriffe, and anchored off the *Puerto de Orotava*.

Dr. Winstock was very anxious that the students should visit this place. Dr. Phelps, the passenger in the Marian, declared that he should spend the winter there; and he was of the opinion that he should bring a dozen patients with him, for, after he had carefully examined the situation, he was satisfied that it was superior to Fayal, Madeira, Nassau, or any other place, as a health resort for persons with weak or diseased lungs.

The doctor's usual party walked out to the town, which is only a couple of miles inland; and Dona Maria insisted upon accompanying them.

"This town is enclosed by mountains, as you see, from three to seven thousand feet high, on all sides except the seaward. It is sheltered from all the bad winds," said Dr. Winstock.

"But this is April; and we can't tell how it feels in the winter," suggested Dr. Phelps, who had joined his professional friend.

"But I have been here in the winter: the glass never falls below fifty, nor gets above eighty-two. It is the most uniform climate in the world," replied Dr. Winstock with enthusiasm.

"But you mention thirty-two degrees variation."

"You have over a hundred variation in the Northern States. But I mentioned the rarest extremes. No average for a month is below sixty-two, or above seventy-two. An invalid may sleep all the year round with his windows open; and fires are never needed."

The two physicians talked over this to them interesting subject; and the students walked about the fields and the town. It was as near paradise as any thing on earth can be.

After remaining at this place for a couple of days, the fleet went to Santa Cruz de Palma for a day, and then sailed for Funchal on the 29th of the month.

CHAPTER XX.

"A YANKEE SHIP AND A YANKEE CREW."

MR. FRISBONE and his wife and Miss Rodwood were none the worse for the benevolent service they had rendered on board of the Castle William. The small-pox patients, as stated before, had been separated by the mate from the rest of the people in the forward part of the vessel. The sanitary measures devised by Mrs. Frisbone, and carried out by her husband, had wrought a wonderful change on board; and, when the vessel arrived at Portsmouth, the condition of the sick had greatly improved. The quarantine regulations were relaxed as much as possible in favor of the devoted nurses; but the ladies, who had been more exposed than the Prince, were not permitted to leave the limits of the hospital for a few days.

As soon as the Ville d'Angers anchored in the harbor of Portsmouth, Gregory sent a message by the steward, that he wished to see the captain. As soon as O'Hara had leisure to attend to the matter, he requested Shakings to bring his prisoners into the cabin, hoping they had repented of the folly which had induced them to "stand out," as they expressed it. The boatswain promptly produced the mutineers, and, touching his cap, was about to retire; but O'Hara desired him to remain.

Gregory appeared, looking more defiant, if possible, than when he was committed. For nearly a week he had been kept in his state-room. The captain had offered to allow him and Clinch to take an airing on the poop-deck every day for a couple of hours, under the eye of the boatswain, who was not to permit them to speak to any of the ship's company; but both of them indignantly declined the proposition, — they would not go on deck as prisoners.

"As I seem to be subject to your will and pleasure, O'Hara, I wish to say that you have carried this thing about far enough," said the ex-first officer, when he came into the presence of the captain.

"That's just my idea," added Clinch, turning up his nose to express his contempt for the young commander of the steamer.

"If you wish to see me in order to intimidate me, I have nothing to say," replied the captain, with dignity; but he was greatly disappointed at the tone and manner of the mutineers.

"I think we were clearly in the right in refusing to do duty when you were running away with the vessel," continued Gregory.

"I do not care to argue the matter," added O'Hara.

"I want to know who is right."

"The principal will decide that in due time."

"The principal is not here to decide any thing."

"We can only wait till we see him."

"I don't intend to wait!" said Gregory angrily. "I shall go on shore."

"At present the steamer is quarantined; and no one is allowed to leave her," answered O'Hara.

"That's another scrape you've got us into!" blustered the rebel.

The captain made no reply to this taunt.

"There has been no show for the officers from the Josephine in this steamer," continued Gregory. "Mr. Shakings, I think you ought to see fair play, at least, when an officer of your own ship is treated in this way."

"All the boatswain has to do is to obey the captain's orders," replied Shakings; but he looked as though he had something else to say if the occasion should require it.

"Come, Clinch, let's go on shore," said Gregory, beginning to move towards the door.

"Mr. Shakings, these officers are still in your keeping," added the captain.

"There is no going on shore for any one in this vessel," interposed the stout forward officer, as he placed himself in front of the rebels. "You will return to your rooms."

"I won't do it!" protested Gregory savagely, as he made a spring towards the door.

"I think you will, my beauty," added the boatswain, as he collared the rebel, and dragged him to his room.

Without any ceremony, he shoved him into the apartment, and locked the door upon him. Clinch had not the pluck to make a forcible resistance; and he went to his room without the assistance of Shakings.

"I don't see that I can do any thing else with Gregory and Clinch," said O'Hara, when the boatswain had secured his prisoners.

"I think you are using them very gently," replied Shakings. "Mr. Fluxion will keep them in the brig a month for this, and send them out of the cabin with the lowest numbers in the ship."

"I only wish to keep them from leading any of the other officers or seamen away from their duty," added O'Hara.

"There is not the least danger of that: every man from the Josephine will stand by you to the end."

As intimated in the newspaper the vice-principal had read at Funchal, Mr. Frisbone was negotiating with the owners of the Castle William for the settlement of the salvage; but little progress was made till the discharge of the Prince from the quarantine, which was done at the end of a week. The vessel and cargo were acknowledged to be worth ten thousand pounds; and the Prince accepted one-half of this sum. The owners of the Ville d'Angers were more exacting, and declined to settle the claim. Proceedings had been instituted as soon as the vessel arrived; and, a few days later, the court decreed that one-half of her value should be paid by the owners to the salvors. The vessel was to be sold at public vendue to determine her value; and the shrewd agent of the owners was satisfied that a French craft, sold in an English port, would bring but a mere song.

The Prince was discharged from quarantine in season to attend the auction. The agent expected no competition in the bidding. His first bid was four thousand pounds; then the Prince added another thousand, and continued to increase upon the agent till the sum of thirteen thousand pounds was reached; and then the first bidder had a cold sweat, for his instructions allowed him to bid no more. The steamer was struck off to the Prince for "a thousand better."

The agent was confounded, and the Prince was in excellent humor. He had to pay only a half of the purchase-money, for the other half belonged to the salvors. But the agent had new instructions when it was too late; and he offered the Prince another thousand, and then two and three, for his bargain, but the buyer declined to sell.

"What do you want of that steamer?" asked Mrs. Frisbone, when he told her what he had done.

"I think we will all go to Madeira in her," replied Mr. Frisbone, laughing. "I have been bothered to know what to do with the ship's company of the steamer; and this settles the question. Besides, the vessel is worth more than I pay for her."

The Prince hastened on board of the Ville d'Angers to inform the officers what he had done, and to have her prepared for the voyage to Funchal. Everybody on board was pleased with the result of the Prince's operations, unless it was the prisoners in their state-rooms.

The steamer was immediately hauled into the dock, her cargo taken out of her, for that had been sold "on account of whom it might concern," and the proceeds had added over eight hundred pounds to the result of the expedition to England. Then she ran up to Southampton, where she coaled and took in a supply of provisions on the most liberal scale. By the morning of the 21st, she was ready to sail; and not a moment was lost in getting under way.

The French and Italian firemen had been discharged, and sent home by the agent of the owners. Another set was employed for the voyage, and two young English engineers were added to the force in the engine-room. In fact, the vessel was fitted out as if she were to go around the world. She had been ballasted so as to put her into the best sailing-trim when the coal in her bunkers should be reduced.

The article in the newspaper had drawn considerable attention to the steamer; and when she sailed there was quite a crowd to witness her departure.

"Where are you bound, captain?" asked a young man, as O'Hara was about to get into the boat which was waiting for him.

"To Funchal, in the island of Madeira," replied the young captain, hardly looking at the inquirer; for he had been tormented with questions ever since he put his foot on the shore.

The person who asked the question was not more than twenty-two years of age, and was accompanied by another young man about his own age. Both of them were dressed in travelling suits of gray; and they appeared to belong to the better class of English people.

"I beg your pardon for troubling you, captain," persisted the inquirer.

"If I can be of any service to you, I shall be happy; but, upon my sowl, I am in a hurry," replied O'Hara pleasantly.

"It's only a moment for another question. Could you by any possibility take a couple of passengers along with you?"

"The steamer is not a passenger-vessel," answered the captain.

"I am well aware of that; but it would be a great accommodation to us; for you see we lost the last steamer to Funchal by a delay caused by a railway accident."

"I do not feel at liberty to take passengers; and I shall be obliged to refer you to the agent of the principal, Mr. Frisbone," added O'Hara.

"This gentleman is Sir Philip Grayner, baronet," said the young man with the applicant for a passage.

O'Hara thought he was rather young to be a baronet, but it was possible to succeed to the title at an early age. But he was not particularly impressed by the fact. The information had been imparted to him as though it was confidential, and he made no use of it.

"Where can I find Mr. Frisbone?" asked the baronet, renewing the attack.

"He is on board of the steamer."

"And how soon do you sail?"

"In the course of an hour."

"Thank you, captain," replied Sir Philip Grayner. "The gentleman with me is Lord Fillgrove," he added in a low tone.

"Another sprig of nobility," thought O'Hara, as he descended to the boat.

The well-trained crew gave way at the order of the coxswain, and the cutter was soon alongside of the Ville d'Angers. The vessel was only waiting for the pilot; but the time fixed for him to be on board had not yet arrived. The cutter was hoisted up at the davits, and secured for the voyage. The other cutter had not yet returned from the shore, where she had gone with a party of the students who had liberty to visit the city. Leave had been freely granted; and in no case had it been abused, so far as the officers were aware. If any of the young men had drank beer, or other dangerous fluids, their condition when they returned did not indicate such indulgence.

About half an hour after the return of the captain, a boat containing the two applicants for passage to Funchal, with their bags and luggage, came alongside. The bringing of their baggage implied that they had a strong expectation of obtaining what they desired. They were permitted to come on board, and presented their application to the Prince.

"We are entirely willing to pay our passage," said the baronet.

"By all means, we shall do that," added the one with the lordly title.

"That is no particular object with us," replied the Prince. "We should not take you for the money you may pay."

"We will at least pay for our diet and the wines we drink," said Sir Philip.

"We don't sell rum on this steamer," replied Mr. Frisbone, very decidedly. "If you can't get along without wine, I think you had better take passage in some other vessel. We don't furnish any thing to drink for anybody; and, what's more, we don't allow any wine or liquor to be used about the steamer."

"That's a matter of no consequence," added Sir Philip, looking at his companion, and giving him a sly wink when he was sure he was not observed.

"We don't care if we never have any thing in the shape of wine or liquor," the young lord agreed.

"What's your name?" asked the Prince bluntly of the first speaker.

"This gentleman is Sir Philip Grayner," said his lordship.

"And my friend is Lord Fillgrove," added the baronet.

"Then you are dooks and lords," continued Mr. Frisbone; but he seemed to be pleased at the idea of meeting them.

"My friend is a viscount," replied Sir Philip.

"And mine is a baronet," said Lord Fillgrove.

"All right!" exclaimed Mr. Frisbone, in his usual loud tone. "I am an American Prince myself."

The Prince talked with Capt. O'Hara and with Capt. Fairfield about the matter; and it was agreed that the passengers would be a pleasant addition to the ship's company. There were some spare state-rooms; for the space between decks, called the "second cabin," had been fitted up for the crew, and it was a very light and airy place for them. They preferred it to the main cabin; and it was more conducive to good discipline to have the officers farther removed from the seamen.

Each of the passengers took his choice of the state-rooms not in use. The Prince introduced them to his wife and her sister under their full titles.

"This is a very unexpected pleasure, Prince Frisbone," said Sir Philip. "I was not aware that we were to have the pleasure of ladies' society on the voyage."

"Prince Frisbone!" exclaimed the worthy machinist, laughing heartily. "That sounds odd."

"I beg your pardon; but I think you told me you

were an American Prince; and, as you did not dispute my title, I am not disposed to deny your claim," answered Sir Philip.

"I suppose your title is a little more regular than mine; but we won't quarrel about these trifles," added the Prince. "This is now a 'Yankee ship and a Yankee crew;' and I have an idea that one man is as good as another on board of her."

"No doubt of it; but I perceive that there is a great difference between the officers and the seamen," suggested Lord Fillgrove.

"Not a bit of difference. No. 24 is just as good as the captain," protested the American nobleman.

"But one commands, and the other obeys."

"That's true; but we don't have any classes of citizens. The day-laborer on town-meeting day is the equal of the man worth a million that hires him; and any fellow before the mast in this vessel may be captain of her the very next month. Here is Capt. O'Hara: when he was at this port last, he was a seaman; and next month he may be a seaman again."

"I hope not," said O'Hara, laughing. "But I heard that the principal and the faculty were getting up a new way to fill the offices on board of the vessels of the squadron; and some of us may slip up when it is applied."

"It's all very democratic," added Lord Fillgrove.

The coming of the pilot put an end to the conversation, though the two young "sprigs of nobility" made themselves as agreeable as possible to the ladies, whom they escorted to the hurricane-deck so as to afford them an opportunity to observe the scenery of "Southampton Water" and "The Solent," as the steamer went to sea.

The anchor had been heaved up to a short stay; and, as soon as the pilot was on the deck, the order was given to man the capstan again. The young tars were wide awake, and the pilot said he had never seen a steamer better handled than the Ville d'Angers was on this occasion.

In a couple of hours the steamer was off the Needles, and the pilot was discharged. Capt. O'Hara was his own navigator, though Tom Speers and first officer Lawring also worked up the problems, and drew off the courses from the chart, to verify the captain's work. The first course was from the Needles, the point of "departure," to Ushant. The weather was delightful, and all on board were happy except the two malecontents in their state-rooms. The extra engineers were intelligent and agreeable men, and the firemen were a great improvement upon the French and Italian ones.

Gregory and Clinch had several times been offered the liberty of the deck, under the charge of the boatswain; and the offer had been declined. But the captain and the instructor did not consider it prudent to allow them to hold any communication with the officers and seamen of the vessel, for Gregory was still in a mood to foment a mutiny.

The steward who carried their meals to the prisoners gave them the current news of the day, so far as he obtained it himself; and they were tolerably well posted. After the sale of the steamer to the Prince, the aspect of the case began to change, as the mutineers viewed it. They had expected that the Ville d'Angers would be given up to the owners, and the ship's company sent to Madeira in a passenger-steamer. That had been the talk before the mutiny. Gregory was confident that the change from the vessel to the packet would afford them an opportunity to escape from the rule of Capt. O'Hara and the instructor.

The ex-first officer was the son of a rich man, an Englishman who had been naturalized in New York. He had a letter of credit for a large amount, and he was fully determined not to return to the squadron. This hope faded away when the steward told him the steamer had been purchased by the Prince, and would sail for Madeira as soon as possible. He was appalled at the idea. He was sure Mr. Fluxion would degrade him to the lowest number in the Josephine; and he was too proud and haughty to tolerate for an instant the thought of such a humiliation.

He wanted to consult with Clinch about the present situation. He knew that the state-room of his fellow-conspirator was next to his own; but he dared not attempt to converse with him through the partition, lest they should be heard by the officers in the cabin, and another room be assigned to one of them. When the steamer began to move, he listened attentively at the door; but no sound came from that direction. The bull's-eye in his room was open, and he could hear voices on the deck above him.

He knocked on the partition to attract the attention of Clinch; and he had often done so before, though the conspirators had been unable to make each other understand more than a few words. His companion in misery promptly replied to his call.

"Make a hole in the partition," said he; and he rapped several times to indicate the place for it.

"All right," replied Clinch.

But they had to repeat what they said several times before they could be understood. Gregory had given his present plan careful consideration. He had selected a spot behind the dressing-case that was fastened to the bulkhead. With his pocket-knife he had removed the screws from the case, and arranged it so that he could restore it at an instant's notice.

Clinch's dressing-case was on the other side of the partition, and the aperture to be made could be concealed on Clinch's side in the same manner as on his own. As soon as the case was removed, he went to work with his knife. The partition was a double one, composed of boards extending diagonally, but from opposite angles in the two rooms.

After half an hour's diligent work he had cut a hole half an inch in diameter through one thickness of the partition. He had spread a towel under the place where he was working, to receive the chips, so that they should not betray him. It was not so easy to cut through the second board; it could be better done by Clinch on the other side. Taking one of the gimlet-screws he had removed from the dressing-case, he turned it with his knife till he had passed it through the second board. He then unscrewed it, and enlarged the hole with a small blade of his knife, till it would admit the lead pencil he carried in his pocket.

The dressing-case consisted of a looking-glass, under which was a rack for bottles and glasses, and a couple of small drawers. He had made the hole where the back of one of these drawers had been. With the lead pencil, he pushed the drawer in Clinch's room out as far as the length of the implement used would permit. His fellow-conspirator observed the movement of the drawer, and removed it from the case. He saw the hole, and fully comprehended the plan of his friend.

"Take out the screws from the dressing-case," said Gregory, with his mouth at the aperture.

Clinch complied with the request without making any reply; for he was afraid he should be heard, and the plan spoiled before it was carried out.

"All right," said he, when he could get his mouth close to the hole.

"Cut out the hole till it is as large as on this side. Put your towel down so as to save the chips," replied Gregory, in a low tone.

Clinch went to work, and in a short time he had made the aperture of the same size all the way through. But half an inch was rather small, and they enlarged it to an inch, which would enable them to talk with less danger of being heard. The dressing-cases were then restored to their former positions. Gregory had improved upon his plan as the work proceeded; and it was necessary to remove only the drawers on each side when they wished to talk together. Each could call the attention of the other by shoving out the drawer. If any one came to the door of either state-room while the contrivance was in use, it could be concealed by restoring the drawer.

"How are you now?" asked Gregory, when the cases had been replaced.

"All right! this is a first-class arrangement," replied Clinch.

"Put your mouth close up to the case, and speak very low," added Gregory, who was as much pleased with his invention as though it had been a useful machine.

"I will," answered Clinch in a whisper. "Can you hear me?"

"Very distinctly. The steamer is in still water now; and we may have to speak louder when she gets to sea."

"I heard some strange voices in the cabin before the steamer sailed. Do you know who they are?" asked Clinch.

"I don't. I have not heard them since the screw began to turn," answered Gregory. "I believe I have heard one of the voices before; but I can't think whose it is now."

"It may be some friend of yours. Your folks are English."

"But they all live in Lancashire; and none of them are likely to be in this part of England."

"We can find out who they are when the steward brings our dinner," added Clinch.

"I don't suppose it makes much difference to us who the strangers are. Things look black enough on this side of the house," said Gregory, in a rather desponding tone.

"So they do on this side," replied Clinch. "We can be a little more sociable than we have been; and that's all."

"I don't give it up yet."

"Give what up?"

"Getting out of this scrape."

"I don't see any way out of it."

A footstep in the cabin caused them both to insert the drawers, and close the conversation.

CHAPTER XXI.

THE SPRIGS OF NOBILITY.

EVERY thing went well with the vessel and her management. The officers and seamen were faithful and attentive to their duty, so far as those in charge could discover. The weather was all that could be desired; and the Ville d'Angers logged from twelve to fifteen knots an hour. The quarter-watches were amply sufficient for the duty of the ship, and the four engineers made it easy work for Alexander and Richards.

The Prince had superintended the provisioning of the steamer, and he had done it in the most lavish manner. The fare was better than that furnished on the vessels of the squadron, good as that was; and the students could not help speaking of the fact.

"We fare better than I ever did at the best hotels in Europe," said O'Hara, when they were seated at dinner.

"You deserve good feed," said the Prince, laughing. "This has been a big expedition we undertook. I was figuring it up before we sailed; and I found we had made twenty-eight hundred pounds, besides the value of the Dangers."

"Besides what?" demanded Mrs. Frisbone.

"The Dangers. Don't you know the name of the steamer you sail in, the Yankee ship with the Yankee crew?" answered the Prince, who pronounced French as it was written, in spite of the frequent admonitions of his educated wife.

"The Ville d'Angers," added the lady, pronouncing correctly the name of the steamer.

"I should have to have my tongue split like a crow, before I could say that; and I don't mean to try. The Dangers suits me better," retorted the Prince good-naturedly. "We were in a good many dangers while we were in her at first; and that's the best name in the world for her. I was saying I had twenty-eight hundred pounds, besides the Dangers, all made out of this cruise to the nor'ard; and, as the young gentlemen have done all the work, I was determined that they should live like fighting-cocks while I had any thing to do with them."

"Thank you, Mr. Frisbone," added O'Hara. "I think we are all in condition to appreciate good living. What are you going to do with this steamer after you have returned us all to the vessels of the squadron?"

"That will be for the principal to say. The steamer belongs to him, and not to me; for it was one of his squadron that picked her up," replied the Prince. "I think he had better use her as one of the vessels of his fleet, and sell out his sailing-vessels. It won't be many years before sails, except with steam, will go out of fashion."

"She will accommodate as many as the two schooners, after she has been fitted up for the purpose," continued the captain. "She is nearly as fast as the Prince; and, if we had been in her when we left Gibraltar, we should have sailed with her."

"Upon my word, I should have liked to be a student in such a vessel when I was a youngster," said Sir Philip Grayner, who sat at the table about opposite the state-room of Gregory.

"You are not much more than a youngster now," added the Prince, laughing at the cool way of the baronet.

"I am two and twenty," replied Sir Philip.

"Then you are not much more than a year older than Mr. Speers, the second officer; and he is a millionnaire at that."

"A millionnaire!" exclaimed the baronet.

"Please not mention that, Mr. Frisbone," interposed Tom, blushing.

"It isn't your fault, my boy; and I don't blame you for it," added the Prince. "He is more than that, Sir Philip: he is a three-millionnaire."

Tom's secret had come out in spite of the vigilance with which he had guarded it. The sprigs of nobility made themselves very intimate with him; and all the students wanted to know about it, for most of them could recollect how careful he was of the small store of money he possessed.

"A millionnaire, is he?" said Gregory, in the stateroom, for the open-work above the door enabled him to hear every word that was said in that part of the cabin. "And he is a great crony with O'Hara."

"I should like to get in with such a fellow," replied Clinch. "But what are we going to do with ourselves?

I have had about enough of this life in a stateroom."

"So have I, to be entirely candid," added Gregory. "The fellows are having a magnificent time, and we are here under lock and key."

"Are you going to back down?"

"There are two kinds of back-downs; and it makes some difference which one you mean. I am not going to kiss O'Hara's great toe, or any thing of that sort; but I am willing to come down a little for the sake of getting out of this scrape."

"All right. Tell the steward that we want to see the captain; and you needn't be so unutterably grand as you were the last time you saw him," replied Clinch.

"I meant to treat him with proper contempt; and, if I ever get hold of him, I shall be even with him in some way," blustered Gregory.

"That's all gas!" exclaimed Clinch, who was rather disgusted with the lofty ways of his companion in rebellion. "What's the use of talking in that way? O'Hara has the weather-gauge of you, and you can't do any thing."

"I know I can't now, while he has Shakings to fight his battles for him," growled Gregory.

"He does just as the principal and the vice-principals do: they never touch a fellow with their own hands; they called on the boatswains."

"If the boatswain had been out of the way, I would have made an end of O'Hara's reign. I am sure I could have got about all the fellows from the Josephine to join our party."

"So much the bigger fool you, for standing out before

you had said any thing to the fellows. Even Stokes backed square down when it came to the scratch."

"I was feeling very badly when I did it. That Burgundy did not agree with me; it made me as cross and sour as a baby at midnight. I did not intend to do any thing till the moment came when I did it."

"It is no use of grumbling about what is past and gone. We are in the scrape; and the question is, how shall we get out of it?" said Clinch, somewhat softened by the confession of his friend.

Gregory told how he intended to manage the matter when the steamer was given up; but this plan had been spoiled by the purchase of the vessel. The one thing he dreaded was being returned to the Josephine. He was conscious that he had been guilty of gross disobedience and insubordination. He had no confidence whatever in the excuse he had offered, that O'Hara was running away with the steamer, and disregarding the instructions of the senior vice-principal. This plea was only an excuse for rebelling against the authority of the captain; and he was sure it would not be accepted by Mr. Fluxion. The voyage to England had been a decided success; and the enterprise had been fully indorsed by all the adults on board.

It was the feeling that he had been snubbed by O'Hara, that the captain had not "made enough" of him, which had excited his wrath. He had come on board of the Ville d'Angers with the expectation that the voyage was to be a sort of pleasure-excursion; and the recitations and the quarter-watches, which practically transferred the work and the discipline of the squadron to the steamer, were exceedingly distasteful to him. But the Burgundy was responsible for his mutinous conduct; and without that he might have got along with the minor difficulty in his path.

He could not tolerate the idea of returning to the Josephine, and taking the penalty of his misconduct. He was ready to resort to the most desperate expedient to avoid the merited punishment. Since the sale of the vessel, he had been cudgelling his brain to devise the plan. He had hoped to become the captain of the Josephine in due time; but now he had given up the idea: the Burgundy had robbed him of all his expectations in connection with the academy squadron. He must get away, and keep away from it.

Clinch listened to all this long story, and confessed that he was in the same boat as his companion. But his father was not a rich man; and he could not cruise all over the world, for the want of the means. But Gregory declared that he had money enough to take them both around the world; and, as long as his friend would stick by him, he should want for nothing. Whatever they did, they were to stick together.

At supper-time Gregory, who did all the planning and scheming, had not settled upon any course of action. The officers of one watch and the passengers were at the table in the cabin. The prisoners, whose time hung heavily on their hands, listened attentively at the doors of their rooms to the conversation. Gregory heard the voice which he believed he had heard before, as he told Clinch. It sounded even more familiar than at dinner.

"You are going off on your travels, I suppose," said the Prince.

"No, sir: I am going to Funchal on a bit of a lark," replied the person with the well-known voice. "I have long wanted to go there; but I could not get away from the university till this spring. I am through with schools for the rest of my lifetime; and now I am going to enjoy myself, if I can."

"Are you going to stop long in Madeira, Sir Philip?" asked the Prince.

"Sir Philip!" exclaimed Gregory to himself; and this was the first time he had heard the name of either of the passengers.

"Only till I get tired of the island. It may be a week, or a month," added the baronet.

"Where are you going then?" inquired the Prince.

"I haven't the least idea. I am opposed to laying out a pleasure-excursion in advance."

"We shall go wherever it suits our fancy to go when we have done the island," added Lord Fillgrove.

"Lord Fillgrove and I are perfectly agreed on this trip," said Sir Philip. "We were in the university together, and we have considered the matter for years."

"Lord Fillgrove!" exclaimed Gregory, as he heard the name of the other passenger.

He listened to the conversation till the close of supper; and, after the steward had given him his evening meal, he opened communication with his fellow-prisoner.

"Did you hear the names of the two passengers, Clinch?" he asked, when his friend had placed his ear at the opening in the partition.

"I did: one is a lord, and the other is a sir," replied Clinch.

"Sir Philip Grayner is my cousin; and I had the biggest lark with him I ever had in my life. It was before I joined the squadron, when I went over to England with my father on a visit."

"Who's the other fellow?"

"He is a friend of my cousin; and I met him in Lancaster when I was there. He is the eldest son of an earl; and I believe they call him a viscount. He is addressed as Lord Fillgrove."

"Do they know you are on board?" asked Clinch, much interested in the information conveyed to him.

"I don't know: I don't suppose they do. But we must get out of this place as soon as we can; and I know my cousin will help us all he can."

"It is easy enough to say, get out; but how will you do it?"

"We must back down,— come clear down," replied Gregory earnestly.

"That don't sound like you, Dave," added Clinch.

"Of course you know what I mean," continued the chief mutineer, apparently annoyed at the remark of his friend. "We are not going to become chaplain's lambs, or any thing of that sort."

"But you must go down on your knees to Capt. O'Hara, the mighty one, who is the supreme authority on board of the Ville d'Angers," answered Clinch, in a contemptuous tone.

"I will even do that, if it is necessary," added Gregory.

"I won't!" exclaimed Clinch.

"Don't be a fool! we must get out of these state-rooms; and that's the only way to do it. But I don't think O'Hara will be very hard on us. Of course he won't attempt to punish us. He has offered us the freedom of the deck under the eye of the boatswain; and we must accept that, if we can't get any thing better. I want to be where I can have a talk with my cousin. I don't expect O'Hara will restore us to our positions as first and third officers, for those places are now filled by fellows from the Josephine. All I want is to get out of this state-room: don't you see?"

"I see; but I don't want to go down on my knees to a fellow from the Tritonia. I will do any thing you say; and I can stand it if you can."

"I can stand it well enough when the thing is done for a purpose," replied Gregory very cheerfully. "I will do the talking when we are before the mighty Capt. O'Hara. Leave it to me."

Clinch was entirely willing to leave it to his friend.

"I have been figuring things up a little since the steamer sailed," continued Gregory. "What day of the month is this, Clinch?"

"The 21st: I heard one of the fellows at the table say so at dinner," replied Clinch.

"Good! then we shall not get to Funchal till the 26th or 27th. At that time the squadron will have been out over a fortnight, nearly three weeks. I have no idea that Mr. Lowington will stay in Funchal so long," argued Gregory. "He will start the fleet for the Western Islands, or wherever he is going next, and leave orders there for the absentees to follow him."

"That may be; and you think he will be gone when we get there?" mused Clinch.

"I am almost sure of it. He will get news by the

regular steamer from the Ville d'Angers; and he won't wait for her. When we reach Madeira, we must get away from the vessel. I am sure my cousin will help us out; and we will join them on their trip."

This was entirely satisfactory to Clinch; and, as soon as he saw the bearing of the "back-down," he was willing even to kiss O'Hara's toe in order to forward the plan.

Gregory was an inventive genius; and, before the first half of the last dog-watch had expired, he had improved upon his plan, and decided to put it in operation at once. He was so impatient that he was not willing to wait till the next day. He did not feel quite as well as usual; and he really wished he was a little sicker than he was. This suggested a way to get at the captain at once. He could easily make himself a little sicker than he was. He had formerly been subject to a certain kind of headache; and he carried in his bag a medicine the family physician had given him before he left home. It always produced nausea to a considerable degree. He took a dose of it; and in a short time he was sick in real earnest. Possibly his confinement in his room had made him more susceptible to nausea.

He knocked loudly on his door; and, when the steward came to inquire what he wanted, he stated that he was sick, and desired to go on deck. The captain was consulted, and the order was promptly given for Shakings to conduct him to the deck. The acting head steward offered his services, and he received every attention his case required. When Mrs. Frisbone heard that he was ill, she went to him.

"I have been feeling badly for some time; and I took some medicine which our family doctor gave me," said the sufferer.

"I think it is quite enough to make one sick, to be shut up in that state-room as you have been, Mr. Gregory," replied the lady, when she had examined into the condition of the invalid.

"I am generally very well, and I have not had occasion to take any of this medicine for a long time," added Gregory.

Mrs. Frisbone spoke to the captain about the case, and expressed her opinion in regard to it.

"I have several times offered to let him go on deck for an hour or two, and he has refused to do so," replied O'Hara.

"Certainly it was his own fault that he has not had any more air and exercise," added the lady.

"I am willing to go still farther," continued O'Hara, who did not wish to injure the health of any student, however guilty he might be. "I will see him in the morning, and will endeavor to give both Gregory and Clinch more liberty than they have had, and without the assistance of the boatswain, for they refused the offer because Shakings was to have charge of them."

The patient was permitted to stay on deck as long as he pleased; but he did not see Sir Philip Grayner, who was playing whist in the cabin with the Prince and the ladies. When he went to his room, and was locked in as usual, he told Clinch what he had been about.

At eight bells the next morning, O'Hara sent for the two prisoners, and they were brought into the cabin by the boatswain. Both of the "sprigs" were there; and

Sir Philip looked him fairly in the eye, but made no sign whatever that he knew him, or had ever seen him. Gregory thought it very strange that his cousin did not recognize him, especially when Capt. O'Hara called him by name.

"I hope you are better this morning, Mr. Gregory," said O'Hara; and he expected a rude, if not an insulting reply.

"I am much better, I thank you, Capt. O'Hara," answered the prisoner. "I wish to say that I am sick, and I can't stand it to be locked up in that room, now that the port has to be closed."

Gregory spoke in a respectful tone; and O'Hara could not but notice the change in his manner.

"I am very sorry that it became necessary to confine you to your room; but I have tried to have you take air and exercise," added O'Hara. "I understand you to object to the attendance of Mr. Shakings."

"I did object; but I do not now. I am willing to do any thing you deem proper, and to confess"—

"I shall not try your case, Mr. Gregory; and it is quite unnecessary for you to make any acknowledgments to me," interposed the captain. "I have a proposition to make to you and Mr. Clinch, which I hope will not be considered humiliating. Both of you shall have the liberty of the vessel, provided you will promise not to speak to any officer or seaman of the steamer."

"It is a very liberal offer; and I am much obliged to you for it, captain. I thankfully accept the proposition, and promise not to speak to any officer or seaman of the vessel," replied Gregory.

"I will do the same," added Clinch.

"I will modify the condition so far as to provide that you hold no private conversation with the officers and seamen. I do not wish to prevent you from speaking on the ordinary topics of the day. You will take your meals with the officers in the cabin; and you are free to talk as much as you please at the table."

"Thank you, captain," replied Gregory meekly.

"Sir Philip, this is Mr. Gregory," said the captain, as the young baronet was about to pass them.

"Mr. Gregory, I am happy to make your acquaintance," replied Sir Philip with no sign of recognition; and the baronet passed out of the cabin.

Gregory was utterly confounded at the conduct of his cousin. The captain soon after presented Lord Fillgrove, whom the ex-first officer had met not more than two years before; but he was as innocent of all knowledge of him as his cousin had been. Neither of them seemed to be inclined to cultivate his acquaintance, perhaps because he was under a cloud just then. After breakfast Gregory went on deck, where he met the "sprigs" again.

"You don't know me, do you, Phil?" demanded Gregory, with considerable indignation in his tones.

"Of course I know you, Dave," replied Sir Philip coldly, as he looked about him to ascertain what officers were in sight. But none were on the poop-deck; for all of them not on duty were attending to their studies.

"You seem to be as stiff as though you were not glad to see me," added Gregory.

"I came on board of this ship on purpose to get you out of this scrape, and I will do it yet; but we had better seem not to know each other very well," replied Sir Philip, gazing at the blue sky above him.. "Wait till we get to Funchal. I want you to go with Fillgrove and me on an excursion of a year or two."

"All right, Phil. I thought by your actions that you intended to cut me," added Gregory, seeing the wisdom of his cousin's precaution. "I want to get out of the academy squadron."

"You shall; and we will have a bigger lark than we did when you were in England before."

"That was a large time," said Gregory, recalling with pleasure the "spree," for that was what it was.

"I met a fellow by the name of Stokes in Southampton, who belonged to the ship; and I asked him about you. He told me you were kept a prisoner in your state-room because you wouldn't kiss the captain's great toe; and I am here to attend to your case," continued the baronet, still looking at the sky. "But let us be any thing but friends."

Gregory assented; but during the rest of the voyage he had some long talks with him. In four days more, the Ville d'Angers arrived at Funchal, — on the morning of the 27th; but the fleet was not there.

CHAPTER XXII.

WHAT THE STUDENTS SAW IN THE AZORES.

ON the last day of the month, the academy squadron sailed into the harbor of Funchal, arriving from the Canaries in advance of the mail-steamer which sailed from Southampton six days before. The vessels anchored off the Loo Rock; for it was intended by the principal to remain only long enough to take on board the ship's company of the Ville d'Angers, when the mail-steamer came in.

She did not appear till afternoon; and no one went on shore till that time, not even Don Roderigue, his wife and daughter; for they had been so hospitably entertained, that they were disposed to prolong their stay on board of the Marian as long as possible. The family were even considering an invitation of Judge Rodwood to visit the Western Islands in the steam-yacht. At two o'clock, when the mail-steamer came into the harbor, Mr. Fluxion and Mr. Pelham, each in the first cutter of the vessel under his charge, went to the packet, to receive his portion of the Ville d'Angers' ship's company.

The two vice-principals went on board of the steamer as soon as it was allowable to do so. Great was their astonishment when the purser informed them that no such passengers as those they described were on board of the packet.

"They went to Portsmouth in the steamer Ville d'Angers, towing the wreck of the Castle William," added Mr. Fluxion.

"Oh, yes! I know all about them!" exclaimed the purser. "They picked up the steamer; and she was sold to settle the salvage. The odd gentleman they called a prince bought her; and the ship's company which brought her there sailed in her for Funchal on the 21st of the month, three days ahead of this packet."

Mr. Pelham was sent to the American Prince to report this news, while Mr. Fluxion hastened up to the city to see the agent of the principal, who was his banker. This gentleman informed the vice-principal that Capt. O'Hara had visited his office three days before; and, when the banker told him the fleet had gone to the Canary Islands, he had departed, leaving no intimation of his intentions. On inquiry later in the day, he learned that the Ville d'Angers had sailed for Santa Cruz, Teneriffe. Mr. Fluxion hastened to the principal with this intelligence. Mr. Lowington was confounded by it.

"Then they are still roaming over the ocean in that steamer," said he. "I have no agent or banker in Santa Cruz; and I left no word there as to the destination of the squadron. O'Hara will not be able to obtain any information as to where we are, or are to be."

"I don't see that any harm can come to them: they are in a good vessel, and have proved, by their voyage to England and back, that they know how to handle it," said Mr. Fluxion, laughing. "I suppose Mr. Frisbone is still with them; at any rate, Capt. Fairfield is; and they are attending to their studies, the same as they would if they were on board of the schooners."

After thinking the matter over, Mr. Lowington was reconciled to the situation. The Ville d'Angers had been gone three days and a half from Madeira. It was time for her to return, even if she followed the fleet to Palma, which had been the last island the squadron had visited. The students were allowed to go on shore in the afternoon, and escort Don Roderigue and his family to their home. A feast was provided for them in the evening, and Dona Maria was as fascinating as ever. But in the evening they bade the family adieu, not expecting to see them again, for they had decided not to go to the Azores in the Marian.

At noon on the following day, as the Ville d'Angers did not appear, the squadron was ordered to sail at once for the Western Islands. The principal left orders with his banker for the steamer to follow him if she put into Madeira again. It was the first day of the month, and the offices were distributed on board of the Prince; but, as one-third of the ship's company of the other vessels were absent, the award of positions was assigned to an early day after the arrival of the Ville d'Angers' people.

"But what shall I do?" asked Judge Rodwood, when the principal had issued the order to sail at once.

"You can do as you think best, judge," answered Mr. Lowington. "If you run over to the Canaries again, you may possibly find this truant steamer."

"As we have just come from there, I don't care to

go again," replied the judge. "I think I shall follow you; for I am sure the truants will find you in the end. I am out for a cruise; and I intended to visit all these islands on my way home."

The Marian followed the squadron; and, after a comfortable run of four days, the fleet anchored off the town of Horta, in the island of Fayal. As the wind was east, the vessels had smooth water; and the students were assembled at once to hear Professor Mapps's talk about the Azores.

"The Azores are about two thousand miles from Boston, the direction being a little south of east. And the Prince or the Marian would make the voyage in six days, while our schooners, with a smashing breeze all the way, would do it in eight or nine. These islands have received various names; and people now call them indifferently the 'Western' and the 'Azores.' They are the most western of the four groups of islands lying nearest to the Western Continent; and this explains the first name. The other word comes from the Portuguese *açor*, a hawk; and I suppose the early settlers found that bird here. The Portuguese word is *açores*, with a mark like a comma under the *c*, which makes it sound like an *s*. They have also been called the Flamingos, or Flemish, the latter being the Portuguese for the former. They were so called from the people of Flanders who settled here.

"It is a little odd that these islands, like those we have lately visited, were discovered by navigators who were driven off their course by heavy weather. In this instance it was one J. Vanderberg, a merchant of the city of Bruges, making a voyage to Lisbon, who had the unfortunate good fortune to discover these islands in the year 1431. When Vanderberg finally reached Lisbon, he was imprudent enough to mention his discovery. At this time Portugal was at the height of the wonderful prosperity I have before described to you; and she was ambitious to acquire all the territory she could. An expedition was immediately fitted out, which first visited the Formigas, near St. Mary, which we saw yesterday morning. In due time the Portuguese obtained full possession of all the islands of the group; and have held it to the present time. The revolutions of the mother-country have extended to these islands; and it is said that the women displayed more of the spirit of resistance than the men in some of them.

"These islands lie between thirty-six and forty, north latitude, and twenty-five and thirty-two, west longitude. They are a province of the kingdom of Portugal, and are represented in the general Cortes, Madeira and the Azores having five deputies. The islands are subdivided into three districts,—the eastern, western, and central,—according to location. You observe that the islands are considerably scattered, and it takes more than a day's sail for a fast steamer to go from one extremity of the group to the other.

"Corvo and Flores form the western district. The latter is the larger island, about ten miles by seven; and the other is about half its size. They are of volcanic origin, like all the group; and are mountainous, some of the peaks being about three thousand feet high. Santa Cruz is the chief town of Flores: it is seldom visited by ships, except whalers, which obtain supplies there cheaper than at the other islands.

"The central district is composed of five islands, of which Fayal and Pico are the principal. It is three and a quarter miles across the channel between them at the narrowest place. Fayal takes its name from *faya*, a beech-tree, and is about a dozen miles in diameter. Of its population of thirty thousand, one-third are here in Horta, and the rest in nine villages in the interior. This place is the capital, and it has the best harbor in the island; but it is exposed to winds from the north and north-east, and from the south-east to the south-west. The south-east gales are the worst ones, and they rake the anchorage so that it sometimes becomes necessary for ships to put to sea to keep out of danger.

"Of course you have noticed the high mountain to the south-east of us; it is the peak of Pico, from which the island takes its name. This island is twenty-five miles long, and from two to nine miles wide. It is covered with extinct volcanoes. The sugar-loaf peak of Pico is over seven thousand feet high. The kind of clouds which gather around the mountain indicate the coming weather, so that it is a barometer to those who have the skill to read the signs. The island contains a large population. By the Statesman's Year Book, I find that the area of these islands is a little less than a thousand square miles, and the population about two hundred and fifty thousand. The grape disease, of which I have spoken before, extended to the Western Islands; and since that time the wine-trade has been very small. The principal production is oranges. The wine from this island was called Pico-Madeira; and it is still manufactured to some extent.

"St. George is thirty miles long, and five wide; and has a peak four thousand feet high in the centre. Griciosa is about seven miles in diameter, and noted for its fertility, producing all kinds of grain in abundance. Terceira was so called because it was the third island discovered by the Portuguese, the word being the feminine of the ordinal 'third.' It is about twenty miles in diameter, and exceedingly fertile. It has been called the principal island of the group. Angra was formerly the capital of the islands, and is a larger place than Horta, containing over ten thousand inhabitants, which is a quarter of the population of the island. Its harbor is sheltered from the west by the promontory of Monte Brazil, over five hundred feet high. It is one of the finest of the Atlantic cities.

"Sao Miguel, or St. Michael, is the largest and most populous of the Azores. Its length is variously given from thirty-five to fifty miles, and from five to twelve miles wide. Like the other islands, it is full of volcanoes, and is remarkable for some curious changes in its surface; as a grassy plain, covered with trees and foliage, was raised two thousand feet by volcanic action in a year. Old craters become lakes; and I hope you will see an example of this kind here in Fayal. In 1811 an island rose out of the sea, less than two miles from the shore, and the English took possession of it; but when they came to look for their new territory, a few weeks later, it 'had gone down to drink,'—had disappeared in the ocean.

"Ponta Delgada is considered the third city of the Portuguese Dominion, and is on the south side of this island; its population has been estimated as high as fifty thousand. It looks like most of the Portuguese cities you have seen. The island is very productive, making a large commerce for this city, which is its principal port.

"One of the principal industries of Fayal is basket-making; and stores for the sale of these wares are to be found in Boston and New York. Lace and fine needle-work are also specialties, for the wages of working-women are only a fourth of what they are in the United States. One hundred and fifty dollars a year will support a Portuguese family, but not an American. These islands are very much resorted to by people from our own country who are troubled with pulmonary complaints, though the climate is hardly so free from changes as that of Madeira, and certainly not as Orotava, in the Canaries. Some of us have seen the bark Kate Williams coming out of Boston Harbor, with her deck crowded with passengers for these islands; and one or two other vessels ply between the same city and Fayal."

The professor finished his talk; and the next morning a boat expedition was organized, in which all the cutters and barges of the fleet took part. Wainwright and Scott, by changing with a couple of officers in the captain's gig of the Prince, obtained places in the same boat with Dr. Winstock, Sheridan, and Murray. The view from the anchorage was magnificent, covering an expanse of green hill-sides and of burnt and blackened mountains, the highest in sight being the peak of Pico.

"Can you tell me where the Praça Constitution is, doctor?" asked Scott, as he gazed at the pretty white houses of the town.

"I think there was no square of that name when I was here before; but very likely they have one by this time," replied the surgeon, laughing. "Of course a Spanish or Portuguese town cannot get along without one. On our right is the castle of Santa Cruz; and this name is quite as indispensable as that of the Constitution. Next to it is the mole, where you will land when you go on shore. The hills, which look so steep and rugged in places, are about five hundred feet high."

"Here is a steep one on the starboard," added Murray.

"That is only half the height I named. It is Monte Queimada, a volcano. Its sides look like a mass of cinders; but the streets and roads of this vicinity are of the same thing, as are many of the sides of the hills. Now we are approaching Monte da Guia. It is nearly five hundred feet high. That building on this side is a chapel."

The boats pulled around the point, and soon came to an opening in the cliffs, not more than an eighth of a mile wide, into which the Prince's gig, leading the way, entered, and proceeded about a quarter of a mile.

"Now we are in the crater of a dead volcano," said the doctor, after the oarsmen had been directed to lie on their oars. "The inside of it has been blown out by the commotion of the elements, and one side of it has caved in so as to form a passage into it. You can see clearly the form of the crater on the land side. We call these extinct volcanoes; but they are liable to break out anew at any time. Nine years ago the earth was fearfully shaken by internal commotions, so that the people left their houses, under whose falling walls they were in danger of being buried, and lodged in tents. But the ground may open and draw them in at any time."

The students gazed with wondering interest at the interior of the crater. The fleet of boats then pulled out and around the Point into Pim Bay, an enclosure formed by the peninsula at the end of which is the Caldeira Inferno, as the burnt-out volcano is called, meaning "the caldron of hell," a name to which it is properly entitled. Pim Bay is only a quarter of a mile wide; but it is perfectly sheltered by the high hills mentioned, and the island, on three sides, but is open on the south-west. It has a castle for its defence; and the streets of the town of Horta extend over to it, so that the port is used for loading small vessels.

The boats returned by noon, and the students were well pleased with the excursion; but most of them were anxious to get out into the country, where the orange-trees were in their glory. After dinner they were permitted to land, and visit the town, or roam on the hill-sides, as they chose.

"Nearly two hundred whale-ships used to come into this port for supplies, and to unload their oil, which was shipped from here to the United States," said Dr. Winstock, when the party had landed at the mole. "A great many of the people of these islands have engaged in the whale-fishery in our ships, which has induced them to emigrate to our country; and there is a part of New Bedford called 'New Fayal.'"

"I think I should emigrate if the ground was liable to open and swallow me up," said Scott.

"The people are used to that sort of thing," added Murray.

"Used to being swallowed up in the earth!" exclaimed Scott. "I believe it would take me a long time to get used to that sort of thing; for I am inclined to think it hurts."

"Used to the liability, I mean," protested Murray.

"That is certainly the case," said the doctor. "One does not heed danger after he gets used to it. There are thousands of people who would not risk themselves on the ocean, as you do every day of your lives without thinking any thing of it at all."

The party walked all over the town without seeing any thing that particularly attracted their attention, or that was worth recording. The next day they went to the Caldron, which is an extinct volcano. The crater is five miles around, the sides sloping uniformly down to the depth of seventeen hundred feet, and being covered with grass and foliage of plants. At the bottom is a lake with a small island in the middle of it. This island is a hill having a hole in the top of it, from which the subterranean fires once poured out.

Another day was given to an excursion over to Pico; and then the regular work of the schoolroom was resumed. The squadron remained a week at the port of Horta, wondering why the Ville d'Angers did not come.

"I am afraid my ward has given you the slip altogether," said Judge Rodwood, when all hands were out of patience at the non-arrival of the steamer.

"I do not think so now; though I had some painful suspicions to that effect in the first of it," replied Mr. Lowington.

"Capt. O'Hara has certainly had time enough to get here," added the judge. "It is not more than a three-days' run from Teneriffe to these islands."

"Unless the Ville d'Angers returned to Funchal, Capt. O'Hara would not know where to look for the squadron," argued the principal. "I have no doubt the students are safe enough, and that they will join us some time.'

"There may have been a row on board," suggested Dr. Phelps. "You remember the captain had some trouble with his crew, according to the English paper which gave us the news."

"I do not apprehend any thing serious on that account; for the boatswain and the carpenter will obey the orders of the captain, whatever happens; and he has the means to conquer any rebellion with their help."

"But we have heard nothing from them since the newspaper account, except that they had sailed for Funchal, and then from Funchal for the Canaries," continued the judge. "Are we to wait here till they come?"

"It is a run of nearly eighteen hundred miles to the Bermudas, which is our next stopping-place; and I should like to see the Ville d'Angers before she sets out on this long voyage," replied Mr. Lowington. "I have my doubts whether Mr. Frisbone, as he has the invalid sister of his wife with him, will care to go any farther than Madeira; and I depend upon him to assist in keeping things straight on board of the steamer."

Another day passed, and the Ville d'Angers came not. Mr. Lowington began to be anxious, and the judge was more impatient than ever. At last, after a long conference, it was decided that the two steamers of the fleet should return to the Madeiras in search of the truants. Before night they were on their way; but they were not ten hours out of Horta when the fog settled down upon them, and they were buried in it till they were near their destination. They went into the harbor of Funchal; but the Ville d'Angers had not returned.

CHAPTER XXIII.

CARRYING OUT THE PROGRAMME.

CAPT. O'HARA went on shore as soon as the Ville d'Angers dropped her anchor in the harbor of Funchal. After considerable inquiry he found the agent of the principal, and was very much surprised to learn that the fleet had sailed for the Canary Islands, leaving no instructions for him. The agent, or banker, knew nothing whatever of the intentions of Mr. Lowington, nor even where the academy squadron was going from the Canaries.

When the fleet sailed from Funchal, Mr. Lowington and the vice-principals had no doubt whatever that the absent students would return to the Madeiras by the mail-steamer which would arrive the last of the month. For this reason the principal had not thought to leave any instructions for O'Hara. They were all confident they should find the party domiciled at a hotel on their arrival from the Canaries, or on board of the packet, if the fleet arrived before her. The problem was simple enough; and there appeared to be no chance for a failure to connect.

O'Hara was on shore a couple of hours in his search for the banker, and in looking up what information he could obtain in regard to the fleet. As soon as the island of Porto Santo was seen from the fore-top of the steamer, Gregory and Clinch began to be very nervous about the prospect ahead. They feared that the Josephine was still at Funchal, in spite of Gregory's theory to the contrary. Whatever disposition was made of the rest of the ship's company of the steamer, they were sure they should be handed over to the senior vice-principal on board of the schooner. They would at once be sent into the steerage of the vessel; and this they regarded as the worst fate that could possibly befall them.

Since they had the liberty of the steamer, they had been planning all sorts of wild expeditions with the "sprigs," who had the highest opinion of the enterprise of Gregory. They did not care for Clinch; but they would rather take him than lose his companion in rebellion. They all desired to see the island of Madeira; and they were willing to stay there a month or more in the springtime. After this, though their plans were not yet clearly defined, they intended to visit other islands of the Atlantic, and then go to the United States. Gregory was at home there, and would be of service to them.

"All this is very nice," said Gregory, after the land had been reported; "but it will be all up with me as soon as we get to Funchal. I shall be sent on board of the vessel to which I belong; and that will be the last you will see of me."

"Nonsense!" exclaimed his British cousin. "We are to get you out of this in some way."

"How are you to get me out of it? That's the

question," replied Gregory. "It is not so easy a thing as you seem to imagine."

"I don't know just how: I had not considered that. We can't very well make the plan till we see the situation."

"There is no situation about it, Phil. After the vessel comes to anchor, I shall be sent on board of the Josephine, and that will be the end of it."

"Don't croak, Dave!" protested Sir Philip, with some impatience in his manner. "The health officer will have to see you and Clinch when he visits the ship, just as they do in those bloody ports up the Mediterranean, where I spent my last vacation. After that, we can fix things all right."

"I don't believe you can," added Gregory dubiously. "If we wait till that time, it will be all up with me."

"Not at all! I will tell you just how I will do it now, for I am beginning to get an idea," continued the Briton. "You are about my size, and don't look very unlike me. I shall pretend I have an ague, or a cold in the head, or something of that kind. After I have said good-by to the ladies and others, I will conceal myself in some part of the vessel. Then you will put on my mackintosh, cap, and muffler. You will cover your face, so that they will not know it is not I, and get into the boat, which we will have at the steps of the gangway beforehand. It shall be a shore boat, and no one will know any thing about the little trick."

Sir Philip Grayner rubbed his hands as though he was delighted with the ingenuity of the plan he had devised, and he thought it was very "clever."

"What will you do?" asked Gregory, who thought the plan might work.

"When you have had time to put yourself into a safe place, I will show myself. Of course they will be surprised to see me; and I shall be obliged to confess that I have played a bit of a Yankee trick upon them."

"Then they will know I have gone."

"No matter if they do, after you are secure on shore. But very likely they will find that you have gone before I show myself. I can get the boatman to come back to the ship after he has landed you, and then I can say that I have come on board again after something I had left in my state-room; and I can leave something there to make it seem all right. Of course you will take all my luggage with you when you go on shore."

"Perhaps that will all work very well, so far as I am concerned; but how about Clinch?" asked Gregory.

"Oh, bother about Clinch!" exclaimed the Briton. "We don't want him any way. He will spoil the whole thing; and this will be a good plan to get rid of him."

"But he has stood by me in all this business; and I can't desert him," answered Gregory. "It would be mean for me to do that."

"But Lord Fillgrove must go in the boat with you, and come back with the boatman. It won't look regular if he don't," protested Sir Philip. "I don't see any way to get Clinch out of the steamer, unless we get him into the boat in some manner before you and Fillgrove get in. You can manage that better than I can; for you know the rules of your bloody ships, and I do not."

"Shakings overlooks every boat that comes to the steamer, or leaves it. We couldn't get Clinch into the boat any more than we could get the engine into it," replied Gregory.

"Then you must leave him on board, unless you are willing to give up the journeys we have planned."

"I am not willing to give them up, or to give up Clinch."

"I'll tell you what we can do. Tell Clinch I have a scheme by which I shall get him out of the ship after you and Fillgrove have gone," suggested the Briton.

"What is the scheme?" demanded Gregory.

"I haven't it ready yet; but I will think of it."

"Then it's only to get rid of him; and I will not consent to that," protested Gregory. But, if he had been entirely candid, he would have admitted that he did not care so much for Clinch's company as he had before, now that he had better associates, — a baronet and a viscount.

"I don't mean to get rid of your friend, though I don't care for him. There are a dozen means of getting him out of the ship; and I shall fix upon one before we reach the harbor," replied Sir Philip. "I see it now! When you get on shore, you can get some young fellow, dressed in poor clothes, to come on board with Fillgrove; and Clinch shall change his uniform for that of the stranger, and go on shore in his place. That will work like a charm!"

The Briton was entirely satisfied with the scheme; and Gregory was rather pleased with it, though he was not so sanguine of its success as his cousin. He had a talk with Clinch on the subject; and that worthy was willing to assent to any thing that promised to release him from his captivity, and save him from the degradation of being sent into the steerage of the Josephine.

It was about noon when the Ville d'Angers dropped her anchor off the Loo Rock. The health officers promptly presented themselves; and all hands were obliged to show themselves on the rail of the vessel, to assure the official that the persons named in the papers were well and hearty. As soon as this formality had been complied with, the captain ordered out his boat to go on shore; for all the surprise and consternation at not finding the academy squadron in the harbor had been expressed before the steamer anchored.

Plenty of shore-boats were within hailing distance of the gangway; and Gregory, as had been arranged, "went into retirement." The mackintosh, cap, and other articles belonging to Sir Philip had been placed where they would be available as soon as the mutineer needed his disguise. Capt. Fairfield was conducting his recitations in the after-part of the cabin; and the exercises were not interrupted by the arrival of the vessel in port, as the watch on deck was sufficient to anchor the steamer. As soon as the health examination was finished, the recitations were resumed. The mutineers had not been asked to attend to their studies, for the reason that it would bring them into too close relations with the members of the starboard watch.

"But the academy vessels are not here!" exclaimed Sir Philip, seeking Gregory in his retirement.

"So much the better!" ejaculated the malecontent.

"But what will the captain of the steamer do? he was confident of finding all the squadron here," added the Briton.

"I don't know what he will do; and he is not likely to take me into his confidence," said Gregory.

"The captain has gone on shore; and I dare say he will do as Prince Frisbone advises him to do."

"I suppose he will."

"Then we will wait till the captain returns before we do any thing," continued Sir Philip.

"Don't do that!" exclaimed Gregory, appalled at the suggestion. "What do you want to wait for?"

"As the squadron isn't here, very likely this steamer will go on to some other place."

"Let it go! I don't care whither it goes if I can only get out of it!" exclaimed Gregory.

"But I rather like this sort of life. I have had a jolly good time since I came on board of the Ville d'Angers; and I am in no hurry to leave her if she is going farther, and the captain, or rather Prince Frisbone, will allow me to do so."

"I don't want to go any farther in her!" protested Gregory, disgusted with the proposition of his cousin. "I am a prisoner on board of this vessel; and, if you intend to remain any longer in her, I shall get out of her before she leaves Funchal if I can. That's the kind of a codfish I am."

"But if the Josephine isn't here, they can't send you back to her, you know," added the sprig.

"That's very true; but if she had been here, the captain wouldn't have gone on shore, and they would have bundled me on board of her before this time," growled Gregory, utterly dissatisfied with the present situation of his affairs. "Don't you see that I can get off twice as well now that the captain and his boat's crew have left the ship?"

"Upon my word, I believe you are more than half right, Dave!" exclaimed the Briton.

"Your plan wouldn't have worked at all, if the fleet had been in the harbor. Don't you see that Fluxion would have been alongside the steamer as soon as the health officer would let him do so? He would miss me at once, for I am one of his officers, and would ask for me. That would bring out the captain's story, and I should be looked up at once. We are in luck as it is; and I am in favor of attending to the business at this very moment, and before the captain gets back."

"All right! and to oblige you, Dave, I will give up the idea of making a longer cruise in the Ville d'Angers," replied Sir Philip. "I will go on deck, and hail a boat."

He had hardly gone before Clinch joined Gregory. They had a conference in regard to Clinch's prospect of getting off if his companion succeeded; and Gregory assured him he was almost sure that the plan relating to his friend would work even better than the one for his own escape. Clinch was satisfied with this answer, and was confident that his companion would stand by him.

On deck Sir Philip found only Speers, the second officer, and four seamen. Capt. O'Hara had taken Raymond with him for the reason that the latter could speak the Portuguese language. The engineers were all busy with the machinery. Speers was studying his lessons in the pilot-house, as he did every moment of the time when he was not on duty. O'Hara, as has been stated before, had spoken of a new method of making the promotions, which had come to his knowledge. The captain and the other officers of the steamer were intensely interested in this information, and they wished to be prepared for it, whatever it proved to be; for they had no knowledge of the nature of the new method.

O'Hara and Speers had been studying with all their might, in order to be ready for any thing. What the new method was, the students had the privilege of guessing; and they could not well help using it. The captain thought it must be a new system of marking the value of the students' work; but the second officer felt very confident that the promotions were to be made by the results of a monthly examination. Each argued for his own view, and each continued to struggle to put himself in condition for any thing.

Sir Philip and Lord Fillgrove ventured to interrupt the studies of the officer of the deck long enough to say good-by to him. Tom shook hands with them, responding to their expressions of good-will, and then resumed his study; for he was in the middle of a difficult problem in navigation, and he did not wish to lose the run of it.

The two sprigs bade farewell to the Prince and the ladies, who were making their preparations to go on shore. They took leave of Capt. Fairfield and the officers of the starboard watch in a body, and then hastened out of the cabin. Calling a boat to the gangway, the steward put their luggage into it; and then Sir Philip hastened below to carry out the more difficult part of the programme. All things worked perfectly, and he did not find it necessary at present to act the farce of being sick or having the ague. The day was quite cool; and this was a good reason for putting on an overcoat, especially as there was considerable sea in the harbor.

"Now we are all ready!" exclaimed the Baronet, in a low tone, as he joined his cousin in the smoking-room, an apartment which had been used during the voyage only by the Britons.

"Who's on deck?" asked Gregory very nervously.

"Mr. Speers is in the pilot-house studying his navigation; and there are some seamen about the deck; but all is working well. I have the luggage in the boat, and Fillgrove has put on his ulster so as to be in keeping with you. Here is the mackintosh, Dave; on with it," continued Sir Philip, taking the coat from the peg where he had hung it.

Gregory put on the garment, and put the muffler around his neck, concealing his face below the nose. Sir Philip jammed his Scotch cap down over his eyes, and it would have been difficult for any one to discover the deception. No one on board would have suspected that the coat did not contain a young baronet.

"Now, here is a sovereign to blind the eyes of the steward if he looks too closely at you," continued the Briton, as he opened the door of the smoking-room. "Don't stop a moment till you are in the boat."

Gregory left the room, and hastened to the gangway, where the steward, who had waited on the sprigs at the table, stood by the side of the other passenger.

"You will be warm enough in that coat and those mufflers," said the steward, as Gregory approached the steps.

"This blasted water is very rough and cold," interposed Lord Fillgrove, turning up the collar of his ulster. "It is best to keep the bloody stuff outside of you."

"So it is, my lord," replied the man.

At this moment Gregory handed the steward the money the baronet had given him for the purpose, though his companion had distracted the attention of the man.

"God bless you, Sir Philip!" exclaimed the grateful steward, as he put the sovereign in his pocket; and no doubt he wished the steamer had more passengers of the same sort, for his lordship had "tipped" him in the same amount.

Gregory hurried down the steps into the boat, and seated himself in the stern-sheets. The Portuguese boatman pushed off, and in a moment more was pulling his fare to the shore.

"This won't do!" exclaimed Gregory, when the boat had gone but a short distance.

"What won't do?" asked Lord Fillgrove.

"The boatman is headed towards the usual landing-place; and the captain's boat is there, waiting for him."

"I don't see that we can help ourselves," replied his lordship.

"Tell the fellow to pull us to some other place!" persisted Gregory, in mortal terror lest Raymond should discover him when he went on shore.

"But you can't land anywhere else; the custom-house blackguards will have to overhaul the luggage, don't you know?"

There was no help for it, and Gregory had to submit to the course of events. But Lord Fillgrove volunteered to do all the talking, and suggested that his companion should pretend to have the toothache, or the ague, or something of that sort. The boat carried them to the usual landing-place; and the boatman handed the baggage out upon the mole. The custom-house officers were very indulgent, and did not detain them beyond a few moments.

The captain's boat was lying near the shore, and Raymond sat in the stern sheets. He could not help seeing the passengers; and his lordship waved his adieus; but the fourth officer of the Ville d'Angers did not seem to be satisfied with this parting, and ordered the bowman to pull the boat in to the shore. The officer landed, and seized the hand of Lord Fillgrove.

"I am sorry you are going to leave us," said he.

"And Sir Philip and I have shed tears at the necessity of saying good-by to you," gushed his lordship.

"But what is the matter with Sir Philip?" asked Raymond, wondering that he was so distant and unsocial, when they had been on excellent terms on board of the steamer.

"You must excuse Sir Philip, for he is in terrible agony with a toothache which has just seized him. He is in such pain, that he can't open his mouth," replied Lord Fillgrove.

With one hand on his jaw, Gregory extended the other to Raymond, who warmly pressed it.

"I am sorry you are in such pain, Sir Philip; but I know what the toothache is, and I will not detain you a moment," added Raymond, shaking the hand he held again.

Gregory hastened away, holding on to his jaw, and groaning audibly to heighten the deception; and, though Raymond had the credit of being a sharp officer, he did not suspect any thing wrong about the passengers. His lordship called a porter (or, rather, he selected one from a dozen who had called themselves), and directed the luggage to be carried to the principal hotel. In a few moments he overtook his companion, who had turned down the collar of his mackintosh, for he had suddenly recovered from his toothache, and seemed to be in good spirits for one who had been such a recent sufferer.

"That was cleverly done," chuckled his lordship, as they followed the porter to the hotel.

"Nothing could have been better done; no Yankee could have managed it more neatly," replied Gregory.

"No, I should say not! If that was a Yankee trick, we Britishers can play a good game at it," said Lord Fillgrove, laughing.

A short walk brought them to the hotel, and they were assigned a room. As soon as the baggage had been brought in, they locked the door.

"Now what am I to do?" asked Gregory. "I am sure to be bagged if I stay here. As soon as I am missed, O'Hara will be after me with a sharp stick; or, more likely, he will send that bear of a Prince Frisbone to look me up."

"You mustn't stay in the town an hour!" exclaimed his lordship. "Have you any money to pay your expenses?"

"I have plenty of sovereigns," answered Gregory.

"Those are the best money to have anywhere on Portuguese territory. Find a horse, and ride till you come to some town or village; and don't let the grass grow under your feet."

A couple of ponies were soon found, and a guide was engaged who spoke English. Thus prepared, Gregory hastened off. Lord Fillgrove returned to the mole, where he obtained a boat, and was pulled off to the ship. He had picked up a porter on his way, and had already given a liberal fee to both him and the boatman. He saw that the captain's boat was still lying at the mole; but he gave it a wide berth this time, for he had no "blackguards of custom-house officers" to bother him. His lordship had brought back the mackintosh and other clothing of his fellow-passenger. Sir Philip put them on. He had Clinch in the smoking-room with him, and in a few moments the porter and the mutineer had exchanged garments. Sir Philip brought a carpet-bag he had left in his state-room, and Clinch was required to carry it to the gangway.

For some reason or other, Speers was on the poop-deck.

CHAPTER XXIV.

A HASTY RUN TO THE CAPE VERDS.

POSSIBLY Tom Speers had finished his difficult problem in navigation, and was making his rounds of the deck of the ship; or possibly the coming of the shore-boat had been reported to him by the lookout, and he wished to assure himself that every thing about the steamer was all right: at any rate, the officer of the deck was there, just where the sprigs did not wish him to be.

"Ah, Sir Philip, I thought you had gone on shore some time ago," said Tom, as blandly as though there was no mischief in him.

"So I did go on shore, Mr. Speers; but I forgot this bloody carpet-bag, and I came back after it," replied the baronet, pointing to the piece of baggage in the hand of the assumed porter.

Speers looked at the bag, and then into the face of the porter, though Clinch turned away, and tried to avoid his gaze.

"Really, Mr. Clinch, I don't think you look so well in that dress as you do in your regular uniform," said Speers, with a pleasant smile.

At the same time he placed himself between the

intended fugitive and the gangway. He looked as mild as one of the chaplain's lambs; and the Britons evidently did not regard his opposition as very serious.

"I will thank you to step out of the way, Mr. Speers, and allow his lordship and myself to get into the boat," said Sir Philip, rather brusquely.

"Certainly, Sir Philip; I have not the slightest objection to your getting into the boat," replied Tom, stepping aside so that the baronet could pass, but still remaining between Clinch and the steps.

"And that porter must carry my bag into the boat, and take it up to the hotel when he gets ashore," continued Sir Philip haughtily.

"I beg your pardon, Sir Philip; but the captain's order is, that no one belonging to the steamer shall be allowed to go on shore," interposed the officer of the deck.

"Into the boat with you, porter!" cried the baronet, who was disposed to carry his point, though he was entirely willing to part company with Clinch, whom he regarded as an undesirable companion for the proposed lark.

Clinch saw that his last chance was to make a rush into the boat, in which Lord Fillgrove had already seated himself. He made a desperate push to get by Tom Speers; but the officer promptly grabbed him by the collar, and crowded him back from the rail.

"Let go of him, or I'll break your bloody head!" exclaimed Sir Philip.

"I should be sorry to strike a baronet; but, if you do, there will be two bloody and broken heads in this vicinity," answered Tom quietly. "Mr. Clinch is an officer of the steamer, and he cannot leave her."

"But he shall leave her!" protested Sir Philip, blustering up to the officer of the deck.

"I think not. — Winchell, pass the word for Mr. Shakings," added Tom, addressing one of the watch who had come up to see what the matter was.

"Pass the word for Mr. Shakings!" called Winchell, hailing the other seamen of the watch on the forecastle.

"Now's your time, Clinch!" shouted Sir Philip. "Into the boat with you before the big boatswain comes!"

Clinch threw the carpet-bag upon the rail, and rushed upon Speers, intent upon crowding him out of the way. But Tom was stout, resolute, and self-possessed; and he easily flung his adversary back. But the Briton on the deck was excited; and he went in to assist the porter. He struck Speers a heavy blow in the face, while he was engaged with Clinch; but, as soon as the mutineer was disposed of, Tom turned his attention to the sprig; and, with a well-directed hit on the nose, sent him over backwards, with his prominent facial organ bathed in gore. The victory was certainly with Tom Speers so far. But Clinch had picked himself up during this diversion, and was about to leap on the rail, when Shakings grabbed him by the collar.

"So you have got a new uniform, my beauty!" exclaimed the big boatswain, as he slung his prisoner back like a basket of bread.

Sir Philip picked himself up; and he was the maddest baronet on the face of the Western Continent. He wanted to fight for revenge now rather than for the possession of Clinch. He was making a rush at

Tom Speers, who stood ready for him, when Mr. Rimmer, attracted by the scuffle, came aft as fast as his slow-moulded nature would permit.

"Hold this fellow, Rimmer," said Shakings, handing Clinch over to him. "I never whacked a baronet yet; but now is my chance!"

Speers had warded off the blow of Sir Philip, and put his left eye in mourning, when the big boatswain seized the baronet by the collar, and tipped him over upon the deck. The sprig struggled with all his might; and the boatswain kept flopping him over and over on the planks, as one deals with an unruly fish he has pulled out of the water. In a few moments the baronet had had enough of this harsh treatment, and he refrained from further struggles.

"Shall I lock him up in a state-room, Mr. Speers?" asked Shakings, as he held his prisoner at arm's length.

"Lock me up in a state-room!" exclaimed Sir Philip, gasping for breath, after his violent struggle. "I am a British subject!"

"But British subjects must behave themselves on board of this vessel, as well as others," replied Shakings, laughing at the bluster of the baronet.

"Hallo! what's all this about?" called the Prince, coming out of the cabin, where he had been disturbed by the noise of the struggle.

Tom Speers pointed to Clinch, in his Portuguese dress, and explained the cause of the trouble.

"You haven't behaved yourself as a barinet should," said the Prince. "If you want to interfere with the discipline of this vessel, you won't feel at home here. — What do you wish to do with him, Mr. Speers?"

"I don't wish to do any thing with him; and I haven't objected to his getting into the boat," replied Speers. "He pitched into me because I would not let Clinch leave the vessel; and I have simply defended myself, though it has cost him a black eye and a bloody nose. Put him into his boat, Mr. Shakings."

The baronet wiped his bleeding member; and, while he was doing so, Shakings hoisted him upon the rail, and gave him a smart shove down the steps. Sir Philip saw that he was making nothing by prolonging the conflict; and now, if not before, he realized that he was fighting for one whom he desired to get rid of. He had done all he could to gratify his cousin's sense of honor, and he went down into the boat. The boatman shoved off, and pulled for the shore.

"Where is Mr. Gregory?" asked Speers, when the boat had gone; for he thought it a little strange that the other mutineer was not in the scrape.

Search for Gregory was made; and of course nothing was found of him, for at this time he was galloping away from Funchal. But in the smoking-room, the Portuguese porter was found, dressed up in Clinch's uniform. Shakings could not help laughing at the figure the swarthy fellow cut in his blue frock, or at the appearance of Clinch in the garments of the Portuguese. Speers ordered them to exchange garments; and directed the boatswain to lock the officer into his state-room till the captain returned.

It was evident that Gregory had escaped from the steamer; and, by comparing notes, it was made plain enough that he had gone off in the mackintosh and cap of the baronet. The officer of the deck called a shore-boat, and sent one of the stewards with a note for the captain to the mole where Raymond was waiting for him. It contained a brief account of what had happened on board during his absence.

O'Hara was very unwilling to leave the harbor without the fugitive; and he stated his case to the consul, who promised to have him arrested as a runaway sailor.

O'Hara had only ascertained that the squadron had sailed for Santa Cruz de Teneriffe six days before. He had no doubt the fleet was there then; and he examined the chart. Satisfied with the promise of the consul to arrest and hold the escaped prisoner, he decided, after consulting the adults on board, to sail for the Canaries. Mr. Frisbone concluded to remain on board, with his wife and her sister; for they had all become in a measure accustomed to the sea, and Miss Louise had wonderfully improved in health.

O'Hara was very confident that he should find the fleet at Santa Cruz; but great was his astonishment when he arrived, to find it was not there. He ordered out the second cutter; and, taking Raymond with him to talk Spanish for him, he went on shore. He inquired at the custom-house, and learned that the squadron, with the Marian, had sailed for Palmas, in the Grand Canary. As at Funchal, the principal had kept his own counsel, and no further information could be obtained. This was the first time he heard that the steam-yacht of Judge Rodwood was with the squadron.

"Tom, my boy, the judge is after you," said O'Hara when he returned to the ship. "He came here with the squadron, in the Marian; and she seems to be a part of the fleet, for she sailed with the other vessels for the Grand Canary."

"Then perhaps my cruise in the Tritonia is nearly up," replied Tom, rather sadly.

"Faix, I don't know that we shall ever find that same fleet!" exclaimed Capt. O'Hara. "It seems to be dodging us, wherever we go."

"I am in no great hurry to find it," added Tom, with a smile, as he turned to his books, which were his constant companions when he was not on duty, and sometimes when he was.

"Well, what's to be done?" asked the Prince, as O'Hara reported to him the latest news.

"I suppose we can do nothing but follow the fleet; and, if it holds still long enough, I have no doubt we shall find it after a while," answered O'Hara.

"But I didn't cal'late to go any further than Me-day-ry. I am over here now to build up the health of Louise; and here we are trapsing all over the ocean with you boys," added Mr. Frisbone, laughing.

"Upon my sowl, the young lady is growing prettier and prettier every day she lives!" exclaimed the gallant captain. "I think you are doing the right thing now for her health."

"Well, I don't know but we are; for sartainly she is gaining every day; and her appetite is as good as one of the hands before the mast."

"I should be sorry to have you leave us, Prince Frisbone; for you have kept my back as stiff as the mainmast of the ship," said O'Hara, who was really very much attached to the eccentric passenger, as well as to the ladies of his party.

"I should be sorry to leave before you find the squadron; but you may chase it clean across the ocean to America."

"Then stay with us, darling; for I may be sent in the steamer to bring you back to whatever port you want to go," replied O'Hara, laughing. "Though I am doing my best to find the fleet, I like the position I hold now very well indeed; and it will be a sorry day when I have to give it up."

"But you ought to see sunthin or other of these islands we go to; and I know my women-folks would like to stretch themselves on shore," added the Prince.

"I shouldn't dare to stop a day anywhere till I find the squadron," said the captain, shaking his head, and looking very serious.

"But perhaps you are running away from it all the time," suggested the Prince.

Capt. Fairfield and Mr. Shakings were called; and they took the same view as the Prince. The fleet had gone to the southward; and very likely it would return in a few days. This consideration induced O'Hara to decide upon a stay of a couple of days; and all hands, except Clinch, were allowed to go on shore. On the 30th of the month, as the fleet did not appear, the Ville d'Angers sailed for Palmas. She arrived the same day; and the captain learned that the squadron had gone to Orotava. After having a look at this city, Mr. Frisbone decided to take his wife's sister there in the fall, and remain all winter.

From this port the fleet had sailed for Santa Cruz de Palma; and the steamer followed her after spending a day at Orotava. On her arrival, the captain learned that the fleet had departed. As none of the vessels were commercial craft, it did not appear that they had entered at the custom-house. As they came from another port in the Canary Islands, they had simply anchored, and the students went on shore to see the town, and what they could of the island, in a few hours. But where had the fleet gone now? for what port had it sailed? The custom-house officials knew nothing about the destination of the squadron. O'-Hara and Raymond wandered about the town in search of information. Where was the pilot? there was no harbor to enter, and they had taken no pilot.

"We don't get ahead any," said O'Hara, after they had continued the search for some time.

"Don't you know what the principal's programme for the voyage among the Isles of the Sea is?" inquired Raymond.

"I don't know: he never gave me a copy of it."

"I have heard it said that the squadron was to go to the Cape Verd Islands after Madeira, and then to the Azores."

"I have heard that same," added O'Hara. "But don't Capt. Fairfield know any thing about it?"

As Capt. Fairfield was on shore with the rest of the ship's company, he was able to speak for himself. He confirmed the impression of the captain and the fourth officer, that the squadron was to go to the Cape Verds. But he did not believe that it had been definitely settled where the vessels were to go; and whether or not they visited certain islands, was to depend upon circumstances. The West Indies had been given up on account of the lateness of the season. While Capt.

O'Hara was talking to the instructor about the matter, a custom-house official spoke to Raymond.

"I am told that you wish to know for what pòrt the two steamers and the two schooners that were here three days ago were bound when they left," said the officer.

"Yes, sir: we desire to know very much," replied Raymond. "Can you give us any information?"

"I can't say that I have any official knowledge; but I heard one of the gentlemen from the smaller steamer say they were bound for Porto Praya, in the Cape Verds."

This intelligence seemed to settle the matter. It was generally understood among the students, that the cruise was to include these islands; and the statement of the custom-house official confirmed it. The officer spoke with Raymond in Spanish; but if he had heard him speak English, or try to do so, he would have been satisfied the islander was not a reliable person to report an English conversation.

"If we are to follow up the fleet, we may as well go to Porto Praya," said O'Hara, when all hands had returned to the ship after their visit to the town.

"I do not see that we can do any other way," replied Tom Speers, to whom the remark was addressed. "If the fleet has been to these islands, it will not be likely to come here again."

"That it will not; and we will sail for the Cape Verds at once."

Just before dark the Ville d'Angers went out of the port, and directed her head to the south-south-west. Shakings knew all about these islands; for he had been in a man-of-war on this station, and the port most used by the African squadron was Porto Praya. The weather was delightful, and the steamer made a quick run in a little over three days. The last was spent in sight of the more eastern of the ten islands forming the group. Capt. Fairfield encouraged the students to study up the geography and history of the Cape Verds, in the absence of Mr. Mapps.

Like some of the other islands they had seen, their appearance from the ship was that of barren wastes of rock and lava. Off Porto Praya a pilot was obtained; for the port has one of the best harbors to be found among the Isles of the Sea, though a heavy sea sometimes breaks in on the shore, which renders it almost impossible to land. It was necessary to coal the steamer here, and while the work was in progress the students were allowed to go on shore. They found much to interest them here, for some things were different from what they had seen in any of the other islands. They took a stroll out of the town, and followed a grassy valley for a couple of miles. Nineteen out of every twenty persons they met in the town and in the country were negroes; and they were very lazy and indolent. They saw plenty of goats, monkeys, and parrots in their walk when they went out of the travelled road. Diminutive donkeys were the only domestic animals. There is scarcely any thing that can be called a tree, except the baobab-tree, which is only twelve or fifteen feet high, but is some twenty feet in diameter, while its thick head of branches is nearly fifty feet through. The fruit is called "monkey-bread." Sugar, cotton, tobacco, rice, and goat-skins are among the principal productions.

Santiago is the largest and most important of these islands. It is about thirty miles long, and half as wide. It has a population of ten thousand, the greater part of which is in Porto Praya. This town is the capital of the islands; but it is a poorly built place, on a hill. The students were not disposed to spend much of their time on shore here. It was a vastly different region from the sunny Canaries; and they were not sorry to leave it.

The fleet was not here. Nothing had been heard from it. It was evident enough, after a full inquiry, that the squadron had not been to the Cape Verds. With the bunkers filled with coal, the Ville d'Angers sailed to the north-west, with the intention of looking into the coaling-station on the island of St. Vincent. A run of half a day brought them between this island and St. Antonio, so that they could look into the bay. No fleet was there; but the lofty peak of San Antonio, nearly ten thousand feet high, was to be seen on the island of this name.

"We shall never find that fleet," said O'Hara, when the ship was out in the open sea, but with the lofty mountain still frowning down upon her.

"I doubt if we ever do," replied Tom Speers.

"I don't know where to go next in search of that same fleet," continued O'Hara. "I think we must hold another council of war. Will you oblige me, Tom, darlint, by asking Prince Frisbone, Capt. Fairfield, and Mr. Shakings to step into the pilot-house?"

In a few minutes the council had assembled, and Capt. O'Hara conducted them into the chart-room adjoining. The large-scale charts, which had been procured at Funchal and elsewhere, of the Cape Verds, had been put away; and the " North Atlantic " lay on the table spread out for use.

"I haven't the slightest doubt now that the fleet went from Funchal to the Western Islands," said Capt. O'Hara, when the adults had assembled.

"I think we may be sartain of that now," added the Prince.

"But the squadron sailed from Funchal on the 21st of last month; and to-day is the 8th of this month, — nearly three weeks ago. Where it is, is the conundrum we have to guess at the prisint moment."

"If the fleet went to the Western Islands on the 21st of last month, it hasn't staid there all this time, I'll warrant," said Mr. Shakings.

"The next isles of the sea the squadron will visit after the Azores will be the Bermudas, I know," continued the captain, as he took up a pencil, and began to figure on a bit of paper.

"Then all we have to do is to run for the Bermudas. How far off are they?" asked the Prince.

"I have not worked up the distance on a great circle; but I should say the distance was about two thousand miles."

"Whew!" whistled the Prince. "That is a long distance."

"It is an eight-days' run for the Ville d'Angers."

"But the fleet may be waiting for us at the Western Islands," suggested Capt. Fairfield.

"That's true for you," replied O'Hara. "It may have gone back to Funchal to look for us."

"And we are in a bad box," laughed the Prince.

"If we run for the Bermudas, the fleet may be looking for us at Funchal, the Canary, or the Western Islands. If we go back to these islands, they may go on to Bermudas, and be waiting for us there."

"Whichever course we take, very likely we shall be sorry we didn't take the other," added O'Hara. "It will require four days to go to Funchal, eight to Fayal, and seven more to Bermudas, making allowance for stops. What do you say, gentlemen?"

"I vote for Bermudas direct," said the Prince.

"So do I," added Shakings.

"*Via* Funchal," Capt. Fairfield followed.

"*Via* Funchal is my judgment," wound up the captain.

"Funchal it is, then. You are the captain," continued the Prince.

After looking the matter over again, Prince Frisbone changed his opinion; and even Shakings admitted that it would be safer to go to Funchal. Capt. O'Hara gave out the course accordingly. But it was agreed by all, that it was useless to put in at the Canaries; and the ship was headed direct for her port in the Madeiras. In four days she arrived at Funchal. O'Hara and Raymond hastened on shore. They went to the consul's office first. The American Prince and the Marian had been there the day before, and had sailed for Fayal again. The principal had left a letter for the captain of the Ville d'Angers. O'Hara took it, and eagerly broke the seal. The missive simply instructed him to run for Fayal, if Mr. Frisbone did not object; and, if the fleet were not there, to remain as long as was necessary for the students to see the island,

and then, if the fleet had departed, to sail for the Bermudas, making a harbor at St. George's. Mr. Lowington stated that the Ville d'Angers had been reported at Santa Cruz de Teneriffe, and that he had ceased to be anxious for the safety of the absentees.

All this was very satisfactory to the captain of the steamer. He asked the consul for his prisoner; but this gentleman stated that Mr. Lowington had settled the case. As soon as possible, the Ville d'Angers was on her way to the Western Islands. The fleet had gone. After a day at Horta, the steamer followed, and reached St. George on the 23d. No fleet was there.

CHAPTER XXV.

THE LAST OF THE ISLES OF THE SEA.

"DON'T you believe those youngsters have gone off on a lark, Mr. Lowington?" asked Judge Rodwood, after they had gone on shore at Funchal, on their arrival from Fayal in search of the missing steamer.

"I do not think so now, though such was my fear in the first of it," replied the principal.

They had been to the banker's, and ascertained all they could about the Ville d'Angers; and were now on their way to the office of the consul.

"I think it must be a great temptation to such young fellows as this O'Hara and Tom Speers," added the judge. "You say that the captain of the steamer has the absolute command of her."

"He has in the absence of any vice-principal; for it does not answer to place a landsman over a sailor at sea," replied Mr. Lowington. "But for all this, Capt. Fairfield, the instructor on board, would have influence enough to prevent the students from going off on a runaway excursion."

"Frisbone would prevent it, if the instructor could not; for he is a very decided man, and, if any thing is wrong, he does not mind cutting through any amount of red tape."

"As a rule, we have a stonger hold on these young men than mere force," continued Mr. Lowington. "Take your ward, for instance: he is ambitious to obtain promotion; and any thing in the shape of a lark would spoil all his chances. He was so interested in his future prospects in the Tritonia, that he has been running away from the vast fortune in store for him; and certainly he would not peril all his hopes by engaging in a runaway expedition."

"But he is under the orders of this O'Hara."

"And O'Hara is controlled by the same motives. My banker has inquired into the condition of the steamer, and ascertained that every thing was regular on board of her. The boat that brought the captain on shore lay at the landing-place two or three hours; and I am told that not a seaman got out of it. That looks like discipline, which would not prevail if the officers and crew were on a lark."

"No doubt you are correct, Mr. Lowington. But it seems very strange to me, that my ward should prefer the strict discipline of one of your vessels to the freedom which I came out here to give him; and I confess that I consider him ten times the man I supposed him to be when I left New York," said Judge Rodwood. "As I said before, the Marian belonged to Mr. Speers, senior, and I intended to turn her over to my ward. You see, the young fellow will have an income of over two hundred thousand dollars a year as soon as he is of age; and that will be in the course of six or eight months."

"Poor fellow!" said Mr. Lowington with a smile.

"As he is fond of the sea, I don't suppose he can spend his money any better than in running this steam-yacht."

"He is getting the right sort of experience now to enable him to handle her," added Mr. Lowington, as they entered a hotel, on their way to the consul's, to see if there were any familiar faces there.

There was one familiar face there, and it belonged to one David Gregory. He was staying at the hotel with his English friends. All three of them sat at a table in the public room, drinking a bottle of wine together; and the mutineer had already had enough to make him rather noisy. The principal immediately turned about so that the runaway did not see him, and led the way out of the hotel.

"What is the matter?" asked Judge Rodwood, when they were in the street. "You act like a man who sees a hard creditor in the distance."

"One of the young fellows you saw at the table drinking wine must have escaped from the Ville d'Angers when she was here," replied Mr. Lowington. "He was the first officer of the steamer, and the one who made the trouble of which we read in the English paper."

"And what are you going to do about it?" inquired the judge.

"I shall have him locked up on board of the American Prince. I see he has made friends here."

At the consul's, the requisite arrangements were made for the arrest of Gregory, and a couple of officers were sent for that purpose. It was necessary for the principal to go with them to identify the fugitive. The party walked into the room where the merry party were still drinking.

"I think I shall be compelled to break up your party, Gregory," said the principal in his mild way.

The mutineer sprang to his feet as though a cannon had been discharged under his ear. Of course he had not expected the American Prince to return to the island, or even the Ville d'Angers. It was no use to contend against the principal and the policemen, though Sir Philip Grayner was inclined to resist.

"Mr. Lowington, I tried to do my duty on board of the steamer; and when O'Hara attempted to run away with the vessel, and make a voyage to England contrary to his orders, I wanted to bring the steamer back. I failed, and here I am," pleaded Gregory.

"I do not care to hear any explanation in this place. On board of the ship I will listen to all you have to say," replied the principal.

The officers sent him on board the Prince, where he was locked up in a suitable apartment under the charge of Peaks, the big boatswain of the vessel. The sprigs doubtless made their tour of the Isles of the Sea and of the United States; but Gregory did not accompany them.

On the day of the arrival of the Prince and the Marian, a clipper schooner came into the port from Teneriffe. She had put into Santa Cruz de Palma; and Mr. Lowington had a long talk with her captain, who reported the Ville d'Angers as having sailed from the latter port on the 3d of the month, for the Cape Verds. The Spanish captain had been on board of the steamer; and he declared that every thing was in perfect order. The students were studying and reciting. Capt. O'Hara was anxious to find the fleet.

"Why did he go to the Cape Verds?" asked the principal.

"Because this fleet was reported as having gone there," replied the Spanish captain.

If the steamer had gone to the Cape Verds, and every thing was in good order on board of her, it was no use to wait for her; and the American Prince and the Marian sailed as soon as they could get up steam.

On the 13th of the month they reached Fayal again, where the schooners were waiting for them. Gregory was sent on board of the Josephine as soon as the anchor of the Prince touched the rocks at the bottom. Mr. Fluxion received him with a smile, for discipline had been victorious in the end. All hands were called; and the uniform was stripped from the recreant officer. Gregory attempted to excuse himself on the plea that Capt. O'Hara was running away with the steamer.

"All you had to do was to obey orders. But you did not believe that Capt. O'Hara was running away with the vessel: you knew better than this. Your number in the Josephine is 36 from this date," said Mr. Fluxion sternly. "But I will say to you, and to all, that the next promotions in all the vessels of the fleet will be made by the results of an examination to be held on the 1st of June. Whatever place you win, you shall have at that time, though your demerits for conduct will be considered in making the award."

The fleet at once departed for the Bermudas. The wind was fair, and the weather generally good, with the exception of a gale, and a two-days' fog, so that the schooners made the passage in ten days. The fleet kept together all the way, and sighted St. David's Head at the same time. This is the north-eastern point of the islands, off which the pilots cruise in good weather, and near which are the two eastern passages into the inner waters, enclosed by an almost continuous reef to the northward and westward of the islands. Each vessel took a pilot, and, going through narrow channels between the reefs, came into the harbor of St. George, the most northern town in the islands.

"Hurrah! hurrah! hurrah!" came from a steamer at anchor, as the Prince went across her bow.

"What's that?" asked the principal.

"It must be the truant steamer," replied Dr. Winstock.

"Three cheers for the Tritonia!" shouted a voice on board of the steamer, as the vessel indicated came into the harbor.

"The Ville d'Angers has got here before us," said Mr. Pelham. "She must have passed us in that fog."

"Three cheers for the Marian!" called Capt. O'Hara, as the beautiful steam-yacht came into view.

They were all given with a will; and there could be no doubt the students on board were glad to see their shipmates after the long separation. In a short time the vessels of the fleet were anchored, and the boats began to drop from the davits into the water.

"Arrah, Tom, my darlint! your guardian has caught you at last!" exclaimed O'Hara, when he saw the barge of the Marian approaching the steamer.

"I shall be as resigned as possible to my fate," replied Tom.

"To the millions of money, you mane!"

"I shall not quarrel with that."

"If you fall out with it, remimber your best frind."

"I shall certainly do that, my dear fellow, whatever happens to me. But I shall not leave the squadron if I can help it."

"Faix, I hope you won't while I am in it!" added Capt. O'Hara, grasping the hand of the second officer. "But here comes his honor the judge. Be ready for him, Tom, and trate him loike a gintleman."

"I shall certainly do that," replied Tom, as he went to the gangway, where the steps had already been rigged, though the steamer had been in port but a few hours.

"Which is my boy?" demanded the judge, as he came on deck.

"Here he is," replied O'Hara, pointing out the second officer.

"Tom, my lad, I am delighted to see you, after wandering all over the ocean in search of you!" exclaimed Judge Rodwood, grasping both the hands of his ward, and giving him a very affectionate greeting. "What do you mean by running away from me?"

"I am very glad to see you, sir; though I do not want to be taken out of the squadron," replied Tom, who found the judge a very different person from what he had anticipated.

He was not a bit like the stern judge he had fancied; and he could not help liking him at first sight.

"You can stay in the squadron till your head is as white as mine, if you like, my lad," protested the guardian warmly. "The Marian, which is not a very ugly craft, is your property, or will be in a few months; and I didn't know but you might like to make a cruise in her. Do as you please, however."

"That alters the case," replied Tom, laughing, and bestowing an admiring glance upon the beautiful steam-yacht. "But I think I should like to remain a while longer."

By this time the principal and the two vice-principals were on board. They greeted the captain with great heartiness; and it was clear enough that he was not under the displeasure of the authorities. O'Hara made his report in full on the spot, detailing all the incidents of the cruise. He sent for the log-books kept by all the officers, and submitted them for examination. The captain had the satisfaction of having his management of the steamer approved.

The meeting between Mr. Frisbone and the principal was a very interesting event; and the ship's company of the Ville d'Angers understood its meaning so well, that they involuntarily gave three cheers as the two gentlemen joined hands on the deck.

"Your boys have been the salvation of myself and those I care a good deal more for than I do for myself, Mr. Lowington!" exclaimed the prince; and the tears gathered in his eyes as he spoke.

"I am glad that they have been of service to you," replied the principal, as they retired to the cabin to see the ladies.

"That Tom Speers, who is worth three millions of dollars now, would weigh down the whole of the money in gold," continued the Prince; and he proceeded to tell the story of Tom's noble conduct in saving the life of Miss Rodwood.

"I hope the money that comes to him will not spoil him. He had been brought up in poverty; and the change may turn his head," added the principal.

"Not a bit of it!" exclaimed Mr. Frisbone. "Tom's head is not one of the sort to be turned by money, or any thing else. He will do more good with that fortune than his uncle ever did; and I thank God it has fallen into good hands."

"Let us hope so."

"And believe so; for I know the young man through and through."

"This is a fine steamer you have, Mr. Frisbone," added the principal, looking about the cabin.

"It is a fine steamer *you* have, Mr. Lowington," yelled the Prince, in his loudest tone. "She belongs to you, every timber and bolt in her! she was saved by your boys, or she would have gone to the bottom. More than this, I have a considerable sum of money from the salvage of the Castle William, which I shall pay over to you, deducting the expenses I have incurred in fitting up the ship, coaling and provisioning her."

The Prince produced his accounts, and insisted upon paying over his balance in sovereigns to the principal; who received it under protest.

"What shall I do with the steamer?" asked Mr. Lowington.

"Use her instead of them two topsail schooners!" screamed the Prince, as he always did when he had a bright idea.

"In due time we will consider that question. Now you are almost back to New York, where you started from; and I understand that you were in quest of health for your wife's sister."

"That's so; but I don't think any thing particular ails her now. We have given her something to think about all the time; and I guess she is pretty much cured now. I shall spend the winter in that place on the back side of the peak of Teneriffe; and if I get there by the 1st of December, it will be soon enough."

"Then this steamer must convey you to your destination," said the principal.

"Well, I sha'n't mind staying with you all summer, if you don't object. This sort of life agrees with my wife and her sister, now they have got used to it; and I don't get sea-sick myself."

The rest of the day was spent in exchanging visits between the vessels; and not much study was done. The Prince and his ladies visited the Marian and the American Prince. Tom Speers went with them; for it could not be denied that he was a prime favorite with the ladies, and especially with Miss Louise. Clinch was sent back to the Josephine, and became No. 35.

The next morning, when things had settled down again, the signal for the lecture was displayed on board of the American Prince. The grand saloon of the steamer was crowded on this occasion, for all the passengers, officers, and engineers of the Marian and the Ville d'Angers were present.

"Before the professor begins his lecture, I wish to say that all the offices of the squadron will be given out in accordance with the results of an examination to be conducted at Hamilton, beginning on the 1st of June. It will include all branches of study and seamanship; and the marks for conduct will be added to the result of the examination," said the principal. "I am sorry I was not able to give this notice to the ship's company of the Tritonia on the 1st of May, as I did in the other vessels."

"But we all knew there was to be a new method adopted; and some of us were sure it was to be an examination," added O'Hara, when he had obtained permission to speak.

"So much the better if you understood the matter. I will add that we have another vessel to officer, and that the examination will be general; that is, the offices will be assigned throughout the squadron, instead of confining the result to a single vessel. The one who stands highest will have his choice of all the places in the squadron; and so on till all the positions are given out. I wish you all to consider the subject during the next week, so that you can choose your places without any delay. I have adopted this method, after consulting the faculty, rather because it affords a little variety than because it is a superior plan to the one we have been using."

The principal retired, and Professor Mapps took his place before the chart he had made of the Bermudas.

"These islands are different in many respects from any you have yet visited," the professor began. "They are coralline, — the most northerly of this type in the world. The rock formed is a gray limestone, which is very soft. They are in latitude thirty-two, twenty; and in longitude sixty-four, fifty. The group consists of five principal islands, and about five hundred small ones, varying in size from a few square feet up to a square mile in extent. The largest island is Bermuda, which is fifteen miles long, and occupies the most southern position in the group. On it is Hamilton, the capital. The land on our starboard side, where you see the town, is St. George, three miles and a half in length; on the other side of us is St. David's, about two and a half miles long. The other two are in the south-west, Somerset and Ireland, each two or three miles in length. None of the islands are more than two miles wide, and in some places you can hardly choose on which side you would fall overboard. The group is twenty miles long; and they contain only twenty-four square miles of land, with a population of about twelve thousand. More than half of the people are negroes.

"There are few wells, or at least few that produce good water. You observe that the houses in the town of St. George are all white or nearly so, including the roofs. They have not been whitewashed, as you may suppose; but they are plastered. This is done to keep them clean; for all the water used is gathered on them, and kept in cisterns or tanks. Where large quantities are required, and the roofs do not afford a sufficient supply, portions of the hillside are plastered in the same manner, and the water that is collected on them is saved. The water from the clouds is the purest that can be had, if it can be kept free from impurities after it falls.

"Agriculture, possibly for the want of labor, is in a very backward state. The negroes are not disposed to work any more than enough to procure the bare necessities of life. You will see little patches of ground spaded up, for they don't often use the plough, as the irregular surface of the land hardly admits it in many places. But it is remarkably fertile and productive.

It yields three crops a year of vegetables, which find a ready market in the neighboring ports of the United States, only six to seven hundred miles distant. The exports of the Bermudas amount to about three hundred and fifty thousand dollars a year. There is a regular steamer to and from New York, but the government has to subsidize the company that runs it.

"This is a very important naval and military station of Great Britain, with extensive magazines and storehouses. On the island of Ireland is a dock-yard, provided with a floating dry dock, built of iron in England, and towed out to the islands. As a naval and military station, the islands are said to be second only to Malta. On account of this interest, the governor, whose authority is little less than supreme, is appointed by the crown of England; and the incumbent is invariably a man of great ability. The two branches of the Legislature are the House of Assembly, which is the popular body, elected by the people of the parishes, and the Council, nominated to the crown by the governor. Though white and black are allowed to vote, there are three times as many voters of the former as of the latter. The voter must own real estate to the amount of sixty pounds; and he must have four times this amount before he can be a member of the House of Assembly. No negro has ever been elected to this office.

"The climate may be said to be delightful; and as a rule the islands are very healthy. When the yellow fever and other diseases have prevailed here as epidemics, it has been entirely owing to the lack of proper drainage, and the neglect of other sanitary measures.

The mercury rarely goes above eighty-five or below forty; and the average is about seventy. It hardly compares with Orotava, and it is too damp for most pulmonary affections.

"I will conclude this brief talk with a word about the history of the islands. They get their name from a Spaniard by the name of Juan Bermudez, who discoverd them about four hundred years ago. But it was not settled by the Spaniards. Very likely the roving buccaneers of the Spanish main had temporary homes here; and there are stories of vast wealth hidden by these worthies. When the more modern settlers took possession of it, they found hogs in vast numbers, though the islands were uninhabited; and there were many evidences of the visits of human beings.

"In 1609, not long after the first settlement of Virginia, a vessel called the Sea Adventure was fitted out in England to convey Sir Thomas Gates, just appointed governor of the Virginia Colony, Admiral Sir George Somers, and other officials, to the scene of their future labors. This vessel went with a fleet, loaded with colonists and supplies for the new home in Virginia. In a terrible storm, the Sea Adventure was separated from the rest of the fleet, and was wrecked on the Bermudas. After suffering great hardships, the shipwrecked party reached the shores of these islands without the loss of a single life. The voyagers found plenty of turtle, fish, and fruit in the island, as well as a most delicious climate; and they were so well pleased with the paradise they had found, that they did not attempt to get away for a year. At the end of this time they had built a vessel, in which they embarked for Virginia, and reached their destination in safety. But the colony were in the utmost need of supplies, being almost in a state of starvation. In this emergency Sir George Somers, who is represented as a noble and unselfish man, willing to peril his life for the salvation of others, procuring a party of volunteers to accompany him, sailed for the Bermudas to obtain a supply of provisions from that land, 'flowing with milk and honey.' Unhappily he died when his vessel reached the locality where we now are; and after him this island was called St. George, though I cannot say when or how he happened to be canonized. After him also the scene of his death received the name of the 'Somers Islands,' as they are often called. The colonists reported so favorably, that settlements were commenced in 1612; and the islands have been under the British Government since that time."

The professor finished his remarks, and the students hastened on shore for the first time.

CHAPTER XXVI.

YOUNG AMERICA HOMEWARD BOUND.

"THE professor did not say this used to be called 'The Isle of Devils,'" said Dr. Winstock, when he seated himself in the stern-sheets of the captain's gig, with Sheridan and Murray. "It was so called because it was such a terrible place for shipwrecks. But the science of navigation had not been carried to such perfection in those days as at present."

"This is a queer old place," said Murray, when he had obtained a view of the town.

"It is not a very progressive place; and things appear here pretty much as they did a hundred years ago. The houses are of the fashion of the past; and I have no doubt that some of them are over a century old. But this is a beautiful harbor; and you will be delighted when you get on the top of some hill, to see the panorama spread out before you. The views in the Bermudas are peculiar. The little islands look like so many green hillocks rising out of the water; and much of the scenery is quite rugged. There is an island off there, with a little white cottage upon it. For my part, I think there is nothing more lovely in the world; and if we could have the society of the States, as they call our country, I should spend the rest of my days here."

The party landed from the boat, and Wainwright and Scott joined them. They walked into the town, taking a general view of it. The houses seem to be scattered about without any regard to order.

"This reminds me of the town of Gosport on the Isles of Shoals, before the hand of improvement touched it," said the surgeon. "Every man built his house where he chose, without heeding any possibility of streets in the present or the future. Here is a pretty cottage with its front garden bordered by a laborer's hovel. During our war a great deal of business was done here in blockade-running; but it don't appear to be very driving in any thing now."

A short time exhausted the streets, or rather lanes, of the town. It contains between two and three thousand inhabitants. The business men rarely live in either St. George or Hamilton, the only towns in the islands; but, when the work of the day is ended, they drive or sail away to their cottages on the islands.

All around St. George are forts to defend the only practicable entrance for large vessels to the interior sea, about twenty-five miles by ten, enclosed by the reefs, in which there are only a few openings, so intricate and dangerous that they can be navigated only by the most skilful pilots.

The doctor's party walked to Cherry-stone Hill, about a mile from the town, which commanded a view of the islands to the eastward, the forts, and the harbor. They sat there for hours, enjoying the prospect of sea and land, and the delicious air of the place.

The next morning the entire squadron, in charge of the pilots, sailed for Hamilton, the capital, where the principal intended to remain for two or three weeks. On the passage, which is about fifteen miles around, through Grassy Bay and Great Sound, up to the head of a considerable inlet, where the capital is situated, the students obtained a full view of the dock-yard and floating dock, which contained a large man-of-war at the time, and of the great store-houses. On the other side, near the shore, at the back of the town, was the governor's house. Threading their way among the multitude of islands, the fleet reached its destination, and anchored in front of the town. It is built on the gentle slope of the hills; and, with its white-roofed buildings, presents a very neat and pretty appearance.

The students were permitted to go on shore as soon as every thing had been made snug on board the vessels. In half an hour more they were wandering through its streets. But there was really little in the place to see; and, as it contains only two thousand inhabitants, it was soon exhausted.

After dinner, the doctor and his party took carriages for a drive. Tom Speers and O'Hara, with Miss Louise, the Prince and his wife, formed another party. These excursions were repeated every afternoon for a week. They visited the southern part of the island of Bermuda, where a hill nearly four hundred feet high afforded them a magnificent view of Port Royal Bay and Great Sound, both sheets of water packed with islands. On some of them are the neat white cottages one sees all over the main islands. In the vicinity of Hamilton there are many more pretentious buildings;

but these little country places are the charm of the landscape. Though some of these structures are very old, they seem to be in good repair; for there is no freezing in the winter to throw a building out of shape, or settle the foundation unequally in different places.

"I see they keep all sorts of animals tied up in this country," said Murray, as the party were out on one of these drives. "There are some hens moored by the leg."

"You see these little gardens in all parts of the islands. They are fenced in with oleander; but a couple of those hens could ruin the hopes of the gardener, after he has planted his onion-seed, or prepared his arrow-root plantation. For this reason all the domestic animals that live out doors are tied to keep them out of mischief," replied the doctor. "Our first onions and tomatoes usually come from these islands."

Sometimes the drive was taken in the opposite direction, towards St. George. Speare and Paynter Hills, in the vicinity of Harrington Sound, afforded the excursionists the desired views of the country. The sound is a beautiful sheet of water. The scenery all around it is enchanting; and there were any number of bowers in the dense growth of tropical trees and shrubs, which were full of interest to the wanderers from the sea.

There is no end of caves in the limestone rock; and caves are a positive glory to boys. Tom Moore lived for a time in this island, and wrote poetry, investing the locality with romance and sentiment; and Moore's "calabash-tree" is still a favorite resort to the visitor. Devil's Hole, or, more poetically, Neptune's

Grotto, is a rocky abyss filled with clear water, and has an underground connection with the sea.

"How full of fish it is!" exclaimed Sheridan, as he discovered that the water was alive with several varieties of fish.

"This is used to keep the fish caught in other waters, at the proper season, to be taken from this storehouse when they are not available elsewhere," answered the surgeon. "You will find a great many ponds in Bermuda applied to this use. You have observed how clear the water is."

"Isn't this a capital road?" said Wainwright, as the carriage moved on towards Hamilton.

"You will find such in all countries where the English people have lived long enough to make them. There are a hundred and fifty miles of these good hard roads in the twenty-four square miles of the Bermudas. You see they have to be cut through the rock in some places," said the doctor, as the carriage passed through such a cutting, the walls on both sides being covered with vines, and with an abundance of plants growing out of the interstices.

Dr. Winstock botanized somewhat with those of his charge who had a taste for the study; and there was abundant material to illustrate the subject. The road all along from the Sound to Hamilton was bordered with flowers; and when the party stopped at a house, to look at its wealth of floral treasures, it was not unusual for the courteous inhabitants to come out, and invite them to enter the grounds, or to accept a hastily gathered bouquet. Indeed, nothing could exceed the courtesy and kindness of the people in town and country.

They all seemed to be interested in the students, and especially in the ladies from the Ville d'Angers.

The excursions were not confined to those made in carriages. The students were roaming all over the islands, during the afternoons, which were wholly given up to sight-seeing. All could not afford carriages; and there were not enough of them to supply all, even if money had been plenty with them. Most of the boys walked; and in their rambles they had a deal of fun among themselves, and with the multitude of negroes that collected whenever the young tars were engaged in a frolic.

Quite as pleasant as the rides in the carriages were the excursions made in the boats of the fleet. On one occasion all the boats of the squadron, sixteen in number, made an excursion to the dock-yard. In the waters of Grassy Bay they gave an exhibition of the skill of the students in handling the cutters, which drew cheers of approbation from the naval officers and others who witnessed it. When the display was over, the boats' crew visited the dock-yard, and one of the men-of-war in port. They were courteously shown all over the yard, and the operation of the floating-dock was explained to them.

On the last day of the month the fleet left the harbor of Hamilton, and sought an anchorage in a retired bay, about three miles from the town. Here the squadron was entirely landlocked, and the water was as smooth as a millpond. The four academical craft were moored alongside each other, so that the professors could pass from one to the others without the use of the boats. Early in the morning the examination was begun. It was continued for three days; but it was understood that the result would give the officers and students their positions for three months, instead of one as before; for such a thorough examination was not possible more than once in a quarter.

All the ambitious students had been at work very diligently for the last two months, preparing for this great event. Tom Speers and Capt. O'Hara had given very little time to frolic and sight-seeing during the time the fleet had been at the Bermudas; but had been studying night and day. The officers of the American Prince had not been so diligent; for most of them had held their positions so long that they felt almost sure of them in the future, whatever system of promotions might be adopted.

On the morning of the fourth day, all hands were mustered under the awnings on the deck of the American Prince to learn the result of the examination. The principal took the rostrum which had been built for this occasion; and an anxious silence followed his appearance. He held in his hand the paper on which the fate of every officer and seaman was written down.

"Young gentlemen," Mr. Lowington began, "I am well aware that the changes proposed to-day will amount to a revolution. About the middle of the month, after the new crews of the several vessel have been trained to their duties under the different order of things, the squadron will sail for Brockway, the former headquarters of the fleet. When we have obtained a new register for the Ville d'Angers, she will be called the Frisbone."

In spite of the anxiety that pervaded the audience of the principal, this announcement was received with the most tremendous applause. The Prince, who was present with his wife and Miss Louise, felt called upon to make a speech, acknowledging the honor conferred upon him. He would rather have his name on the stern of a vessel used for the purpose to which the "Frisbone" was to be applied, than on that of the biggest ocean steamer that could bear it to the most remote regions of the earth.

"The Frisbone will take the place of the Josephine and the Tritonia, after she has been properly fitted for the purpose. With the two steamers, which will not have to wait for any sailing-vessels, we may make a voyage around the world; for I intend to re-organize the squadron, on a much more extensive plan of study. But this will not be done till the end of the quarter upon which we have now begun.

"The Frisbone will now be officered in the same manner as the schooner, with a captain, four lieutenants, and four masters. The office of purser and midshipman on board of the Prince will be abolished, so that there will be only nine cabin officers on board of each vessel. The two engineers of the Frisbone will be relieved from further duty in that department. The Prince will have forty-eight petty officers and seamen, and each of the other vessels thirty-six. Since the late Commodore Cantwell left the academy squadron, the office he held has not been filled, for the reason that those who came out the highest preferred the more active position of captain. We shall in future dispense with this ornamental figure-head.

"In addition to the choice of offices, each student will be entitled to elect in which of the four vessels he will serve for the coming quarter, until the complements are complete. Some exchanges may be allowed in the end, for I am not disposed to separate friends unnecessarily; but all such must be on equal terms, and by agreement between those exchanged."

The principal paused to put on his glasses, and the students improved the opportunity to applaud the plan laid down.

"The first name on the list is Sheridan," continued Mr. Lowington; and the usual demonstration when popular officers obtained good positions was made. "Capt. Sheridan, I congratulate you on the high rank you have won; and you have the right to choose any position in the fleet."

"I prefer to remain where I am," replied Sheridan. And Mr. Pelham made a record of his choice.

"The next name is that of Thomas Speers," said Mr. Lowington.

The announcement seemed to create as much surprise as when the same name had been mentioned in the harbor of Gibraltar, two months before. But all the ship's company of the Ville d'Angers manifested a tremendous enthusiasm.

"Good boy, darlint!" screamed O'Hara, grasping Tom's hand, and wringing it with hearty good-will. "That's what all your hard study manes; and I rather you had this place than have it myself."

"What place do you elect?" asked the principal.

"I am sure you will come next, and I shall take the position of first lieutenant of our steamer," whispered Tom to his late captain.

"Bother with you! don't do any thing of the sort!

my name may not come till the fortieth, and then where shall we be?" protested O'Hara. "He will take the place of captain of the Frisbone," he added, turning to the principal.

"You must speak for yourself, Mr. Speers," said the principal, with a smile.

"Will you tell me what name comes next on the list, Mr. Lowington?" asked Tom.

"I cannot do that," replied the principal, shaking his head. "And I hope no student will give way for another."

"Captain of the Frisbone," replied Tom, who would gladly have given up the position in favor of O'Hara.

Wainwright came in third, and selected his present office in the Tritonia.

"O'Hara is the fourth on the list," the principal proceeded.

Tom Speers engineered a very warm demonstration in favor of his friend, when the announcement was made, as O'Hara had done when his own was mentioned.

"I am knocked out of my place!" exclaimed Vroome, the captain of the Josephine.

But O'Hara, without an instant's hesitation, selected the position of first lieutenant of the Frisbone, and then he wanted to hug Tom.

"Murray," read the principal from the list.

The Josephines shook again; but Murray preferred his old place as first lieutenant of the Prince, for he and the captain were very dear friends, and were always together with the doctor when they went on shore. Vroome fortunately came next, and the Josephines were put out of misery.

The principal went through the list, and it was found

by the students, that the officers were not very different from what they had been before, except in the few cases where extraordinary efforts had been made. With hardly an exception, they preferred to remain in the vessels they had belonged to before. Scott came out third lieutenant of the Tritonia, and Blair recovered his lost place in the cabin, Richards having fallen out of it. Gregory and Clinch were seamen, and chose to serve in the Prince.

"Tom Speers, you are ten times the man I took you to be," said Judge Rodwood, grasping the hand of his ward, when he got near enough to him to do so. "I am sure your uncle's fortune, or that part of it that came to you, will go to the right place. I congratulate you, Capt. Speers, and I know you are worthy of the place you have won."

"Thank you, sir," replied Tom, glowing with excitement. "I set out for the position, or one just like it, and I have got it. Of course you will not expect me to leave the squadron now?"

"Certainly not; but as soon as you are twenty-one I shall hand the Marian over to you; and any time before that, when you choose to leave the command of the Frisbone, she is at your service."

Capt. Speers decided not to make any use of her at present. In the afternoon the new officers were put into position on board of the vessels of the fleet. Tom took possession of the captain's cabin; and O'Hara "gushed" all the afternoon, he was so pleased with the present order of things on board.

On the 15th of the month, the fleet, including the Marian, sailed for Brockway. After a pleasant June passage, the vessels arrived.

And now, having taken the academy squadron twice across the Atlantic, our series of stories comes to an end. In the course of the summer the principal reorganized his squadron, as he had intended. In November Tom Speers, as captain of the Frisbone, as she was now legally named, conveyed Mr. Frisbone, his wife, her sister, and Dr. Phelps, to Orotava, in the island of Teneriffe, where they had decided to spend the winter. When he had landed his passengers, he sailed for Havana, where the American Prince was to join him; and the two vessels were to spend the winter in the West Indies.

Early in the spring the two steamers went to the Canaries again; where a happy meeting between Tom and Miss Louise occurred, and it was rumored that they were in very great peril of becoming more nearly related in a few months or years. At this point Tom concluded, that, as he was twenty-one, he would retire from the command, and go on a cruise in the Marian. The last we heard of him, he was in the China Sea, with O'Hara, who had graduated in the fall of the same year as Tom, still sticking to him like a brother. The young millionaire does not spend all his income upon himself, and the poor and the needy have good reason to thank God that old Tom Speers gave half of his colossal fortune to his nephew.

Having taken our readers all over Europe, we bid them all good-by as we step ashore from our voyage among "The Isles of the Sea."

Franklin Press: Rand, Avery, & Co., Boston.

www.ingramcontent.com/pod-product-compliance
Lightning Source LLC
Chambersburg PA
CBHW030356230426
43664CB00007BB/620